India-Pakistan Relations with Special Reference to Kashmir

VOLUME II

Edited by

K.R. GUPTA

ATLANTIC
PUBLISHERS & DISTRIBUTORS

Published by
ATLANTIC PUBLISHERS AND DISTRIBUTORS
B-2, Vishal Enclave, Opp. Rajouri Garden, New Delhi-110027
Phones : 25413460, 25429987, 25466842

Sales Office
7/22, Ansari Road, Darya Ganj, New Delhi-110002
Phones : 23273880, 23285873, 23280451
Fax : 91-11-23285873
web : www.atlanticbooks.com
e-mail : info@atlanticbooks.com

ISBN 81-269-0270-1 (Vol. II)
ISBN 81-269-0271-X (Set)

Typeset at
APD Computer Graphics, Delhi
Printed in India at
Nice Printing Press, Delhi

PREFACE

The two states of India and Pakistan were born in August 1947, when India was partitioned at the end of British colonization. India had to agree to partition under compelling circumstances. The British Rulers were following the policy of Divide and Rule and by supporting Muslims they had created a situation in which India had to agree to the creation of Pakistan for obtaining Independence without any further delay. After India got Independence, it should have taken steps to undo the mischief of the British Rulers by bringing home to Muslims the damage done to them by the Britishers.

We may in this context learn a lesson from China. As soon as China consolidated its position in the country, it started looking around for Chinese territories which were separated from them by circumstances beyond their control. China had even to fight a war with India to annex some territories which they claimed to be theirs. China got Hong Kong included in their country. Now China is making every possible efforts to gain control of Taiwan which separated from their mainland.

As regards undoing partition of India, had the country shown some courage, things would have been much easier immediately after partition, particularly, when Pakistan provided an excuse to us by sending its forces in Kashmir. The Pakistan army at that time was weak and the job could have been done at a minimum cost. The second opportunity arose in 1965 when Pakistan again attacked Kashmir, we fought and won the war with the blood of our army but returned all occupied areas to Pakistan under the Tashkent Agreement. We did not have the courage to tell the world that we had accepted the mischief of Britishers in the creation of Pakistan under compelling circumstances. Even now it is not too late to tell the world of this fact and take necessary measures. But the operation now would be much more costlier in terms of men and war materials because the Pakistan has built a strong army and developed nuclear power over the long period provided to them by India's rulers. But this cost may still be less than the cost we are incurring from continued hostility and cross-border terrorism in the form of continuous military deployment and killings of civil and military persons.

The foundation of Pakistan was laid on the hatred for Hindus and India. This hatred against India has continued to be the major plank for ruling Pakistan for every party that comes to power.

Despite India's completely legal and valid position on Jammu & Kashmir, in order to find a solution to the situation created by Pakistan's aggression, India had accepted the option of holding a plebiscite in J&K. It had, however, been made clear by the Indian leaders that holding of such a plebiscite would be conditional upon Pakistan fulfilling Parts (I) & (II) of the UNCIP resolutions of 13 August 1948, which *inter alia,* required that all forces regular and irregular under the control of both sides shall cease-fire; Pakistan would withdraw its troops; it would endeavour to secure withdrawal of tribesmen and Pakistan nationals and India will withdraw bulk of its forces once the UNCIP confirms that the tribesmen and Pakistan nationals have withdrawn and Pakistan troops are being withdrawn.

The Government of Pakistan wrecked any possibility of plebiscite being conducted by not implementing part II of the resolution, perhaps because it was fully aware of what the result of such an exercise would be. The Pakistani troops, which were to withdraw from the state, did not do so. As a result normal conditions under which a plebiscite could be held were never created.

India should drop 'no first use' policy against a country which repeatedly threatens first use of nuclear weapons. The first use of nuclear weapons by Pakistan may be so massive and widespread that it may disable India to use the nuclear weapon.

If India drops its 'no first use' option of nuclear weapons, Pakistan would stop blackmailing India and may even be deterred venturing terrorism in India.

The Volumes include viewpoints of a number of eminent experts on Indo-Pak relations. These include views not only of Indian experts but also of Pakistani experts. The Volumes contain texts of all the documents, in original, relating to Indo-Pak relations since the partition of India in 1947.

It is hoped that the Volumes would be found useful by the students and research scholars concerned with international relations. The Volumes would also be useful to the parliamentarians and executives of India and Pakistan concerned with the formulation and execution of foreign policy of their country.

Common readers interested in Indo-Pak Relations would also find the Volumes useful and interesting.

K.R. GUPTA

CONTENTS

30

President of the Security Council's brief on the dispute over Jammu and Kashmir

New York, 7 May 2001

Ambassador Shamshad Ahmad Khan, today, called on the President of the Security Council, US Ambassador James Cunningham, to brief him on the current regional situation in the context of the Kashmir dispute and Afghanistan problem.

Ambassador Shamshad apprized the President of the Security Council that Pakistan was making efforts for resumption of dialogue with India. Despite its repeated offers to India, even at the level of Pakistan's Chief Executive, for resumption of dialogue at any time, at any place and at any level, India had shown no positive response and remained intransigence. Ambassador Shamshad re-affirmed Pakistan's commitment for purposeful dialogue with India for a final settlement of Kashmir dispute in accordance with UN Security Council resolutions and in conformity with the legitimate aspirations of the Kashmiri people.

On the Afghanistan issue, Ambassador Shamshad underlined the importance of achieving durable peace in that war-torn country through dialogue and conciliation. While he re-affirmed Pakistan's commitment to abide by the UN Security Council resolutions on Afghanistan, Ambassador Shamshad told the President of the Security Council how important it was for the world community to engage in a constructive political process in Afghanistan rather than pursuing the blind track of punitive measures. He also emphasized the need for the international community to seriously address the current humanitarian crisis in Afghanistan in order to prevent internal displacement and further influx of refugees into Pakistan. The Pakistan's Permanent Representative also informed the President of the Security Council on the discussions which held the UN High Commissioner for Refugees (UNHCR) with the Chief Executive and the Foreign Minister of Pakistan on the Afghan refugee situation.

Pakistan's Permanent Representative also briefed the President of the Security Council, Pakistan's imminent participation in the United Nations Mission in Sierra Leone (UNAMSIL).

The President of the Security Council thanked Ambassador Shamshad Ahmad for his briefing and promised to convey his views to the Security Council. The President also expressed appreciation for Pakistan's commitment to UNAMSIL.

31

Government to embark upon political dialogue with all sections of peace loving people of Jammu & Kashmir

New Delhi, 6 April 2001

The Government of India had declared unilaterally a policy of Non-Initiation of Combat Operations in Jammu and Kashmir with a view to lowering the levels of violence and creating an atmosphere conducive to commencement of a peace process in the troubled State. Despite the continuing violence on the part of some predominantly non Kashmiri terrorist groups, the Government is gratified to note that there is an unmistakable ground swell for peace among the people of J&K. In order to promote a vigorous movement towards establishment of peace and tranquility, the Government have decided to embark upon a political dialogue with all sections of the peace loving people of the state including those who are currently outside it.

The dialogue from the side of the Government of India will be held by Shri K.C. Pant, Deputy Chairman, Planning Commission. It is hoped that representatives of all walks of life from among the people of J&K will be partners in this dialogue. More specifically it is expected that, beside the J&K Government, all Political Parties, Non-Government Organisations, Trade Unions, Social and Religious bodies from all the regions of the State will participate. The Government invites people of goodwill who desire restoration of peace and normalcy in the State to come forward to participate in the dialogue.

The Government notes that the APHC has all along taken the position that talks should be unconditional. Now that the Government has agreed to hold talks in the interest of early restoration of peace, it is for the APHC to consider whether it would not be inconsistent for them to set pre-conditions for the dialogue. The doors are open for them to join in the talks. The doors are also not closed for Kashmiri Organisations which are currently engaged in militancy in the State but are desirous of peace. The Agenda for the dialogue briefly stated is 'Peace and how it may be attained in the troubled State'. All aspects bearing on this theme will be relevant to the dialogue.

The Government of India takes note of the frequently repeated requests from Pakistan that they are eager for a dialogue with India on J&K. The Government of India re-affirms its faith in such a bilateral dialogue and hopes that Pakistan will help in its resumption by curbing cross-border terrorism and putting an end to the vicious anti-India propaganda emanating from Pakistan. This will be in accordance with the Shimla Agreement and the spirit of the Lahore Declaration.

The road to peace is not without serious obstacles : one such is continuing violence against the innocent people of J&K. To reduce this violence security forces have been directed to vigourously conduct operations against those who disturb the peace and victimise the innocent people of J&K, while at the same time ensuring that the population at large is spared undue hardships or harassment. The Government expects that all right thinking people in the State will join hands with the Government and march purposefully in quest of the peace which has eluded them for the last 12 years. It is only in an atmosphere of peace that an agreed solution for the J&K issue can be evolved.

32

Prime Minister Vajpayee's statement in Lok Sabha regarding Jammu & Kashmir

22 February 2001

As Hon'ble Members would recollect, Rashtrapatiji during his address to the Joint Sitting of both the Houses of Parliament had given voice to the Government's approach to the whole question of Jammu & Kashmir. He had then, amongst other things, shared with the Honb'le Members of Parliament that :

"The Government is pursuing a multi-pronged strategy to bring peace and normalcy in Jammu and Kashmir. As part of this, it launched a major peace mission on November 19, 2000, by announcing a unilateral non-initiation of combat operations in the State during the holy month of Ramzan. This bold initiative was extended twice up to February 26, 2001. As anticipated, this was warmly welcomed by the people of Jammu & Kashmir, who are longing for an end to militancy and violence in their beautiful State. The international community has also given overwhelming support, because it sees in it yet another demonstration of India's sincere commitment to a peaceful and permanent solution to the Kashmir issue."

Rashthrapatiji had also then informed the Hon'ble Members that :

"Militancy in Jammu & Kashmir is now increasingly confined to foreign mercenary groups. This has widened the scope for democratic activity in the State. The people of the State participated enthusiastically in the recent Panchayat elections.

I reiterate the Government's readiness to have talks with every group in the State that abjures violence."

The Government has decided to pursue this path by initiating talks with various groups in J & K.

The Government has seriously addressed the question of continuing with the peace process and further extending the period of non-initiation of combat operation by our security forces. In this regard, the Government has benefited by the detailed briefing of and consultations with all political parties that it had on February 21, 2001.

Having examined all aspects of the question in its totality, the Government has decided to further extend the period up till the end of May. Let this opportunity not be missed by all those that desire peace, for our patience is not infinite.

I wish to make it abundantly clear that the peace process is only for those that wish to benefit from it. We will not let this process be derailed, diluted or misused. For such organisations or elements, as have vowed to disrupt the peace process, or intend to continue with violence and the killing of innocents in J & K, my message is unequivocal and clear. If you inflict injury on any Indian citizen in the State of Jammu and Kashmir, or elsewhere, or commit any act of violence or terrorism then the security forces have clear instructions to act decisively and to defeat such intentions. Law and order shall be maintained. Those who think that our security forces are less determined today to put an end to terrorism are only deluding themselves.

It is my hope that Pakistan will act, even now, and adjure violence, give up their continuous hostile propaganda against India, stop promoting and aiding cross-border terrorism, take the path of peace through bilateral talks as enshrined in the Simla Agreement and the Lahore Declaration, thus creating a conducive atmosphere so that the comprehensive dialogue process can be resumed resulting in a lasting solution to the problems.

The process of peace is to enable our citizens in Jammu &

Kashmir to live peacefully. It is their voice that has to be heard, not of the militants or foreign mercenaries.

Peace is our objective, to peace and dialogue we remain committed because that, above all, is what the people of Jammu & Kashmir need most.

33

Ministry of Foreign Affairs Press Statement

Islamabad, 22 February 2001

The announcement made today by the Indian Prime Minister on an extension of the period of "non-initiation of combat operations" by Indian forces in Occupied Kashmir is yet another attempt by India to mislead world opinion. Instead of responding positively to the initiatives taken by Pakistan for the reduction of tension and the commencement of a peace process on Kashmir, India has repeated its old allegations against Pakistan and sought to malign the freedom struggle that the people of Kashmir have been waging against India's illegal occupation of the State and against the terror and violence unleashed by the Indian forces against the Kashmiri people.

During the sham cease-fire which has now been in operation for nearly three months, there has been no lessening of repression or violence by India against the Kashmiri people. Instead, there has been escalation in extra-judicial killings, disappearances, torture and other atrocities. Peaceful demonstrators, including women and children, have been fired upon by the Indian Army and other occupation forces. The massacres at Haigam and at Maisuma are only the latest examples of shooting by the Indian forces on unarmed civilians.

India's false claims about the situation in Occupied Kashmir are also belied by the large-scale demonstrations last week for the right to self-determination in Occupied Kashmir in which the Kashmiri people braved curfews and firings by Indian forces to show their support for the freedom struggle. Some of the scenes of the brutality with which Indian forces sought to suppress these demonstrations have been carried by TV channels all round the world.

Wire service reports have quoted Indian official sources as saying that under today's extension of the so-called cease-fire, Indian forces will be free to carry out "search and seize operations" and conduct "targeted attacks against militant groups." These remarks expose the Indian claim of non- initiation of combat operations as lacking any credibility.

The Government of Pakistan calls upon the Government of India to realise the futility of its effort to impose a military solution on Kashmir and join Pakistan in a sincere effort to resolve the dispute. To this end, India must halt its repression, violence and terror against the Kashmiri people, respect the right of the Kashmiri people to self-determination, respond positively to the Pakistani initiatives for peace, permit the APHC delegation to visit Pakistan and enter into a meaningful dialogue with Pakistan for a peaceful settlement of the Kashmir dispute in accordance with the relevant UN Security Council resolutions.

34

Prime Minister Vajpayee's statement on the situation in Jammu & Kashmir

Udupi, Karnataka, 18 January 2001

The recent spurt in terrorist violence in Jammu & Kashmir and elsewhere in India, unleashed by Pakistan-based militant organizations has vitiated the atmosphere for resumption of talks between India and Pakistan. Terrorist attacks on our security forces and civilians have increased both in number and in their gravity. The incidents at the Red Fort and Srinagar airport, combined with the threat to strike at the Prime Minister's Office, show that militant outfits, which are opposed to peace and normalcy in the State are alarmed at the prospects of fruitful dialogue between India and Pakistan.

What is particularly surprising and distressing is the fact that the leadership of Pakistan continues to do nothing to restrain these terrorist organizations, which operate from Pakistani soil, even as it professes its eagerness to resume talks with India. Its argument that violence will stop once talks begin is strange, to say the least. It convinces neither India nor the international community. There cannot be meaningful talks for resolving outstanding issues and normalizing bilateral relations when the guns of terrorist outfits continue to do their own talking.

India's readiness to have talks with Pakistan at any level, including at the highest level has been well established. We have also strongly demonstrated our sincerity to create a conducive atmosphere for talks through specific confidence-building measures, such as unilateral cessation of combat operations in Jammu & Kashmir. However, the continuation of terrorist activities in and outside the State shows that the purpose of our taking these unilateral initiatives is not being fulfilled.

I urge the leadership of Pakistan to demonstrate its sincerity and commitment to the dialogue process by unequivocally condemning terrorist violence by Pakistan-based militant groups and effectively checking their anti-India activities. The onus of creating a positive atmosphere for bilateral talks rests clearly with Pakistan.

35

Prime Minister Vajpayee's statement in both the Houses of Parliament regarding peace-initiatives in Jammu & Kashmir

New Delhi, 20 December 2000

Before the Winter Session of the Parliament concludes, and the House rises for the festivals of Christmas and Id, I wish to take this opportunity and share with Hon'ble Members the Government's assessment of the situation in J&K, also along the LoC.

Following my announcement of 19 November, that during the holy month of Ramzan our security forces would not initiate operations against the militants, also expressing a hope that along the LoC, too, infiltration would cease, there have been some encouraging developments. Certain other aspects, however, remain as our continuing concerns.

The Government is greatly heartened by the response of the citizens, political parties and other organisations in the State of J&K. Our peace initiative has been widely welcomed there. A distinctly different and a more optimistic mood now prevails in that State. The constituency for peace has expanded significantly.

There has also been a decline in incidents of terrorist violence in that state. Activities, however, of organisations like Lashkar-e-Tayaaba and Harkat-ul-Mujahedin continue, resulting in most unfortunate and regrettable loss of innocent civilian lives, also of the personnel of our security forces. The Government remains firm in its resolve to combating these and other challenges, also to defeating their inhuman and nefarious designs.

There has been a recognizable decline, too, in attempts at cross-LoC (line of control) and cross-IB (international border) infiltration of terrorists. This must cease entirely. The Government is committed to achieving this end.

Along the LoC, we have witnessed a marked improvement in incidents of exchange of fire. Relative peace has prevailed all along the LoC, ever since my announcement of 19 November, barring some incidents in the early stages.

After careful consideration of all aspects the Government has, therefore, taken a decision to extend the period of 'no initiation of combat operations' by another month. After Republic Day 2001, the Government will review the position again.

As the initiator of the dialogue process with Pakistan, India remains committed to it. The existence of a suitable environment for such a process is self evidently necessary. As part of our continued commitment to the Shimla Agreement and the Lahore Declaration, the Government will initiate such exploratory steps as are considered necessary, by it, so that the 'Composite Dialogue Process' between the Governments of India and Pakistan could be resumed.

Let me inform the House that the government's unwavering commitment to meeting the challenge of terrorism remains undiluted. Whereas we will continue to exercise maximum restraint in face of grave provocations, national interests will never be compromised.

I wish to assure Hon'ble Members that we remain steadfast in our commitment to restoring lasting peace and to enabling all our citizens from J&K to join as equal partners in India's march to prosperity.

36

Statement by the Prime Minister Atal Behari Vajpayee on the situation in Jammu & Kashmir

New Delhi, 19 November 2000

The people of India are heartened by the steady improvement in the situation in Jammu & Kashmir. Our sisters and brothers in the State have always longed for the return of peace and normalcy, which is now happening steadily and perceptibly. The true complexion of the forces of terrorism and separatism, as also their growing isolation in the State, are now clearer than ever before. The entire world now knows who is misusing the name of Islam to prolong the agony of the people of Jammu & Kashmir.

India has always stood for a peaceful resolution of the Kashmir issue. Events of the past two years have further underscored India's credentials for peace. They have also once again proved, beyond a shadow of doubt, that India has both the resolve and capability to defeat any attempt to transgress India's security or challenge our unity and integrity.

During my visit to Srinagar on August 3 this year, I had underscored the need for resolving all issues in the spirit of insaniyat (humanism). Mine was a sincere appeal for cooperation to bring to an end the long trail of violence, which has claimed so many precious lives and inflicted untold misery on all sections of the State's population — Muslims, Hindus, Buddhists and Sikhs alike.

We have continued our efforts to normalise the situation in the State and to hold talks with all those who are prepared for a dialogue. The holy month of Ramazan, during which Prophet Mohammed exhorted one and all to live in peace and harmony, is soon approaching. The Government has, therefore, instructed the security forces not to initiate combat operations against militants in Jammu & Kashmir during this most pious month in the Islamic calendar. I hope that our gesture will be fully appreciated and all violence in the State and infiltration across the Line of Control and the international border will cease and peace prevail.

37

Address by the Chief Executive (Pakistan) to the OIC Contact Group on Jammu and Kashmir at the Summit Level, Ninth Islamic Summit, Doha, Qatar, 13 November 2000

Mr. Chairman,
Excellencies,
Honourable Secretary General,
Distinguished delegates,

It is a privilege and honour for me to be speaking to the OIC Contact Group on Jammu and Kashmir. Its meeting, today, at the Summit level, testifies to the importance that the OIC and the Islamic Ummah attach to the success of the just struggle of the Kashmiri people for self-determination. It also reflects the concern of the Islamic countries at the serious implications for global and regional peace and security arising from the failure to resolve this long-outstanding dispute between Pakistan and India.

For the convening of this important meeting of the Contact Group, I wish especially to thank you, Mr. Chairman, and our Secretary General. Throughout his tenure, Secretary General, His Excellency Mr. Azeddine Laraki, took keen interest in developments relating to Kashmir. He expressed concern, time and again, on behalf of our Organization, at the gross violations of human rights in Indian Occupied Kashmir and expressed solidarity with the Kashmiri cause.

I salute the courageous sons and daughters of Kashmir who

have been resisting India's illegal occupation, undeterred by India's ruthless effort to suppress them. Their heroic defiance of India's armed might and their sacrifices have set a shining example of valour which we all admire and respect.

I wish to pay the highest tribute to the Kashmiri leadership and to the courage and fortitude of the freedom struggle, especially the All Parties Hurriyet Conference. In the face of relentless repression, they have remained steadfast in demanding their inalienable fundamental right to self-determination, which is sanctified by the United Nations. I welcome Mir Waiz Umer Farooq and Maulana Abbas Ansari who have been able to represent the Hurriyet, while their other APHC colleagues who were invited could not do so because of denial of permission to travel.

The right of the Kashmiri people to self-determination is derived from international law, which the international community expressly guaranteed to them through the UN Security Council. India itself made a solemn commitment for holding a plebiscite under United Nations auspices. It refused to honour that promise when it realized that it would not be able to manipulate such a plebiscite in its favour.

Since then, India has used both force and manipulation to maintain its hold on Kashmir. Its response to the Kashmiri freedom struggle has been an exponential escalation of violence and repression against innocent and unarmed Kashmiri people. Today more than 700,000 Indian military and paramilitary forces in Kashmir are engaged in an effort to subjugate ten million Kashmiris. There is no parallel in recent history for such a massive concentration of forces to quell a freedom movement.

There are daily reports of the killings of Kashmiris at the hands of the Indian occupation forces. More than 75,000 of them have embraced martyrdom since 1989. To say that Indian forces are guilty of large-scale human rights violations would be an understatement. The tragedy approaches genocide. For India, every Kashmiri who wants freedom is a "militant" who must be eliminated.

In its frustration at its inability to suppress the freedom struggle, India now seeks to malign the noble and heroic struggle of Kashmiris by telling the world that those who resist Indian illegal occupation of the State are "terrorists" or "Islamic fundamentalists." This argument will have a familiar ring. The Palestinians who fight against the occupation of their land have also been given the same appellation. This is no coincidence. Not long ago, a Minister of the Indian Government visiting Israel also spoke of the common threat of "Islamic terrorism" faced by the two countries. Not surprisingly, too, India has sought the help of the same country in suppressing the Kashmir freedom movement.

The real terrorists, of course, are not those who struggle against injustice and oppression but those who perpetrate atrocities against a civilian population which does not submit to the illegal occupation of its land. It is the Indian occupation forces who are engaged in state sponsored terrorism against the people of Kashmir.

India has misread international trends, if it feels encouraged in seeking a military solution of Kashmir or rejecting dialogue with Pakistan. Kashmiri aspirations for freedom will not be extinguished, nor can the international legality established by the UN resolutions lapse.

The Kashmir question, which involves the life and future of the millions of people of the State, has also been the root cause of tensions in South Asia as recognized by the world community. Its settlement is an indispensable pre-requisite for peace and stability in the region. Pakistan is firmly committed to seeking a peaceful solution of the Kashmir dispute in accordance with the wishes of the Kashmiri people and international norms of justice.

Mr. Chairman,

The Kashmiris are a peace-loving people. They were forced to resort to an armed struggle when their peaceful freedom struggle for self-determination was met with brute force. The Kashmiris are also a freedom-loving people. What is more, they are a determined people. They are firmly resolved to achieve their right to self-determination which India has sought to usurp. India's efforts to deprive them of their freedom are bound to fail, as have the efforts of others colonial and occupying powers.

The Twentieth Century saw the emancipation of scores of peoples from colonial domination and enslavement on the basis of their inalienable right to self-determination. This right was recently reaffirmed by the UN Millennium Summit. Today, Kashmir is among the few legacies of the colonial era. We are confident that our Kashmiri brethren too would soon realize their long cherished goal of freedom.

This meeting of the Contact Group at the Summit level is a manifestation of our solidarity with the Kashmiri cause and also a testimony to your resolve to stand steadfast in support of Islamic causes. We should, once again, demand an immediate end to the Indian repression in the occupied Kashmir as well as respect for the fundamental human rights of the Kashmiri people. We need to act in concert and take concrete measures to safeguard, protect and uphold the Kashmiri struggle for freedom and press India to chose the path of dialogue and peaceful settlement. I am confident that the resolutions adopted by the Summit would represent a powerful voice in support of the just Kashmiri cause and in solidarity with the Kashmiri people.

I thank you, Mr. Chairman.

38

Statement by the Home Minister L.K. Advani on situation in Jammu & Kashmir in Parliament

New Delhi, 9 August 2000

On July 24, 2000, the Hizbul Mujahideen announced a unilateral ceasefire and publicly expressed a willingness to initiate talks with the Government of India. The Government of India responded positively to the offer.

The people of Jammu & Kashmir enthusiastically welcomed the development.

Yesterday's announcement by Hizbul Mujahideen that the ceasefire has been withdrawn has naturally come as a deep disappointment to all those who were looking forward to a return of peace to J&K state.

The nature, location, context and content of the announcement by Hizbul Mujahideen leader Syed Salahuddin can leave no doubt in anybody's mind that it is Pakistan which has sabotaged the prospects of peace in the State.

The offer of ceasefire was made by Majid Dar, a leader of Hizbul Mujahideen, in Srinagar. It was withdrawn by Salahuddin in Islamabad.

It is clear that the voice that made the announcement may have been Salahuddin's, but the words came from the ruling establishment in Islamabad which is the arch patron for numerous militants groups engaged in State sponsored cross border terrorism in J&K and other parts of India.

The Hizbul Mujahideen leader has said that his organisation withdrew from the proposed talks because of India's unwillingness to invite Pakistan as the third participant in the talks. This has precisely been the demand of Pakistan's military establishment, which it has expressed on several occasions in the past but most shrilly after Hizbul Mujahideen announced its ceasefire and its readiness to have talks with the Government of India.

Indeed all statements from Islamabad since July 24 made it obvious that the ceasefire did not fit in with Pakistan's design of continuously promoting terrorism in J&K.

Pakistan's determination to sabotage the talks became known with deadly clarity when extremists trained and armed on its soil created a mayhem of massacres in J&K on August 1 & 2 leaving over 100 innocent persons dead.

It is not difficult to know why Pakistan struck terror on such an unprecedented scale and soon thereafter sabotaged our initiative for talks with some representatives of our own people. The rules of Pakistan are terrorized by the prospect of peace in J&K. They were similarly terrorized by the prospect of friendship with India following Prime Minister, Shri Atal Behari Vajpayee's historic peace initiative in Lahore.

Kargil war was the result of their fear of peace in 1999. The brutal killing of the Amarnath Yatris and other innocent people is the result of their fear of peace in 2000.

Just as India could not be frightened by the war inflicted by Pakistan in Kargil, we shall not be frightened by the intensification of proxy war by Islamabad now. Pakistan had to face a humiliating and self-damaging defeat in the Kargil war. Similar will be its fate in its proxy war against India.

India's sincere desire for restoration of peace and normalcy in J&K and a comprehensive and lasting solution to the issue of Kashmir are now clearly established.

Not only the people of Kashmir but also people all over the world now clearly know who is for peace and who is for hostilities; whose is the voice of sanity and humanity and whose is a voice of subterfuge and sabotage.

The Hon'ble Members of this House must also have noticed the negative role played by the Hurriyat leadership in this entire episode. From the beginning, their response to the Hizbul initiative was not just cold, they even labeled it as a 'hasty' move. Perhaps they forgot that Jammu & Kashmir has been in a bloodied turmoil for the last more than a decade. Under the circumstances how could this peace initiative be called 'hasty'? It seems that the Hurriyat leadership was acting under pressure from Pakistan. They certainly did not act in the interest of Jammu & Kashmir and thus compromised the well being of the people of the State.

In the days and months to come India will not deviate from its chosen course of talks with all those in Kashmir who eschew the path of terror and violence and our simultaneous battle against all those who continue to stick to that path. We shall persist with our policy of firmness and flexibility.

Our security forces are ready to face the challenge and threat of renewed militancy in the State of Jammu & Kashmir. In fact, it is the militant outfits which should worry because they have the Indian security forces and the never-say-die spirit of the Indian soldier to face. More importantly they have the strength of Indian democracy to contend with.

India has all along maintained that the question of a dialogue with Pakistan is a separate issue. Prime Minister, Shri Vajpayee has made it clear that India is willing to talk with Pakistan on all matters of bilateral concern when Islamabad demonstrates its resolve to end cross border terrorism.

39

Prime Minister Vajpayee's statement in Parliament regarding the recent massacre in Jammu & Kashmir

New Delhi, 4 August 2000

I visited Pahalgam and Srinagar on Thursday to study the situation arising out of recent massacre in various places in Jammu and Kashmir and of pilgrims at Pahalgam. I am thankful to Smt. Sonia Gandhi, Shri Somnath Chatterjee, Shri Mulayam Singh Yadav, Shri Yerrannaidu and Shri Ghulam Nabi Azad for agreeing to join me at such short notice. My colleagues Shri George Fernandez, Ms. Mamta Bannerjee and Shri Chaman Lal Gupta also joined me along with Chief of Army Staff.

From Srinagar the Governor and the Chief Minister of Jammu and Kashmir accompanied us. Our visit was also intended to assure people of the state that the entire nation stood by them at this hour and to share their grief over the inhuman behavior of the terrorists against innocent people belonging to the state as well as many from other parts of the country on pilgrimage to Amarnath.

The briefing which we were given by the chief of unified command and security forces, made it clear that perpetrators of these heinous crimes were foreigners. Arms and ammunitions recovered from them clearly establish their links with Pakistan based Lashkar-e-Toiba.

Delegations of local population as well as pilgrims met me

and spoke to me about the difficulties many were facing in the wake of the killings.

The house, I am sure, is one with me in assuring the people of Jammu and Kashmir and the nation that we will not yield before terrorism. I may add that while the fight against terrorism will be continued, India will not give up efforts for restoration of peace in Jammu and Kashmir.

I made it clear at Srinagar that the dialogue with Hizbul Mujahideen is a part of this effort. Other groups who have chosen the path of violence should also realize that the people of Jammu and Kashmir want peace in the state. It is futile for them to continue on the path of violence. They should come forward for talks with the government for redressal of their grievances.

40

An Update on Terrorist Killings in Jammu & Kashmir

3 August 2000

Prime Minister Atal Behari Vajpayee, accompanied by main Opposition Congress leader Sonia Gandhi and Defense Minister George Fernandes, visited some of the areas in Jammu & Kashmir where militants killed more than 100 people. He told reporters that groups owing allegiance to Pakistan had sought to derail the peace process.

"We have come here to express our solidarity with the people who have been killed. The militants are behind these killings. This is a conspiracy by Pakistan and no one should have doubts about it," Vajpayee told reporters.

"There will be a court of inquiry set up to probe the killings so that no doubts remain. All people should condemn the barbaric incident. The Hizbul Mujahideen has already condemned it ... other militant organizations should also come forward."

Prime Minister Vajpayee speaking in the Parliament yesterday has said, the government will not succumb to the pressure unleashed by Pakistan-controlled terrorist outfits to hamper the peace process in Jammu and Kashmir.

The Home Minister, Mr. L.K. Advani said the government would continue its efforts for a dialogue on Jammu and Kashmir. Making a detailed statement in both Houses, Mr. Advani described the massacre as a determined bid by those upset at the prospects of peace. He asserted if Haizbul Mujahideen remains firm on the peace initiatives, the government will respond positively. Mr. Advani said the incidents are part of the continuing proxy war being waged by Pakistan against India.

Earlier President K.R. Narayanan and Vice-President Krishan Kant condemned the killings. The President said he was shocked and deeply grieved to learn of the mindless killings of innocent people. “To kill pilgrims, laborers, ordinary and innocent men and women in the name of Jehad is the height of barbarism and inhumanity,” he said. “We must all stand together and condemn such violence which is against our culture and ethos,” Mr. Narayanan said.

The security scenario in Jammu and Kashmir was reviewed at a high level meeting held in Srinagar. The State has been put on high alert following the killings. The Chief Minister, Dr. Abdullah along with the Governor Mr. G.C. Saxena visited the massacre sites.

The State government says there is enough evidence to suggest that the Lashkar-e-Toiba was behind the latest series of killings in the State. In New Delhi, an information cell has been opened at the Jammu and Kashmir Resident Commissioner’s Office to give information on the Pahalgam massacre.

The US President, Mr. Bill Clinton telephoned Prime Minister, Mr. Atal Behari Vajpayee last night to convey his deepest sympathies and support for India following the massacres in Jammu and Kashmir in the last 24 hours. He added that he would speak to the leaders of Pakistan and do everything possible to contain such activities. President Clinton also expressed his admiration for the Prime Minister’s positive response to the ceasefire offer of the Hizbul Mujahideen.

41

Press Release Issued by the Ministry of External Affairs on Pakistan's Support to Cross-border Terrorism

New Delhi, 10 November 1999

Our strong concerns at the anti-India tirade witnessed during the annual congregation of the terrorist organisation, Lashkar-e-Tayyaba, held at Muridke from November 3-5, 1999, were conveyed to the Deputy High Commissioner of Pakistan, who was summoned to the Ministry of External Affairs today.

He was told that it was particularly reprehensible that open threats against India were made during the congregation by the terrorists and that the Pakistani authorities had taken no action against those who had made these threats and had used provocative language. This was yet another manifestation of Pakistan's support to international terrorism. The Pakistan Deputy High Commissioner was also told that the Government of India once again called upon the Pakistani authorities to abandon their irresponsible support of cross-border terrorism.

42

Pakistani Prime Minister Nawaz Sharif's Address to the Nation, 12 July 1999, during the Kargil Crisis

My dear Countrymen, not everyone will know of the tensions that we have gone through and the circumstances we have braved during the last month and a half. It is a fact and no secret anyway that the deterioration in Pakistan-India relations brought our two countries to the brink of war. While there is no doubt that the Kashmiri Mujahideen through their sacrifices and battle successes wrote out a new chapter in their freedom struggle, the situation on the diplomatic front became so complicated that it was no easy task to straighten it out or control its adverse fallout.

Dear brothers and sisters, by the grace of God, Pakistan is not a wall of sand or a child's plaything. We have the ability to deal befittingly with aggression. Had war been imposed on us, the invader would have lived to regret the day. However, we do not wish to make war, nor have we looked for it. We know that in a nuclear conflict there can be no victors.

It is my considered opinion that by going to war Pakistan and India can only multiply their problems without solving even one of them. I have repeatedly said that the Kashmir dispute should be resolved amicably. I am also aware of the record of those who vowed to fight for a thousand years. I know what their aims were. Their only gift to the nation was ignominy and lasting regret. After taking stock of past events and making an objective study of history, I have come to the conclusion that our principal national priority should be making Pakistan a great self-reliant economic power. Only then can we achieve our supreme national objectives.

After the Lahore Declaration in February this year, not only the people of Pakistan and India but the international community as well had begun to hope that after their long history of discord, our two countries had chosen the path of peace. Prime Minister Vajpayee of India visited the Minar-i-Pakistan in Lahore and what he said on the occasion was a good augury for the future since it showed that he wanted to begin a new chapter in our relations, with the bitterness of the past forgotten and old attitudes abandoned. I welcomed this. While we were preparing for negotiations in line with the Lahore Declaration, the Indian Lok Sabha was dissolved and fresh elections were announced. On the other hand, the Kashmir freedom struggle which has been underway for the last eleven years entered a new and intensified phase with the freedom fighters gaining control of the Kargil mountains.

Prime Minister Vajpayee phoned me, expressing his concern at these developments. I suggested a meeting between local commanders while pointing out that we should resolve this matter at a local level, as in the past so that there should be no escalation. He agreed with me and the next day the two local commanders met but, simultaneously, India turned its heavy guns on us, while the Indian air force began to pound the Mujahideen-held positions. This sudden escalation was unexpected. It is true that the Mujahideen were present on several Kargil heights but it was part of their long freedom struggle and inseparable from it. For example, you all know that the Mujahideen took control of the Hazratbal shrine in Srinagar once. Now there is no way in which Pakistan could have come to their aid there. The shrine was surrounded by Indian troops and yet the Mujahideen took it over and held it for several days. Once the world took notice of what their action and the unresolved question of Kashmir became duly highlighted, they vacated their occupation of the shrine. It is for the same reasons that the Mujahideen must have occupied those heights in Kargil. Once the Mujahideen had succeeded in drawing world attention to Kashmir, it is understandable that they would wish to disengage.

Had we tried, this matter could have been resolved peacefully; but India set the fires of war alight instead of dealing with the situation through negotiations. It also chose to engulf the entire country in a war frenzy. However, Pakistan remained unprovoked and we saw to it that there was no war hysteria in the country. We also ensured that there would be no break in mutual contacts. Since the start of the crisis in Kargil, up to this day, I have spoken to Prime Minister Vajpayee on the phone several times. I also sent my Foreign Minister over though his visit proved fruitless. Given all this, it is unfair to allege that we stabbed anyone in the back. It has been my constant effort that our countries be spared the horror of a nuclear war. Only a desire for collective suicide can prompt us to take such a step. I have no such intention. I believe Prime Minister Vajpayee has no such intention either. However, going by the attitude of India, it did seem to us that New Delhi was rapidly moving towards war. The use of air and land power in Kargil by India was on a scale associated with a large and regular war only. Pakistani positions were shelled from across the Line of Control resulting in the death of innocent civilians and armed forces personnel who were merely defending themselves.

The number of troops deployed by India on our borders was again warlike. Its naval power was moved close to our shores and its nuclear missiles turned towards us. The Indian air force was put on red alert. I salute the armed forces of Pakistan which took all necessary steps to deal with the expected Indian attack with exemplary efficiency and speed. I also wish to pay tribute to all those innocent citizens who fell victim to Indian shelling. Those who suffered material loss as a result of Indian actions have my full sympathy. The government will soon take steps to give them due compensation. I also salute those martyrs of the Pakistan army who fell while performing their duties on the Line of Control. Those who suffered injury also have my heartfelt sympathies. Their courage, valour and resoluteness will serve as an example to the world. They surprised a military power several times their size on the world's most inhospitable and difficult front by dint of their grit and determination. They resisted the unrelenting attacks of the Indian air force and infantry in an admirable manner. They proved that they were prepared to go to any extent for the sake of their freedom. I take this occasion to pay tribute to the gallant freedom fighters of the All Parties Hurriyet Conference.

My dear Countrymen, we have decided to give diplomacy another chance. This decision is neither hasty nor has it been taken under pressure or out of nervousness. It has been said that it takes more courage to extricate oneself from war than to start one. For many years and with time it has gained in intensity and strength. Kargil has been a part of that struggle. We were constantly in consultation with our friends as the fighting continued. When the clouds of war began to draw closer, we intensified our contacts. At the same time, we did not snap contact with the Indian government. I was busy trying to press every entity, every individual, in aid of our cause and its furtherance. I was in touch with President Clinton. When American representatives came to Pakistan, we made it clear to them that the problem would not be solved by putting out the fires in Kargil but to get to the heart of the problem. We argued that, the Kashmiri urge for freedom was like molten lava in the belly of the earth which would always find other points of eruption.

Even if we succeeded in capping the fire-spitting mountains of Kargil, unless the basic problem was addressed, there will be outbreaks elsewhere. If the Kashmiri people were not given their right of self-determination, there would be other Kargils. Neither we, nor India, would be able to stop that. The only way to stop more Kargils from happening was to do justice to the Kashmiris. The promises made to their had to be fulfilled. That was the message I carried to America and I am glad that President Clinton agreed that unless the basic issue of Kashmir was resolved, the clouds of war would continue to hover over the

Subcontinent. This was the backdrop of the joint statement issued in Washington. The statement clearly stated that as soon as the situation on the Line of Control returned to normal, negotiations between India and Pakistan would begin in order to resolve all outstanding issues, including Kashmir. President Clinton extended the assurance that lie would riot only encourage all moves aimed at settling all outstanding disputes through dialogue, but he would take a personal interest in these efforts in order to ensure that they were intensified.

This assurance, coming from the head of a great power like the United States is no ordinary matter. It is clear that after this unequivocal commitment from President Clinton in particular and the international community in general, the world will pay serious attention to Kashmir, being now aware of its importance and sensitivity. That is why we appealed to the Mujahideen to come down from the heights they were occupying in Kargil and give diplomacy a chance so that it could carry forward and complete the mission for which they had made so many sacrifices. I am grateful to the Mujahideen for having accepted our appeal. The outcome of every war leads to negotiated decisions which is the route we have also taken and I am sure that truth and justice will prevail in the end.

My dear Countrymen, true leadership is that which is riot interested in merely staying in office but in ensuring national security and public welfare. True leadership does not hesitate from sacrificing office or popularity if it is the security of the country and the people which is at stake. You will recall that in my first term as Prime Minister, the shadows of the Gulf war lay across this region. Kuwait had been occupied and the Allied forces were preparing to invade Iraq, at that time, many of our political parties, leaders amid even individuals in the service of the state tried to gain cheap popularity by inciting the people and playing with their sentiments. They kept the facts hidden front the masses in order to advance their own political careers. They led processions and fell no hesitation in jeopardizing the national interest as long as it won them popular following. You know well that had I allowed myself to be swept away by emotion and begun to raise sentimental slogans to please die masses, the consequences for my country and its people would have been grave. Those who conspire to attain power and advance their political careers are the very same people who end up pushing their country and their nation over the precipice. Whatever decision I took, I took to protect the interest of my country and my people. During the Gulf war I chose what in my view was the right course. I was riot swayed by considerations of personal power.

I did not follow the popular upsurge, if you recall. The results are there for everyone to see. If you have faith, you should only take those decisions which in your judgment are correct.

Dear Countrymen, I want to declare that the Kashmiri urge for freedom cannot be stifled by force. The Kashmiri people's struggle will continue. Freedom is their fundamental right and unless they Win that right, the people of Pakistan will continue to be with them, shoulder to shoulder. We will never abandon the Kashmiris.

My dear Countrymen, it has always been my dream to take Pakistan to the highest pinnacle of glory and in the pursuit of this dream, I have not been held back by fear or self-interest. You will recall that when India was firing off its missiles and the world instead of restraining that country was putting every possible pressure on Pakistan not to join the race, I resisted and went on to test the Ghauri and Shaheen missiles. There were many other pressures on us subsequently but I refused to buckle under them. Can anyone forget the crass Indian bid to establish its overlordship over this region after detonating nuclear bombs on 11 and 13 May 1998! Highly provocative statements were issued and it was said that Pakistan would have to come to terms with its reduced status. While we were being subjected to intense external pressure and threats, inside the country there were some to whom the lure of dollars was more attractive than the attainment of self-sufficiency and freedom. They were terrified of sanctions but it was I who stood firm and went ahead to conduct our nuclear tests. Thereafter, sanctions were indeed imposed on us but I stood my ground. Such hard decisions can only be taken by a person who has the supreme interest of his people and the fear of God at heart. You know that whatever Nawaz Sharif does, he does in order that you and your children live in peace and security, enjoy prosperity and walk with honour. For me my country always comes first. Pakistan and Nawaz Sharif are one. Pakistan is a part of my being and I am part of Pakistan. Each breath that I take is like a prayer for the security of Pakistan and the progress and well-being of my people.

My dear Countrymen, I want to thank you today because at this most delicate point in our history, you have not fallen into the emotional traps laid out for you and you have not allowed yourselves to be fooled by any political party. You have refused to hit the streets for the sake of the those who have chosen the path of negativism. You have demonstrated that the Pakistani nation is not willing to act frivolously when the questions involved carry grave national consequences. You have shown that you have complete trust in your elected leadership.

Let me assure you that given the help of God, I will never betray your trust.

My dear Countrymen, during the Lahore summit, I told Indian Prime Minster Vajpayee that we had gained nothing by fighting wars. Every war had led to the next one. I say again today that in the last fifty years, Pakistan and India, despite having fought several wars, despite having put their armies in direct face-to-face confrontation with each another, despite spending billions of rupees on armaments, and despite having trained their nuclear weapons at each another, have failed to resolve any of their disputes through conflict. Is that not a pity!

Because of the failure to resolve the Kashmir dispute, we have not been able to give the people of the Subcontinent a single day of peace. Can we not solve this problem and thereby guarantee a peaceful, tranquil and secure future to the one billion people who live here! How many more Kashmiris have to die at the hands of India before this reality dawns upon that country! How many more Kashmiri homes have to be laid waste! How many more Indian soldiers have to die pursuing an unjust war! How many more Kashmiri youth have to perish! How many more Kashmiri women still need to be outraged! How any more mothers in Indian cities are fated to shed tears over the dead bodies of their sons!

My dear Countrymen, world opinion will have to decide how long this drama of blood and fire is to be played in Kashmir. Why the delay in resolving the Kashmir problem! The United Nations conferred the right of self-determination on the Kashmiris over fifty years ago. India promised to implement those resolutions. It was not Pakistan which passed those resolutions : it was the United Nations. India neither implements those resolutions nor does it enter into any meaningful or result-oriented discussions with Pakistan. Is this how problems are resolved in this world! Where lies the gain in sticking to a single recalcitrant position! How can anything be resolved amicably if such diehard attitudes are allowed to prevail! Because of its intransigence, India has suffered. It has been left behind, and so have we. It is in the interest of both India and Pakistan to give up the old, obstinate, unbending attitudes of the past and make an honest attempt to settle the Kashmir dispute amicably through negotiations.

How long can we snatch food from the mouths of our people to buy guns?

How long will we go on jeopardizing the future of our children by buying the shells that go into these guns?

How long will we allow our resources to go up in gun smoke and add to the number of our unemployed?

India should learn a lesson from history. No liberation movement has ever been crushed through the use of military force. Bullets do indeed draw blood but in the process become blood drenched themselves. How long will India continue to tell the world that it is Pakistan which is interfering in Kashmir! No outside power can sustain a movement for eleven years through the use of infiltrators.

My dear Countrymen, you will remember that during my election campaign I had promised to end all disputes with India and establish good relations with that country. I want that the mandate which the people have given me should be used for their welfare. I want to settle the long-standing question of Kashmir so that I can forever secure the future of my country and its people. The people of India also need peace. India too has to move ahead. I ask Prime Minister Vajpayee to step forward and talk to us. Let's save our people from the scourge of war and give them peace and security. Let us sit across the negotiating table and begin our search for a better future for our people. A great deal of time has passed. Let no more time pass. In the end, I pray for the solidarity, strength and well-being of Pakistan and its people. May God be our strength and our support.

Long live Pakistan.

43

Indian Prime Minister Atal Behari Vajpayee's Address to the Nation during the Kargil Crisis

7 June 1999

My dear Countrymen,

You are well aware of the situation which has developed in Kargil :

It is a serious situation;

It is a situation fraught with danger;

It is a situation that has arisen from one simple fact : the decision of Pakistan to cross the Line of Control, to send its men and materials to occupy our territory.

No government can tolerate such an incursion — our Government certainly will not.

Countries the world over have recognised that we have the full right to evict these intruders from our soil. But for me, and for my Government this is not just a matter of our having a right. It is our duty to rid our sacred Motherland of every single intruder.

For this reason, as you have seen, our armed forces have launched a major operation to drive them back. No one should entertain the slightest doubt : they shall not stop till they have completely attained their objective. No one shall stop them till they have done so.

You know well that our relations with Pakistan, as with all our neighbours, were improving rapidly :

The Prime Ministers and other ministers of the two countries were in regular contact;

Dialogue among officials of the two countries was proceeding constructively, and satisfactorily;

Areas of co-operation had been identified, and at various levels, plans were afoot to work together on each of them;

Most important, people-to-people contacts and exchanges had opened up as never before in fifty years — there had been an outpouring of goodwill on both sides.

In the midst of all this, regulars of the Pakistan Army and infiltrators have been sent across. Fomenting insurgency here was heinous enough. But this time Army regulars have been sent. They have been sent to occupy our territory. And, having occupied it, to choke off our links with other parts of our country — in particular with Siachin and Ladakh.

This step has been taken after a great deal of preparation. It was a preplanned operation.

It is a repudiation of the letter and spirit of the Lahore Declaration. It is a violation not just of one article of the **Simla Agreement**, but an eightfold violation of that solemn Agreement.

The Simla Agreement binds each side to respect the territorial integrity, sovereignty, and independence of the other. The Clauses repeatedly enjoin that neither side shall use the threat of force or force to affect the territorial integrity of the other.

The Agreement deals specifically with the Line of Control. It lays down that the Line of Control resulting from the cease-fire of December 17, 1971 shall be respected by both sides. Furthermore, that "Neither side shall seek to alter it unilaterally". The Agreement goes a step ahead and specifies, "Both sides further undertake to refrain from the threat or the use of force in violation of this Line."

And yet that is exactly what Pakistan has done : it has used force in an attempt to unilaterally alter the Line of Control.

This having been done, it has now been said that the Line of Control is vague. This is nothing but an ex-post artifice to justify aggression. After Agreement in Simla in 1972, the military authorities of the two sides went over the Line of Control — section by microscopic section. The salients, the locations, the co-ordinates were marked out on detailed maps. The exercise was done thoroughly : five months were expended on delineating the maps so that no ambiguity may remain.

Not just that, at no time in the last 27 years has the Line of Control been called in question — not once, not on a single occasion.

The new assertion, therefore, is just a contrivance to explain away the aggression. It will fool no one. And I do want to make it plain : if the stratagem now is that, the intrusion should be used to alter the Line of Control through talks, the proposed talks will end before they have begun.

India is always open to talks. But the talks must have a definite, specific purpose. In the present instance, the subject is one, and one alone : the intrusion, and how Pakistan proposes to undo it. To discuss this, our doors are always open, and all dates are convenient to us. India wants peace. We are at peace with all other neighbours of ours. We were taking major steps with Pakistan also — towards undoing the fifty-year history of bitterness. Our people desire it. Our Government is committed to it. We have travelled quite some distance for it.

I remain confident that the people of Pakistan too yearn for peace and harmony. They know the possible costs of hostilities — of how these will push economic gains even further beyond the horizon. They know that in today's world whosoever launches aggression of any kind will get isolated in the international community.

Moreover, both India and Pakistan are nuclear powers. Our responsibilities in this regard are all the greater.

Therefore, I once again urge the Government of Pakistan : undo the armed intrusion.

We must hope, my countrymen, that even now reason will prevail, that those within Pakistan who see the folly of aggression will have their way.

But till that happens, we have a job on our hands.

Our first thought, and our last thought must be for our jawans, for our airmen and our officers who are fighting back the intruders. I want each one of them to know : the entire country stands with you, every Indian is grateful to you. The whole operation has been thrust upon us. To ensure victory, you would not be wanting in your requirements.

Our jawans and officers are laying down their lives. Should we be continuing our petty squabbles at such a time? We should stand by them and avoid unnecessary debates.

Let us use this occasion to learn from our defence forces : let us translate into our own conduct some of the discipline for which they are renowned. The whole world is watching how our brave armed forces are defending the Motherland in inhospitable hilly terrain and at grave risks to their lives. In this hour of crisis, we must maintain an equanimity and act with confidence.

We should not be disheartened by some momentary mishap. We must realise the gravity of the situation and emulate the fortitude with which our fighting men take such events in their stride.

Have confidence in the ability of our armed forces.

The armed forces shall accomplish this task and ensure that no one dares to indulge in this kind of misadventure in future.

Jai Hind.

44

The Lahore Declaration (21 February 1999)

The following is the text of the Lahore Declaration :

The Prime Ministers of the Republic of India and the Islamic Republic of Pakistan :

Sharing a vision of peace and stability between their countries, and of progress and prosperity for their people;

Convinced that durable peace and development of harmonious relations and friendly co-operation will serve the vital interests of the people of the two countries, enabling them to devote their energies for a better future;

Recognising that the nuclear dimension of the security environment of the two countries adds to their responsibility for avoidance of conflict between the two countries;

Committed to the principles and purposes of the Charter of the United Nations, and the universally accepted principles of peaceful co-existence;

Reiterating the determination of both countries to implementing the Simla Agreement in letter and spirit;

Committed to the objective of universal nuclear disarmament and non-proliferation;

Convinced of the importance of mutually agreed confidence building measures for improving the security environment;

Recalling their agreement of 23rd September, 1998, that an environment of peace and security is in the supreme national interest of both sides and that the resolution of all outstanding issues, including Jammu and Kashmir, is essential for this purpose;

Have agreed that their respective Governments :

— shall intensify their efforts to resolve all issues, including the issue of Jammu and Kashmir.

— shall refrain from intervention and interference in each other's internal affairs.

— shall intensify their composite and integrated dialogue process for an early and positive outcome of the agreed bilateral agenda.

— shall take immediate steps for reducing the risk of accidental or unauthorised use of nuclear weapons and discuss concepts and doctrines with a view to elaborating measures for confidence building in the nuclear and conventional fields, aimed at prevention of conflict.

— reaffirm their commitment to the goals and objectives of SAARC and to concert their efforts towards the realisation of the SAARC vision for the year 2000 and beyond with a view to promoting the welfare of the people of South Asia and to improve their quality of life through accelerated economic growth, social progress and cultural development.

— reaffirm their condemnation of terrorism in all its forms and manifestations and their determination to combat this menace.

— shall promote and protect all human rights and fundamental freedoms.

(Sd/-)	(Sd/-)
ATAL BEHARI VAJPAYEE	MUHAMMAD NAWAZ SHARIF
Prime Minister of the Republic of India	Prime Minister of the Islamic Republic of Pakistan

Dated : 21-02-1999.

JOINT STATEMENT

The following is the text of the Joint Statement issued at the end of the Prime Minister, Mr. A. B. Vajpayee's visit to Lahore :

In response to an invitation by the Prime Minister of Pakistan, Mr. Muhammad Nawaz Sharif, the Prime Minister of India, Shri Atal Behari Vajpayee, visited Pakistan from 20-21 February, 1999, on the inaugural run of the Delhi-Lahore bus service.

2. The Prime Minister of Pakistan received the Indian Prime Minister at the Wagah border on 20th February 1999. A banquet in honour of the Indian Prime Minister and his delegation was hosted by the Prime Minister of Pakistan at Lahore Fort, on the same evening. Prime Minister, Atal Behari Vajpayee, visited Minar-e- Pakistan, Mausoleum of Allama Iqabal, Gurudawara Dera Sahib and Samadhi of Maharaja Ranjeet Singh. On 21st February, a civic reception was held in honour of the visiting Prime Minister at the Governor's House.

3. The two leaders held discussions on the entire range of bilateral relations, regional co-operation within SAARC, and issues of international concern. They decided that :

(a) The two Foreign Ministers will meet periodically to discuss all issues of mutual concern, including nuclear related issues.

(b) The two sides shall undertake consultations on WTO related issues with a view to co-ordinating their respective positions.

(c) The two sides shall determine areas of co-operation in Information Technology, in particular for tackling the problems of Y2K.

(d) The two sides will hold consultations with a view to further liberalising the visa and travel regime.

(e) The two sides shall appoint a two member committee at ministerial level to examine humanitarian issues relating to Civilian detainees and missing POWs.

4. They expressed satisfaction on the commencement of a

Bus Service between Lahore and New Delhi, the release of fishermen and civilian detainees and the renewal of contacts in the field of sports.

5. Pursuant to the directive given by the two Prime Ministers, the Foreign Secretaries of Pakistan and India signed a Memorandum of Understanding on 21st February 1999, identifying measures aimed at promoting an environment of peace and security between the two countries.

6. The two Prime Ministers signed the Lahore Declaration embodying their shared vision of peace and stability between their countries and of progress and prosperity for their people.

7. Prime Minister, Atal Behari Vajpayee extended an invitation to Prime Minister, Muhammad Nawaz Sharif, to visit India on mutually convenient dates.

8. Prime Minister, Atal Behari Vajpayee, thanked Prime Minister, Muhammad Nawaz Sharif, for the warm welcome and gracious hospitality extended to him and members of his delegation and for the excellent arrangements made for his visit.

Lahore,
February 21, 1999.

MEMORANDUM OF UNDERSTANDING

The following is the text of the Memorandum of Understanding signed by the Foreign Secretary, Mr. K. Raghunath and the Pakistan Foreign Secretary, Mr. Shamshad Ahmad, in Lahore on Sunday :

The Foreign Secretaries of India and Pakistan :

Reaffirming the continued commitment of their respective governments to the principles and purposes of the U.N. Charter;

Reiterating the determination of both countries to implementing the Shimla Agreement in letter and spirit;

Guided by the agreement between their Prime Ministers of 23rd September 1998 that an environment of peace and security is in the supreme national interest of both sides and that resolution of all outstanding issues, including Jammu and Kashmir, is essential for this purpose;

Pursuant to the directive given by their respective Prime Ministers in Lahore, to adopt measures for promoting a stable environment of peace and security between the two countries;

Have on this day agreed to the following :

1. The two sides shall engage in bilateral consultations on security concepts, and nuclear doctrines, with a view to developing measures for confidence building in the nuclear and conventional fields, aimed at avoidance of conflict.
2. The two sides undertake to provide each other with advance notification in respect of ballistic missile flight tests, and shall conclude a bilateral agreement in this regard.
3. The two sides are fully committed to undertaking national measures to reducing the risks of accidental or unauthorised use of nuclear weapons under their respective control. The two sides further undertake to notify each other immediately in the event of any accidental, unauthorised or unexplained incident that could create the risk of a fallout with adverse consequences for both sides, or an outbreak of a nuclear war between the two countries as well as to adopt measures aimed at diminishing the possibility of such actions, or such incidents being misinterpreted by the other. The two side shall identify/establish the appropriate communication mechanism for this purpose.
4. The two sides shall continue to abide by their respective unilateral moratorium on conducting further nuclear test explosions unless either side, in exercise of its national sovereignty decides that extraordinary events have jeopardised its supreme interests.

5. The two sides shall conclude an agreement on prevention of incidents at sea in order to ensure safety of navigation by naval vessels, and aircraft belonging to the two sides.
6. The two sides shall periodically review the implementation of existing Confidence Building Measures (CBMs) and where necessary, set up appropriate consultative mechanisms to monitor and ensure effective implementation of these CBMs.
7. The two sides shall undertake a review of the existing communication links (*e.g.*, between the respective Directors- General, Military Operations) with a view to upgrading and improving these links, and to provide for fail-safe and secure communications.
8. The two sides shall engage in bilateral consultations on security, disarmament and non-proliferation issues within the context of negotiations on these issues in multilateral fora.

Where required, the technical details of the above measures will be worked out by experts of the two sides in meetings to be held on mutually agreed dates, before mid-1999, with a view to reaching bilateral agreements.

Done at Lahore on 21st February 1999 in the presence of Prime Minister of India, Mr. Atal Behari Vajpayee and Prime Minister of Pakistan, Mr. Muhammad Nawaz Sharif.

(Sd/-)
K. RAGHUNATH
Foreign Secretary of the
Republic of India

(Sd/-)
SHAMSHAD AHMAD
Foreign Secretary of the
Islamic Republic of Pakistan

45

Joint Statements and Joint Press Statements

JOINT STATEMENT

The Foreign Minister of Pakistan Mr. Sartaj Aziz and the Minister of External Affairs of India, Shri Jaswant Singh met today on the sidelines of the 21st Session of the SAARC Council of Ministers at Nuwara Eliya, Sri Lanka.

They reiterated the historic significance of the Lahore Declaration which embodies the vision of the Prime Ministers of the two countries for ending the legacy of tensions and conflicts of the past fifty years and for ushering a new era of peace, security and prosperity. They discussed ways and means to build on the Lahore Declaration which commits the two countries to build trust and confidence, develop mutually beneficial co-operation and intensify their efforts to resolve all outstanding issues including Jammu and Kashmir.

The two Foreign Ministers agreed on the urgency of taking concrete measures for implementation of the Lahore Declaration, the Memorandum of Understanding and the Joint Statement issued during the Lahore Summit. In this context, the Ministers agreed that the composite and integrated dialogue process must be intensified.

The Ministers agreed to the following :

(i) The meetings of Experts for implementation of the Memorandum of Understanding will be held over the next two months.

(ii) The next round of the composite and integrated dialogue process in accordance with the agreed agenda will commence in May 1999 in New Delhi and Islamabad and will be held over a period of six weeks.

(iii) They will meet shortly after the conclusion of the May-June round of the composite and integrated dialogue process.

(iv) The Committee on humanitarian issues composed of Minister of State for Foreign Affairs of Pakistan and the Ministers of State of External Affairs of India set up the Prime Ministers at the Lahore Summit will meet in April 1999 to formalize the agreement on the issue of release of civilian prisoners as well as to discuss other humanitarian issues.

(v) That both sides have agreed to relax the visa regime for several categories of visitors. The specific visa relaxation measures shall be announced by the two Governments shortly.

(vi) Delegations of experts from India shall visit Pakistan during April 1999 for identifying areas of co-operation in information technology, Y2K and WTO-related issues.

Sri Lanka
March 19, 1999.

JOINT STATEMENT

The Prime Ministers of India and Pakistan held a bilateral meeting on the sidelines of UN General Assembly in New York on 23rd September, 1998.

Their discussions covered the whole range of bilateral relations. The two Prime Ministers also carried out a detailed review of new developments in the region during the past few months.

They reaffirmed their common belief that an environment of durable peace and security was in the supreme interest of both India and Pakistan, and of the region as a whole. They expressed their determination to renew and reinvigorate efforts to secure such an environment. They agreed that the peaceful settlement of all outstanding issues, including Jammu and Kashmir, was essential for this purpose.

The two leaders reiterated their commitment to create conditions which would enable both countries to fully devote their resources, both human and material, to improving the lives of their people, particularly the poorest among them.

The two Prime Ministers noted with satisfaction the agreement reached between the Foreign Secretaries on operationalizing the mechanism to address all items in the agreed agenda of 23rd June, 1997 in a purposeful and composite manner. They directed the Foreign Secretaries, accordingly, to resume the dialogue on the agreed dates.

New York
September 23, 1998.

JOINT STATEMENT

The Foreign Secretary of India, Shri K. Raghunath, and the Foreign Secretary of Pakistan, Mr. Shamshad Ahmad, met in New York on 23rd September 1998.

Pursuant to the agreement set out in para 4 of the Joint Statement issued at Islamabad on 23 June 1997, the Foreign Secretaries agreed as follows :

(i) The mechanism to address all the outstanding issues listed in para 4 (i) of the Joint Statement would now be made operational.

(ii) As stipulated in para 4 (ii) of the Joint Statement, all the issues shall be addressed substantively and specifically through the agreed mechanism in an integrated manner.

(iii) All outstanding issues shall be dealt with at the levels indicated below :

  (a) Peace and Security including CBMs At the level of Foreign Secretaries.

(b) Jammu and Kashmir Foreign Secretaries.

(c) Siachen Defence Secretaries.

(d) Wullar Barrage/Tulbul Navigation Secretaries, Water & Power Project.

(e) Sir Creek Additional Secretary (Defence)/Surveyors General.

(f) Terrorism and Drug Trafficking Home/Interior Secretaries.

(g) Economic and Commercial Cooperation Commerce Secretaries.

(h) Promotion of friendly exchanges Secretaries, Culture in various fields.

(iv) The detailed composition of the official teams is left to the discretion of each side.

The above mentioned subjects of this composite dialogue process will be discussed at the indicated levels in separate meetings. The dates of these meetings will be determined by mutual consent. At each round, the Foreign Secretaries will hold separate meetings on :

(a) Peace and Security including CBMs and

(b) Jammu and Kashmir and review the progress of the dialogue process.

The Foreign Secretaries will commence the substantive dialogue with separate meetings on :

(a) Peace and Security including CBMs and

(b) Jammu and Kashmir in Islamabad on 15-18 October, 1998. The remaining six subjects *i.e.*,

(c) Siachen,

(d) Wullar Barrage/Tulbul Navigation Project,

(e) Sir Creek,

(f) Terrorism and Drug Trafficking,

(g) Economic and Commercial Cooperation and

(h) Promotion of friendly exchanges in various fields, shall be taken up in substantive and separate meetings in New Delhi in the first half of November 1998.

The cycle of meetings of the Foreign Secretaries will be continued on this pattern on agreed dates.

New York
September 23, 1998

JOINT STATEMENT

Mr. Shamshad Ahmad, Foreign Secretary of Pakistan and Mr. K. Raghunath, Foreign Secretary of India, met in Islamabad on 15-18 October 1998. They held separate meetings on agenda item (a) Peace and Security, including Confidence-building Measures, and (b) Jammu and Kashmir, on the basis of the 23rd June 1997 Agreement. The talks were held in a cordial and frank atmosphere within the framework of the composite and integrated dialogue process.

The deliberations between the Foreign Secretaries were guided by the shared belief of their Prime Ministers as expressed in their joint Statement of 23 September 1998 that an environment of durable peace and security was in the supreme interest of both countries, and the region as a whole, and that the peaceful settlement of all outstanding issues, including Jammu and Kashmir, was essential for this purpose.

The Foreign Secretary of India called on the Prime Minister of Pakistan Mr. Nawaz Sharif, and conveyed to him a message of goodwill from Prime Minister A.B. Vajpayee. The Prime Minister of Pakistan warmly reciprocated the Indian Prime Minister's good wishes. The Indian Foreign Secretary also called on Foreign Minister Sartaj Aziz.

The meeting on 16th October, 1998 discussed issues of peace and security, including Confidence Building Measures. Both sides underscored their commitment to reduce the risk of a conflict by building mutual confidence in the nuclear and conventional fields.

The meeting on 17th October discussed Jammu and Kashmir. The two sides reiterated their respective positions.

The two Foreign Secretaries agreed that the next round of talks on the issues of Peace and Security and Confidence Building Measures and Jammu and Kashmir, respectively, and a review of the round would be held in the first half of February, 1999 in New Delhi.

Islamabad
October 18, 1998

JOINT PRESS STATEMENT

As part of the composite and integrated dialogue between India and Pakistan on the basis of the agreed agenda of 23rd June 1997, Wullar Barrage/Tulbul Navigation Project was discussed in New Delhi on 5.11.1998. The Indian delegation was led by Shri Z. Hasan Secretary to Government of India, Ministry of Water Resources and the Pakistan delegation was led by Syed Shahid Husain Secretary to Government of Pakistan, Ministry of Water and Power.

Syed Shahid Husain will call on Shri B.C. Mishra, Principal Secretary to the Prime Minister of India.

The discussions were held in a frank and constructive atmosphere. While reaffirming their continued commitment to the Indus Waters Treaty of 1960, both sides exchanged views and took note of the previous discussions on the subject from October 1987 to August 1992.

It was agreed that the discussions would continue at the next round of the dialogue process with a view to finding a solution to the issue consistent with the provisions of the Treaty.

New Delhi
November 5, 1998

JOINT PRESS STATEMENT

As part of the composite and integrated dialogue process between India and Pakistan on the basis of the agreed agenda of the Joint Statement of June 23, 1997, discussions were held on the Siachen issue in Delhi on November 6, 1998. The Indian delegation at these discussions was led by Defence Secretary, Shri Ajit Kumar and the Pakistani delegation by Defence Secretary Lt. Gen. (Retd.) Iftikhar Ali Khan.

The Pakistan Defence Secretary also called on Raksha Mantri (Defence Minister), Shri George Fernandes.

Discussions were held in a frank and cordial atmosphere. The two sides stated their respective positions on the issue.

It was agreed to continue discussions on the issue during the next round of the dialogue process.

New Delhi
November 6, 1998

JOINT PRESS STATEMENT

As part of the composite and integrated dialogue between India and Pakistan on the basis of the agreed agenda of 23 June 1997, Sir Creek was discussed in New Delhi on 9th November 1998.

The Indian delegation was led by Lt. Gen. A.K Ahuja, Surveyor General of India and the Pakistan delegation was led by Rear Admiral M. Jameel Akhtar, Additional Secretary, Ministry of Defence.

The discussions were held in a frank and cordial atmosphere. The two sides stated their respective positions.

It was agreed to continue discussions during the next round of the dialogue process.

New Delhi
November 9, 1998

JOINT PRESS STATEMENT

As part of the composite and integrated dialogue process between India and Pakistan on the basis of the agreed agenda of June 23, 1997, discussions were held on Economic and Commercial cooperation in Delhi on November 10, 1998. The Indian delegation at these discussions was led by Commerce Secretary, Shri P.P. Prabhu, and the Pakistan delegation by Commerce Secretary, Mr. Mohammad Sulaiman.

Mr. Mohammad Sulaiman will call on Commerce Minister, Shri R.K. Hegde at 1600 hrs. today

The discussions were held in a frank and cordial atmosphere.

They exchanged views on various aspects of Economic and Commercial Co-operation and decided to continue discussions at the next round of the dialogue process.

New Delhi
November 10, 1998

JOINT PRESS STATEMENT

As part of the composite and integrated dialogue between India and Pakistan on the basis of the agreed agenda of 23 June 1997, Terrorism and Drug Trafficking were discussed in New Delhi on 12 the November 1998.

The Indian delegation was led by Shri B.P. Singh, Home Secretary and the Pakistan delegation was led by Mr. Hafeezullah Ishaq, Secretary, Ministry of Interior.

The discussions were held in a frank and cordial atmosphere. The two sides stated their respective positions.

It was agreed to continue discussions during the next round of the dialogue process.

New Delhi
November 12, 1998

JOINT PRESS STATEMENT

As part of the composite and integrated dialogue between India and Pakistan on the basis of the agreed agenda of 23rd June 1997. Promotion of Friendly Exchanges in Various Fields was discussed in New Delhi on the 13th November 1998. The Indian delegation was led by Dr. R.V. Vaidyanatha Ayyar, Secretary, Department of Culture, and the Pakistan delegation was led by Syed Roshan Zamir, Secretary of Culture, Sports and Youth Affairs of the Government of Pakistan.

Syed Roshan Zamir will call on Dr. Murli Manohar Joshi, Minister for Human Resources Development.

The discussions were held in a frank, cordial and constructive atmosphere.

Both sides exchanged views on various aspects of Promotion of Friendly Exchanges between India and Pakistan and agreed to continue discussions at the next round of the dialogue process.

New Delhi
November 13, 1998

46

Composite Dialogue

Between March 1997 and September 1998, the Foreign Secretaries of India and Pakistan met on several occasions to work out the details for a new format to conduct India Pakistan bilateral talks.

An agreement on the new format was formally announced at New York on September 1998 following a meeting between the Indian and Pakistani Foreign Secretaries. Under the new format both sides agreed to a broad based approach that aimed at building trust and confidence, developing mutually beneficial cooperation and address outstanding issues between India and Pakistan through a Composite Dialogue of eight subjects, at levels specified in the Joint Statement. All subjects were to be given equal importance so as to move the India-Pakistan relations forward over a broad front. The new format was a significant departure from the earlier format under which India-Pakistan talks were conducted at the Foreign Secretary level without any fixed agenda.

Under the agreed format, discussions were to be conducted on 8 identified subjects in the following manner :

(a) Peace and Security including CBMs at the level of Foreign Secretaries.

(b) Jammu & Kashmir at the level of Foreign Secretaries.

(c) Siachen at the level of Defence Secretaries.

(d) Tulbul Navigation Project at the level of Secretaries, Water & Power.

(e) Sir Creek at the level of Additional Secretary (Defence)/ Surveyor General.

(f) Terrorism and Drug Trafficking at the level of Home/ Interior Secretaries.

(g) Economic and Commercial at the level of Cooperation Commerce Secretaries.

(h) Promotion of Friendly Exchange At the level of in various fields Secretaries Culture.

The Foreign Secretaries of India and Pakistan met in Islamabad on 15-18 October 1998 for separate discussions on Peace and Security including CBMs, and on Jammu & Kashmir. Discussions on the other 6 agenda items were held at New Delhi between 5-13 November the same year.

47

Home Secretary's Statement on India-Pakistan talks on the subject of Terrorism-Narcotics — 12 November 1998

As part of the composite dialogue process between India and Pakistan, which is aimed at building a relationship of trust and confidence, putting in place a structure for mutually beneficial co-operation in various fields, and addressing outstanding issues, India and Pakistan today held discussions on Terrorism & Drug-Trafficking.

2. During the talks, India pointed out that terrorism and drug-trafficking posed a direct challenge to democratic societies and political systems everywhere. In this connection, we drew Pakistan's attention to the incontrovertible and irrefutable fact that it had consistently used terrorism as an instrument of state policy against India. We pointed out that Pakistan's sponsorship and instigation of terrorism directed against India included recruiting, training, financing, arming, infiltrating and controlling terrorists, foreign mercenaries and assorted underworld criminal elements, with a view to using them in very way possible for destabilizing the Indian State. It was emphasized that such activities violated all established norms and canons of inter-state conduct, and were contrary to fundamental rights, civil liberties and freedom.

3. Pakistan's overt and covert involvement in terrorism directed against India is a matter of record. It is well documented and acknowledged by neutral international observers, including

the media, and corroborating evidence is found in the Pakistani media itself. During these talks, we drew Pakistan's attention to these facts, and also presented overwhelming evidence of its involvement, and that of its official agencies, in terrorism in the Indian states of Punjab and Jammu & Kashmir, as also elsewhere in India. In this connection, we also handed over to Pakistan a document containing material evidence of Pakistan's involvement in terrorism.

4. Pakistan Delegation tried to deny their involvement in states sponsorship of terrorism in India on the alibi that they are only giving moral support to the so-called freedom struggle in the State of Jammu and Kashmir. It was pointed out to Pakistani side that terrorism anywhere cannot and should not be justified by any civilised society on basis of such definitional quibbles. The pretense of Pakistan only providing moral support to terrorists in J&K was also exposed by the fact that as many as 243 Pakistani and 48 residents of Pakistan Occupied Kashmir belonging to various fundamentalist/terrorist organisations have been killed by Indian security forces in the last few years and as many as 91 Pakistani and 34 residents of Pakistan Occupied Kashmir are in Indian jails in connection with the terrorist crimes. Further, recoveries of over 47,000 sophisticated fire arms and over 30,000 kg. high explosives from Pakistan trained militants on the international border and elsewhere in other parts of the country also indicates Pakistan's involvement in sponsoring terrorist activities in India. Lionisation in Pakistan of mercenaries killed in Jammu & Kashmir by organizations like Lashkar-e-Taiba, Al Badr etc. is also proof of Pakistan's involvement.

5. It was made abundantly clear to the Pakistan side that Jammu & Kashmir is an integral part of India and not a disputed territory as claimed by Pakistan. Successive democratic elections in the State of J&K to ascertain the popular will as well as to install democratically elected Governments bear testimony to this fact. Pakistan's suggestion for involvement of United Nations Military Observers Group (UNMOGIP) in India and Pakistan or some other international observers along the border in J&K to

verify India's allegations regarding Pakistan's involvement in terrorism in India was firmly rejected. India is firmly opposed to any third party involvement in such matters and the Shimla agreement clearly provides that all differences between the two countries should be resolved bilaterally. Pakistan's allegation that though the roots of sectarian violence lay elsewhere but that India was taking advantage of the same was categorically rejected. Even the people and media in Pakistan attribute the growth of sectarian strife in Pakistan to Pakistan's own patronage to nurseries of terrorism like Markaz-Dawa-wal-Irshad (MDI), Hizbul Mujahideen and Harqat-ul-Mujahideen etc. who have become breeding grounds for home grown militias that have turned Pakistan cities into battle fields.

6. We also underlined the fact that the menace of terrorism had assumed serious proportions through its nexus with narco-terrorism and drug trafficking. Pakistan today is a major source of supply and a transit route for illicit drugs including heroin. There was agreement on both sides to further strengthen existing bilateral cooperation between the Narcotic Control Bureau of India and Anti-Narcotics Force of Pakistan for combating drug trafficking.

7. Both sides also agreed to set up a mechanism for regular meetings and exchange of operational information between the Central Bureau of Investigation of India and Federal Investigation agency of Pakistan for expeditions assistance to each other for combating various types of crimes including counterfeiting of currency, cyber crimes etc.

8. We urged Pakistan to stop its relentless but futile pursuit of destabilising India through state-sponsored terrorism. We believe that for creating a right atmosphere for bilateral relations, and as a responsible country, it is incumbent upon Pakistan to cease these activities which are not in the interests of either country. Accordingly, we proposed the following steps to be taken by Pakistan.

(i) Abandon the policy of state sponsorship of terrorism against India and dismantle totally the infrastructure existing in Pakistan for indoctrinating, recruiting, training, arming financing and infiltrating militants for the purpose of terrorist violence in India.

(ii) Close down more than 30 training camps for terrorists functioning in PoK/Pakistan.

(iii) Hand over immediately to India terrorists and underworld operators of Indian origin currently sheltered in Pakistan and against whom international warrants of arrest have been issued by Interpol.

(iv) To deny use of their territory of other facilities to fundamentalist and militant organizations who have been propagating the cult of religious violence, training militants and raising funds for 'Jehad'.

9. Our discussions were held in a frank and cordial manner. We urged Pakistan to abandon the policy of sponsoring terrorism against India. We pointed out that a stable structure of cooperation between the law enforcing and security agencies of both countries for expeditious assistance to each other in combating terrorism, organized crime and drug trafficking would be useful. We have also made it clear to Pakistan that its proxy war will not succeed under any circumstances, and that it would be best to renounce this path and, instead, seek mutually beneficial cooperation in the areas of combating terrorism and its associated evils which pose a threat to both our societies.

48

Declaration on Jammu and Kashmir adopted at the OIC Co-ordination meeting of Ministers of Foreign Affairs held at the United Nations in New York on 2 October 1997

Recalling all OIC resolutions as well as Security Council Resolutions pertaining to Jammu and Kashmir;

Seriously concerned over the intensification of repression and continued violations of the human rights of Kashmiri people including the denial of their inalienable right to self-determination;

Noting the Memorandum submitted by the True Representatives of the Kashmiri people;

1. Reaffirms all OIC Summit and Ministerial Resolutions on Jammu and Kashmir dispute.

2. Calls for a peaceful settlement of the Jammu & Kashmir issue in accordance with relevant UN resolutions.

3. Urges the international community to take effective steps for safeguarding the human rights of the Kashmiris including their right to self-determination.

4. Supports the ongoing efforts of the Government of Pakistan to seek a peaceful solution to the Kashmir issue through all possible means including substantive bilateral talks with India.

49

Memorandum presented by the Special Committee of the National Assembly of Pakistan on Kashmir on 15 August 1997 to the Secretary-General of the United Nations

The principles embodied in the UN Security Council resolutions 47 (1948) of 21 April 1948, 51 (1948) of 3 June 1948, 80 (1950) of 14 March, 1950 and 91 (1951) of 30 March 1951, and the United Nations Commission for India and Pakistan resolutions of 13 August 1948 and 5 January 1949 expressly state that the final disposition of the State of Jammu and Kashmir will be made in accordance with the will of the people expressed through the democratic method of a free and impartial plebiscite conducted under the auspices of the United Nations.

The Prime Minister of India, Jawaharlal Nehru, reiterated before the Indian Parliament on 26 June 1952, "if after a proper plebiscite, the people of Kashmir said, We do not want to be with India, we are committed to accept that. We will accept it, though it might pain us. We will not send in any army against them. We will accept that, however hurt we might feel about it."

The Special Committee of the National Assembly of Pakistan on Kashmir recall that tragically despite the passage of over four decades, the oppressed people of Indian Held Kashmir (IHK) continue to struggle for their very basic and fundamental right *i.e.*, the right to self-determination. Instead of fulfilling its promises to the people of Kashmir and its obligations to the international community, India has reacted with violence to the legitimate demands of the Kashmiri people.

Over the past 8 years, 60,000 innocent Kashmiri men, women and children have perished at the hands of the 600,000 strong Indian security forces present in Kashmir. A reign of terror has been let loose, characterized by extra-judicial executions, indiscriminate killings, random and mass arrests for political reasons, forced relocation of population, gang rapes of women and systematic efforts to obliterate the ethnic, social and cultural identity of the Kashmiri people. Kashmir is in flames. A threat to regional and global peace looms large on the horizon.

The denial by India of the inalienable right of self-determination to the people of Kashmir cannot be permitted and the atrocities being perpetrated on them by the Indian security forces cannot be condoned. It is for all civilized and responsible member states of the international community of nations to send a loud and clear message to India condemnation of the grave human rights violations and the necessity of upholding the sanctity of UN resolutions.

To ensure peace and stability in South Asia in particular and the world in general, it is pertinent to stand by the Kashmiris in their just cause — their demand for the right of self-determination pledged to them by the international community and by India and Pakistan in the form of UN resolutions, and to support Pakistan in its moral and legal stand based on its commitment to peaceful settlement of the Kashmir dispute in accordance with UN resolutions.

Let the word go forth from the United Nations that :

(i) Injustice anywhere is a threat to justice everywhere.

(ii) Massive violations of the human rights of 'the Kashmiris including their right of self-determination in accordance with UN resolutions is flagrant transgression of Charter principles and civilized norms.

(iii) Indian repression of the Kashmiris must be stopped.

The Chairman and the Members of the Kashmir Committee urge the United Nations :

(a) To hold a plebiscite in Jammu and Kashmir, without further delay, in accordance with the Security Council resolutions.

(b) To demand that India withdraws its army of occupation from Jammu and Kashmir to end its repression of the Kashmiri people.

(c) To urge India to continue the dialogue with Pakistan with Sincerity and seriousness and to peacefully resolve all outstanding issues between the two countries including the Jammu and Kashmir dispute.

To enhance the number and role of the United Nations Military Observer Group in India and Pakistan (UNMOGIP) for facilitating its crucial functions of guaranteeing the inviolability of the line of Control in Kashmir. Since the establishment of UNMOGIP in 1949 it has played, in your own words "a very useful role" and therefore needs the whole hearted support of the international community.

(d) To demand that international human rights organizations are given full access to Jammu and Kashmir.

The appointment of a Special Rapporteur on Jammu and Kashmir by the Human Rights Commission.

We urge the Secretary General actively encourage, facilitate and support efforts leading to a peaceful resolution of the Jammu and Kashmir issue in accordance with the relevant Security Council resolutions as well as to exercise the mandate entrusted to him by Charter of the United Nations and under relevant international instruments to safeguard the fundamental rights and freedoms of the oppressed Kashmiri people.

Ch. Muhammad Sarwar Khan, MNA,
Chairman,
Pakistan's National Assembly Special Committee on Kashmir.

Islamabad, 15 August 1997

50

OIC Declaration on Kashmir : Special Declaration of the Extraordinary Session of the Islamic Summit of the Organization of the Islamic Conference on Jammu and Kashmir held in Islamabad, Islamic Republic of Pakistan, 14 Dhul Qi'dah 1417h (23 March 1997)

Bismillah Ar Rahman Ar Rahim We, the Sovereigns, Heads of States and Governments of the Member States of the Organization of the Islamic Conference, gathered in Islamabad, Islamic Republic of Pakistan for the Extraordinary Session of the Islamic Summit Conference on 14 Dhul Qi'dah 1417H (23 March, 1997),

Deeply concerned over the situation in Jammu and Kashmir, especially the suffering of the Kashmiri people and the consequent tensions in the region.

Reaffirming all OIC Summit and Ministerial resolutions on the Jammu and Kashmir dispute.

Declare :

1. Our commitment to promote a just and peaceful solution to the Jammu and Kashmir dispute in accordance with the United Nations resolutions;
2. Our support to the fundamental human rights of the Kashmiri people including their right of self-determination;

3. Our condemnation of the oppression and massive violations of the human rights of the Kashmiri people;
4. Our support for the efforts of the government of Pakistan to resolve through a substantive and meaningful dialogue the Jammu and Kashmir dispute which is the basic cause of the tensions between India and Pakistan.

51

An Act further to amend the Jammu and Kashmir Constitution Act, 1996. Act No. XVII of 2008

Whereas it is expedient further to amend the Jammu and Kashmir Constitution Act, 1996, with a view to bring it in accord with the spirit of Proclamations dated 5th March 1948, 20th June 1949 and 20th April 1951 and the changes brought about in the actual governance of the State, in the manner hereinafter appearing :

Now, therefore, in exercise of the powers reserved under Section 5 of the J&K Constitution Act, 1996, read with the Proclamation issued by His Highness and published in the Extraordinary issue of the Government Gazette, dated 7th Har 2006, Yuvaraj Shree Karan Singh ji Bahadur is pleased to enact as follows :

Short title and Commencement .... (1) This act may be called the Jammu and Kashmir Constitution (Amendment) Act, 2008. (2) It shall come into force at once,

Amendment of section 4, Act XIV of 1996. 2 : In Section 4 of the Jammu and Kashmir Constitution Act 1996 (hereinafter referred to as the 'said act') for the words "except in so far as may be otherwise provided by or under this Act, or as may be otherwise directed by His Highness", the words "on the advice of the Council except in so far as may be otherwise provided by or under this Act and except in regard to those matters enumerated in List I in the Seventh Schedule to the Constitution of India with respect to which the Parliament of India has power to make law for the State" shall be substituted.

Omission of section 5, Act XIV of 1996. 3 : Section 5 of the said Act shall be omitted.

Amendment of section 6, Act XIV of 1996.4 : In section 6 of the said Act for the words and figures "Subject always to the provision of sections 4 and 5 subject also to such rules of business and allocation of portfolios and such other directions as to consultations with or reports to and confirmation by His Highness on special matters as His Highness may give from time to time by general or special orders in that behalf", the words "Subject to the Provisions of this Act" shall be substituted.

Substitution of section 7, Act XIV of 1996. 5 : For section 7 of the said Act, the following section shall be substituted, namely :

"Constitution of the Council-7. The Council shall consist the Prime Minister appointed by His Highness and such other Ministers of the State as His Highness may appoint on the advice of the Prime Minister. The Prime Minister and other Ministers shall be collectively responsible to the Legislative Assembly of the State. The Prime Minister shall be the President of the Council."

Amendment of section 9, Act XIV of 1996.6 : In section 9 of the said Act, for the words "The Prime Minister may with the previous sanction of His Highness", the words "The Council may" shall be substituted.

Insertion of new sections 9-A and 9-B in Act XIV of 1996.7 : After section 9 of the said Act, the following sections shall be inserted namely :

Appointment of Deputy Ministers — 9-A :

1. His Highness may on the advice of the Prime Minister appoint Deputy Ministers to work in such Ministeries as the Council may consider necessary.
2. The Deputy Ministers shall be selected from amongst the members of the Legislative Assembly.

3. The Deputy Ministers before entering on the duties of the office shall take an oath of office before the Prime Minister in the form set out in Schedule I.

Salaries of Ministers and Deputy Ministers — 9-B :

1. The salaries and allowances of Ministers shall be such as the Legislative Assembly may from time to time by Act determine and until the Legislative Assembly so determines, Ministers shall draw such salaries and allowances as they were drawing immediately before the commencement of the Legislative Assembly.
2. The salaries and allowance of Deputy Ministers shall be such as may be determined by the Legislative Assembly from time to time and until the Legislative Assembly so determines, the salaries and allowances of Deputy Ministers shall be as set out in Schedule II.
3. Amendment of section 10, Act XIV of 1996.8 : After subsection (3) of section 10 of the said Act the following sub-section shall be added namely :
4. The Council may make rules not inconsistent with this Act is regard to the duties of the Advocate General.

Omission of section 12, Act XIV of 1996.9 : Section 12 of the said Act shall be omitted.

Substitution of words "Legislative Assembly" for the words "Praja Sabha" in part III, Act XIV of 1996. 10. In Part III of the said Act, for the words "Praja Sabha" wherever they occur the words "Legislative Assembly" shall be substituted.

Substitution of section 13, Act XIV of 1996.11 : For section 13 of the said Act, the following section shall be substituted namely :

"Legislature : 13

1. The Legislature of the State shall consist of His Highness and a House to be known as the Legislative Assembly.
2. Notwithstanding anything contained in this Act, the powers of the Legislative Assembly under this Act shall, until other provision is made by or in accordance with

a law made by the Constituent Assembly set up under the Proclamation dated 20th April 1951, be exercisable by the said Constituent Assembly and references in this Act to the Legislative Assembly shall be construed accordingly.

3. The Legislative Assembly may make rules and standing orders, subject to the provisions of; this Act for regulating their procedure and conduct of their business.

4. Until rules are made under sub-section (3), the rules of Procedure and standing orders in force in relation to the Praja Sabha shall apply to the Legislative Assembly, subject to such modifications and adaptations as may be made therein by the Speaker of the Legislative Assembly."

Omission of section 14, Act XIV of 1996. 12 : Section 14 of the said Act shall be omitted.

Substitution of section 15, Act XIV of 1996. 13 : For section 15 of the said Act, the following section shall be substituted, namely :

"Summoning of the Legislative Assembly : 15

1. The Legislative Assembly shall be summoned to meet at least twice in a year and more than six months shall not intervene between its last sitting in one session and the date appointed for its first sitting in the next session.

2. Subject to the Provisions of this section, the Speaker of the Legislative Assembly may from time to time :

   (a) summon the Legislative Assembly to meet at such time and place as he thinks fit;

   (b) prorogue the Legislative Assembly."

Amendment of section 16, Act XIV of 1996. 14 : In section 16 of the said Act.

(i) In clause (b) the words "or any other Minister" shall be omitted, and

(ii) In clause (c) for the words "the President" the word, "the Speaker" shall be substituted.

Amendment of section 17, Act XIV of 1996. 15 : In section 17 of the said Act, for the words "President" the words "the Speaker" shall be substituted.

Substitution of section 19, Act XIV of 1996. 16 : For section 19 of the said Act, the following section shall be substituted, namely :

"Speaker and Deputy Speaker : 19.

(1) The Legislative Assembly may choose two members of the Assembly to be respectively Speaker and Deputy Speaker thereof and so often as the office of the Speaker or Deputy Speaker becomes vacant, the Assembly may choose another member to be the Speaker or the Deputy Speaker, as the case may be.

Until the Legislative Assembly elects a Speaker and Deputy Speaker, as provided in sub-section(1), the President of the Constituent Assembly shall act as Speaker and Deputy Speaker of the Legislative Assembly."

Amendment of section 20, Act XIV of 1966.17 : In section 20 of the said Act :

(i) sub-section (1) shall be omitted;

(ii) sub-section A shall be renumbered as sub-section (i) and in the sub-section as so renumbered.

(a) for the words "Deputy President" the words "Deputy Speaker" and for the words "the President", wherever they occur, the words "the Speaker" shall be substituted, and

(b) the words "with the approval of the Council" shall be omitted; and

(iii) for sub-section (3) the following sub-section shall be substituted, namely :

"(2) During the temporary absence of the Speaker and the Deputy Speaker from a meeting of the :

Legislative Assembly such person shall act a Speaker as may be determined by the Rules of Procedure of the Legislative Assembly or if no such person is present such other person as may be determined by the Assembly".

Amendment of section 21, Act XIV of 1996. 19 : In section 2 of the said Act, for the words "Deputy President" the words "the Speaker or the Deputy Speaker" shall be substituted.

Substitution of section 22, Act XIV of 1996. 19 : For section 22 of the said Act, the following section shall be substituted, namely :

"Parliamentary Secretaries-22.

(1) The Council may appoint from among the members of the Legislative Assembly as many Parliamentary Secretaries for such period and on such term and conditions as the Council may think fit.

(2) The Council may make rules not inconsistent with the provisions of this Act in regard to the duties of Parliamentary Secretaries".

Substitution of section 23, Act, XIV of 1996. 20 : For section 23 of the said Act, the following section shall be substituted namely :

"Legislative power of the Legislative Assembly-23, Subject to the provisions of the Act the Legislative Assembly may make laws for the whole or any part of the State and for the State subjects, wherever they may be, except in regard to those matters enumerated in List I in the seventh Schedule to the Constitution of India with respect to which the Parliament of India has power to make laws for the State."

Omission of section 24, Act XIV of 1996. 21 : Section 24 of the said Act shall be omitted.

Amendment of section 25, Act XIV of 1996. 22 : In Section 25 of the said Act :

(i) in sub-section (l) for the word "President" the word "Speaker" shall be substituted, and

(ii) in sub-section (3) for the words "one fifth", wherever they occur, the words "one fourth" shall be substituted.

Omission of Section 26, 27, and 28, Act XIV of 1996. 23 : Sections 26, 27 and 28 of the said Act shall be omitted.

Substitution of section 30, Act, XIV of 1996. 24 : For Section 30 of the said Act, the following section shall be substituted, namely :

"Allowances and Salaries : Section 30. The Speaker, the Deputy Speaker and the members of the Legislative Assembly shall receive such salaries and allowances as may be determined by an act of the Legislative Assembly and until that Act is passed such salaries and allowances shall be as set out in Schedule III."

Amendment of section 31, Act XIV of 1996. 25 : In sub-section (3) of section 31 of the said Act, for the words "In English" the words "both in Urdu and English shall be substituted.

Amendment of section 32, Act XIV of 1966. 26 : in section 32 of the said Act, the proviso shall be omitted.

Substitution of section 38, Act XIV of 1996.28 : For section 38 of the said Act, the following section shall be substituted, namely :

"Expenditure charged on the revenues of the State — 43

The following expenditure shall be the expenditure charged on the revenues of the State :

(a) Allowances of His Highness and other expenditure relating to his office;

(b) Debt charges for which the State is liable including interest, sinking fund charges and Redemption charges and other expenditure relating to the raising of loans and service redemption of debt;

(c) Salaries, allowances and pensions payable to or in respect of the Judges of the High Court and the Members of His Highness Board of Judicial Advisers;

(d) Expenditure relating to Constituent Assembly and its staff;

(e) Any sums required to satisfy and judgement decree or award of any court or arbitral tribunal;

(f) Any other expenditure declared by this Act or any Act of the Legislative Assembly to be so charged."

Amendment of section 45, Act XIV of 1996.32 : In Section 45 of the said Act;

(i) at the end of sub-section (1) fullstop shall be deleted, and the following words shall be added, namely : "but nothing in this sub-section shall be construed as preventing the discussion in the Legislative Assembly of any of these estimates."

(ii) Provisions to sub-section (2) shall be omitted.

Substitution of section 46, Act XIV of 1996.33 : For section 46 of the said Act, the following section shall be substituted, namely :

"Supplementary Expenditure. — Section 46 : If in respect of any financial year a further expenditure from the revenues of the State becomes necessary over and above the expenditure authorised for that year the Council shall have the power to author) se that expenditure. A statement of the Legislative Assembly along with the financial statement for the following year and the provisions of the preceding sections shall have effect in relation to that statement of the expenditure as they have in relation to the annual financial statement."

Amendment of section 48, Act XIV of 1966. 34 : In sub-section (b) of section 48 of the said Act for the words "one or more Judges" the words "two or more other Judges" shall be substituted.

Amendment section 49, Act XIV of 1996.35 : In section 49 of the said Act, for the figures "55" the word "Sixty" shall be substituted and the first proviso shall be omitted.

Amendment of section 51, Act XIV of 1996. 36 : In section 51 of the said Act for the words "British India" wherever they occur, the word "India" shall be substituted.

Substitution of section 72. Act XIV of 1996. 37 : For section

72 of the said Act the following section shall be substituted, namely;

"Prerogative : Section — 72. Nothing in this Act shall derogate from the prerogative of His Highness to grant pardons reprieves, respites of remissions of punishment."

Amendment of section 75, Act XIV of 1996.38 : In section 75 of the said Act, the words "Subject to the provisions of Section 5" shall be omitted.

Omission of sections 77 and 78, Act XIV of 1996. 39 Sections 77 and 78 of the said Act shall be omitted.

52

Parliament Resolution on Jammu and Kashmir

22 February 1994

"This House

Notes with deep concern Pakistan's role in imparting training to the terrorists in camps located in Pakistan and Pakistan Occupied Kashmir, the supply of weapons and funds, assistance in infiltration of trained militants, including foreign mercenaries into Jammu and Kashmir with the avowed purpose of creating disorder, disharmony and subversion :

Reiterates that the militants trained in Pakistan are indulging in murder, loot and other heinous crimes against the people, taking them hostage and creating an atmosphere of terror;

Condemns strongly the continued support and encouragement Pakistan is extending to subversive and terrorist activities in the Indian state of Jammu & Kashmir;

Calls upon Pakistan to stop forthwith its support to terrorism, which is in violation of the Simla Agreement and the internationally accepted norms of inter-State conduct and is the root cause of tension between the two countries reiterates that the Indian political and democratic structures and the Constitution provide for firm guarantees for the promotion and protection of human rights of all its citizens;

Regard Pakistan's anti-India campaign of calumny and falsehood as unacceptable and deplorable.

Notes with deep concern the highly provocative statements emanating from Pakistan urges Pakistan to refrain from making statements which vitiate the atmosphere and incite public opinion;

Expresses regret and concern at the pitiable conditions and violations of human rights and denial of democratic freedoms of the people in those areas of the Indian State of Jammu and Kashmir, which are under the illegal occupation of Pakistan.

On behalf of the People of India,

Firmly declares that —

(a) The State of Jammu & Kashmir has been, is and shall be an integral part of India and any attempts to separate it from the rest of the country will be resisted by all necessary means;

(b) India has the will and capacity to firmly counter all designs against its unity, sovereignty and territorial integrity;

and demands that —

(c) Pakistan must vacate the areas of the Indian State of Jammu and Kashmir, which they have occupied through aggression; and resolves that —

(d) all attempts to interfere in the internal affairs of India will be met resolutely."

The Resolution was unanimously adopted.

Mr. Speaker : The Resolution is unanimously passed.

February 22, 1994

53

Letter written by a former Governor of Jammu and Kashmir, Mr. Jagmohan, to the Former Prime Minister and the President of Congress, Mr. Rajiv Gandhi, 21 April 1990

Dear Shri Rajiv Gandhi,

You have virtually forced me to write this open letter to you. For, all along, I have persistently tried to keep myself away from party politics and to use whatever little talent and energy I might have to do some creative and constructive work, as was done recently in regard to the management and improvement of Mata Vaishno Devi shrine complex and to help in bringing about a sort of cultural renaissance without which our fast decaying institutions cannot be nursed back to health. At the moment, the nobler purposes of these institutions, be they in the sphere of executive, legislature or judiciary etc. have been sapped and the soul of justice and truth sucked out of them by the politics of expediency.

You and your friends like Dr. Farooq Abdullah are, however, bent upon painting a false picture before the nation in regard to Kashmir. Your senior party men like Shiv Shankar and N.K.P. Salve have, apparently at your behest, been using the forum of the Parliament for building an atmosphere of prejudice against me. The former raked up a fourteen-year old incident of Turkman Gate and the latter a press interview an interview that I never gave to hurl a barrage of accusations of communalism against my person. Mani Shankar Iyer, too, has been dipping his poisonous darts in the columns of some magazines. I, however, chose to suffer in silence all the slings and arrows of this outrageous armoury of disinformations. Only rarely did I try to correct gross distortions by sending letters to the editors of newspapers and magazines. My intention was to remain content with a book, an academic and historic venture which, I believed, I owed to the nation and to history.

But the other day some friends showed to me press clippings of your comments in the election meetings in Rajasthan.

That, I thought, was the limit. I realised that, unless I checked your intentional distortions, you would spread false impression about me throughout the country during the course of your election campaign.

WARNING SIGNALS. Need I remind you that from the beginning of 1988, I had started sending "Warning Signals" to you about the gathering storm in Kashmir? But you and the power wielders around you had neither the time, nor the inclination, nor the vision, to see these signals. They were so clear, so pointed, that to ignore them was to commit sins of true historical proportions.

To recapitulate and to serve as illustrations, I would refer to a few of these signals. In August 1988, after analysing the current and undercurrents, I had summed up the position thus : "The drum-beater of parochialism and fundamentalism are working overtime. Subversion is on the increase. The shadows of events from across the border are lengthening. Lethal weapons have come in. More may be on the way". In April 1989, I had desperately pleaded for immediate action I said : "The situation is fast deteriorating. It has almost reached a point of no return. For the last five days, there have been large-scale violence, arson, firing, hartals, casualties and what not. Things have truly fallen apart." Talking of the Irish crisis, British Prime Minister Disraeli had said : "It is potatoes one day and Pope the next". Similar is the present position in Kashmir. Yesterday, it was Maqbool Bhat; today it is Satanic Verses; Tomorrow it will be repression day and the day after it will be something else. The Chief Minister stands isolated. He has already fallen-politically as well as administratively; perhaps, only constitutional rites remain to be performed. His clutches are too soiled and rickety to support him. Personal aberrations have also eroded his public standing. The situation calls for effective intervention. Today may be timely, tomorrow may be too late. Again, in May, I expressed my growing anxiety : "What is still more worrying is that every victory of subversionists is swelling their ranks, and the animosity is being diverted against the central authorities". But you chose not to do anything. Your inaction was mistifying. Equally mistifying was your reaction to my appointment for the second term. How could I suddenly become communal, anti-muslim and what not?

When I resigned in July 1989, there was no rancour. You wanted me to fight, as your party candidate, election for the South Delhi Lok Sabha seat. Since I had general revolusion for the type of politics which out country had, by and large, come to breed, I declined the offer. If you had any serious reservation about my accepting the offer of J&K Governorship for the second term, you could have adopted the straight forward course and apprised me of your views. I would have thought twice before going into a situation which had virtually reached a point of no return. There would have been no need for you to resort to false accusations.

May be you do not consider truth and consistency as virtues. May be you believe that the words inscribed on our national emblem — *Satyameva Jayate* — are mere words without meaning and significance for motivating the nation to proceed in the right direction and build a true and just India by true and just means. Perhaps power is all that matters to you — power by whichever means and at whatever cost.

REALITY. In regard to the conditions prevailing before and after my arrival on the scene, you and your collaborators have been perverting reality. The truth is that before the imposition of Governor's rule on January 19, 1990, there was a total mental surrender. Even prior to the day (December 8, 1989) of Dr. Rubaiye Sayeed's kidnapping, when the eagle of terrorism swooped the state with full fury, 1600 violent incidents, including

351 bomb blasts had taken place in eleven months. Then between January 1 and January 19, 1990, there were as many as 319 violent acts — 21 armed attacks, 114 bomb blasts, 112 arsons, and 72 incidents of mob violence.

You, perhaps, never cared to know that all the components of the power structure had been virtually taken over by the subversives. For example, when Shabir Ahmed Shah was arrested in September 1989, on the Intelligence Bureau's tip- off, Srinagar Deputy Commissioner flatly refused to sign the warrant of detention. Anantnag Deputy Commissioner adopted the same attitude. The Advocate-General did not appear before the Court to represent the state case. He tried to pass on the responsibility to the Additional Advocate General and the Government council. They, too, did not appear.

Do you not remember what happened on the day of Lok Sabha poll in November 22, 1989? In a translating gesture, TV sets were placed near some of the polling booths with placards reading "anyone who will cast his vote will get this". No one in the administration of Dr. Farooq Abdullah took any step to remove such symbols of defiance if authority.

Let me remind you that Sopore is the hometown of Gulam Rasool Kar, who was at that time a Cabinet Minister in the State Government. It is also the hometown of the Chairman of the Legislative Council, Habibullah, and also of the former National Conference MP and Cabinet Minister, Abdul Shah Vakil. Yet only five votes were cast in Sopore town. In Pattan, an area supposedly under the influence of Iftikar Hussain Ansari, the then Congress (I) Minister, not a single vote was cast. Such was the commitment and standing of your leaders and collaborators in the State.

And you still thought that subversion and terrorism could be fought with such political and administrative instruments.

Around that point of time, when the police set-up was getting rapidly demoralised, when intelligence was fast drying up, when infiltration in services was bringing stories of subversives plan like TOPAC, your protagonist, Dr. Farooq

Abdullah was either going abroad or releasing 70 hardcore and highly motivated terrorists who were trained in the handling of dangerous weapons, who had contacts at the highest level in Pakistan occupied Kashmir, who knew all the devious routes of going to and returning from Pakistan and whose detention had been approved by the three member advisory board presided over by the Chief Justice. Their simultaneous release enabled them to occupy key positions in the network of subversion and terrorism and to complete the chain which took them again to Pakistan to bring arms to indulge in killings and kidnappings and other acts of terrorism. For example, one of the released persons, Mohd. Daud Khan of Ganderbal, became the Deputy Commander-in-Chief of a terrorist outfit, Al-Bakar, and took a leading part in organising a force of 2,500 Kashmiri Youths. Who is to be blamed for all the heinous crimes subsequet}y committed by these released 70 terrorists? I would leave this question answered by the people to whom you are talking about the "Jagmohan Factor".

The truth, supported by preponderance of evidence, is that before January 19, 1990, the terrorist had become the real ruler. The ground had been yielded to him to such an extent that dominated the public mind. He could virtually swim like a fish in the sea. Would it matter if the sea was subsequently surrounded?

LABELLING ANTI-MUSLIM. In your attempt to hide all your sins of omission and commission in Kashmir and as a part of your small politics which can not go beyond dividing people and creating vote banks, you took special pains to demolish all regards and respects which the Kashmiri masses, including the Muslim youth, had developed for me during my first term from April 26, 1984, to July 12, 1989. Against all facts, unassailable evidence, and your own precious pronouncements, you started me labelling me as anti-Muslim.

May I, in this connection, also invite your attention to three of the important suggestions made in my book, *Rebuilding Shahjahanabad : The Walled City of Delhi*. One pertained to the creation of the green velvet between Jama Masjid and Red Fort; the second to the construction of a road linking Parliament House with the Jama Masjid complex, and the third to the setting up of a second Shahajhanabad in the Mata Sundari road-Minto road complex, reflecting the synthetic culture of the city, its traditional as well as its modern texture. Could such suggestions I ask you, come of an anti-Muslim mind?

FORUM OF PARLIAMENT. How you and your associates use the forum of Parliament undermine my standing amongst the Kashmiri Muslims, was evident from what N.K.P. Salve, MP did in the Rajya Sabha on May 25, 1990.

Referring to the so called interview to the *Bombay Weekly,* "The Current" — an interview which I never gave — Salve chose wholly unjustified expressions; "There was a patent and palpable attitude if very disconcerting communal bias and, therefore, he (Governor) was happy under the garb of eliminating the terrorist, the saboteurs and the culprits, in eliminating the whole community as it were; now the Governor has himself given profuse and unabashed vent to his malicious malignity, hate and extreme dislike, branding every member of a particular community as a militant".

I know Salve. I do not think, if left to himself, he would have done what he did. Clearly, he was goaded to say something which was against his training and background. But the elementary precaution which any jurist, at least a jurist of Salve's imminence, would have taken, was to first check up whether any such interview weekly had been given by me, and if so, whether the remarks attributed to me were actually made. The unseemly haste was itself revealing. The issue was raised on May 25, while the weekly was dated May 26-June 2, 1990. You yourself rushed a letter to the President on May 25, on the basis of the interview that in reality did not exist. You explained that V.P. Singh had appointed a person with "Rabid Communalist Opinion as Governor. You also got your letter widely published on May 25 itself."

Since your party men did not allow me to have my say in

the Rajya Sabha, even when an opportunity came my way to speak on the subject, I was left with no other option but to file a 20 Lakhs damage suit against *The Current Weekly* in the Delhi High Court. The case may take a long time and I may donate the damages, if and when awarded, to charity, but I intend sparing no effort to expose all those who have played dirty roles in the disinformation-drama.

ARTICLE-370. You created a scene on March 7, 1990, at the time of the visit of the All Party Committee to Srinagar, and made it a point to convey to the people in 1986 I wanted to have Article 370 abrogated. At that critical juncture, when I was fighting the forces of terrorism with my back to the wall beginning to turn the corner after frustrating the sinister designs of the subversives from January 26, 1990 onwards, you thought it appropriate to cause hostility against me by tearing the facts out of context. Whether this act of yours was responsible or irresponsible, I would leave to the nation to decide.

What I had really pointed out in August-September 1986 was : 'Article 370' is nothing but a breeding ground for the parasites at the heart of the paradise. It skins the poor. It deceives them with its mirage. It lines the pockets of the "power elites". It fans the ego of the new sultans, in essence, it creates a land without justice, a land full of crudities and contradictions. It props up politics of deception, duplicity and demagogy. It breeds the microbes of subversion. It keeps alive the unwholesome legacy of the two-nation theory. It sufficates the very idea of India and fogs the very vision of a great social and cultural crucible from Kashmir to Kanyakumari. It could be an epicentre of a violent earth-quake, the tremors of which would be felt all over the country with unforeseen consequences.

I had argued, 'The fundamental aspect which has been lost sight of in the controversy for deletion or retention of Article 370 is its misues. Over the years, it has become an instrument of exploitation in the hands of the ruling political elites and other vested interests in bureaucracy, business, judiciary and bar. Apart from the politicians, the richer classes have found it convenient to amass wealth and not allow healthy financial legislation to come to the State. The provisions of the Wealth Tax, the Urban Land Ceiling Act, the Gift Tax etc, and other beneficial laws of the Union have not been allowed to be operated in the State under the cover of Article 370. The common people are prevented from realising that Article 370 is actually keeping them impoverished and denying them justice and also their due share in the economic advancement.'

My stand was that the poor people of Kashmir had been exploited under the protective wall of Article 370 and that the correct position needed to be explained to them. I had made a number of suggestions in this regard and also in regard to the reform and reorganisation of the institutional framework. But all these were ignored. A great opportunity was missed.

Subsequent events have reinforced my views that Article 370 and its by product, the separate Constitution of Jammu and Kashmir must go, not only because it is legally and constitutionally feasible to do so, but also because larger and more basic considerations of our past history and contemporary life require it. The Article merely facilitates the growth and continuation of corrupt oligarchies. It puts false notions in the minds of the youth. It gives rise to regional tensions and conflicts and even the autonomy assumed to be available is not attainable in practice. The distinct personality and cultural identity of Kashmir can be safeguarded without this Article. It is socially regressive and causes situations in which women lose their right if they marry non-State subjects and persons staying for over 44 years in the State are denied elementary human and democratic rights. And, above all, it does not fit into the reality and requirement of India and its vast and varied span. What India needs today is not petty sovereignties that would sap its spirit and aspirations and turn it into small "banana-republics" in the hands of 'tin-pot dictators', but a new social, political and cultural crucible in which values of truth and rectitude, of fairness and justice, and of compassion and catholicity, are melted, purified and moulded into a vigorous and vibrant set-up which provides real freedom, real democracy and real resurgence to all.

I must also point out that when other States in the Union ask for greater autonomy, they do not mean separation of identities. They really want decentralisation and devolution of power, so that administrative and development work is done speedily and the quality of service to the people improves. In Kashmir, the demand for retaining Article 370 with all its 'pristine purity', that is, without the alleged dilution that has taken place since 1953, stems from different motivation. It emanates from a clever strategy to remain away from the mainstream, to set up a separate fiefdom, to fly a separate flag, to have a Prime Minister rather than a Chief Minister, and Sadr-i-Riyasat instead of a Governor, and to secure greater power and patronage, not for the good of the masses, not for serving the cause of peace and progress or for attaining unity amidst diversity, but for serving the interests of 'new elites', the 'new Sheikhs'.

All those aspiring to be the custodians of the vote-banks continue to say that Article 370 is a matter of faith. But they do not proceed further. They do not ask themselves : What does this faith mean? What is its rationale? Would not bringing the State within the full framework of Indian Constitution give brighter lustre and sharper teeth to this faith and make it more just and meaningful?

In a similar strain, expressions like 'historical necessity' and 'autonomy' are talked about. What do these mean in practice? Does historical necessity mean that you include, on paper, Kashmir in the Indian Union by one hand at a huge cost and give it back, in practice, by another hand on the golden platter? And what does autonomy or so called pre-1953 or pre-1947 position imply? Would it not amount to the Kashmiri leadership say in : 'you will send and I will spend; you will have no say even if I build a corrupt and callous oligarchy and cause a situation in which Damocles' sword of secession could be kept hanging on your head'?

KASHMIRI PANDITS. You and the like of you have made India

a country which has lost capacity to be true and just. Anyone trying to be fair is dubbed communal. The case of the Kashmiri Pandits bears eloquent testimony to this fact.

Whatever be the vicissitudes of the Kashmiri Pandits' history and whatever unkind quirks their fate might have brought to them in the past, these all pale into insigficance in companison to what is happening to them at present. The grim tragedy is compounded by the equally grim irony that one of the most intelligent subtle, versatile, and proud community of the country is being virtually reduced to extinction in free India. It is suffering not under the fanatic zeal of mediaeval Sultans like Sikander or under the tyrannical regime of Afghan Governors, but under the supposedly secular rule of leaders like you, V.P. Singh and others who unabashed search for personal and political power is symbolised by calculated disregard of the Kashmiri migrants' current miserable plight and the terrible future that stares in their eyes. And to fill their cup of pain and anguish, there are bodies like 'Committee for Initiative on Kashmir' which are over-anxious and over active to rub salt into their wounds, and to label anyone who wants to stand by them in their hour of distress as communal.

In a soft, superficial, permissive and, in many ways, cruel India which has the tragic distinction of creating over one lakh refugees from its own flesh and blood and then casting them aside like masterless cattle to fend for themselves on the busy and heartless avenues of soulless cities, chances for Kashmiri Pandits to survive as a distinct community are next to nothing. Split, scattered and deserted practically by all, they stand today all alone, looking hopelessly at a leaking, rudderless, boat at their feat and extremely rough and tumultuous sea to face before they can reach a safe shore across to plant their feet firmly on an assured future.

The deep crisis through which the Kashmiri migrants, or for that matter, the entire Kashmir, is passing is really the crisis of Indian values — the perversion, in practice, of its constitutional, political, social and moral norms. If I visited the camps of the refugees and tried to extend the firm hand of justice to a community in pain, if I instructed that, instead of cash doles, the migrant Government servants should be given leave salary, and if I conceded the demand of a widow of the person brutally killed by a terrorist, for allotment of a house on payment, I became communal, a known anti-Muslim, about whom concoted stories were planted in the press. If, on the other hand, someone falsely accused the Indian Army and the Governor's administration, if he assailed Jagmohan in particular, of giving inducements through provisions of plots and trucks, without giving particulars either of plots or of trucks, his accusations got published all over the press, his reports were flaunted in national and international forums and were copiously quoted in Parliament by the members of your party and he was labelled as secular and progressive and champion of human rights and what not. Hard Evidence about 'Jagmohan Factor'. I do not like to refer to anything that looks like indulging in self-praise. But not to let you get away with your calculated campaign of disinformation, about Jagmohan communal factor, I must invite attention to some hard evidence about what the people of the Valley actually thought about me before you and your proteges started the smear campaign on my appointment for the second term.

Your principal propritor of current politics of Kashmir, Dr. Farooq Abdullah, was not to be left behind in the drive launched to create an 'anti-Muslim' image of mine. In his interview published in the *Times of India* of August 30, 1990, he said, "A known anti-Muslim was appointed as Governor of a Muslim majority state". How untrue, how unfair, was the propaganda, should be obvious from the fact that on November 7, 1986, at the time of his swearing-in-ceremony, Dr. Farooq Abdullah, in a public speech for which the records exist, said : "Governor Sahib, we should need you very badly. It is, indeed, amazing that such remarkable work could be done by you in a short time through an imbecile and faction-ridden bureaucracy. If today three ballot boxes are kept — one for the National Conference, one for the Congress and one for you, your ballot box would be full while the other two ballot boxes would be empty".

The misfortune of our country is that we have leaders like Dr. Farooq Abdullah who have no regard for facts or truth and whose superficiality is matched only by their unprincipled politics.

Incidentally, did it not strike you that Dr. Farooq was virtually accusing your late mother of being anti-Muslim because she was the Prime Minister when, in April 1984, a 'known anti-Muslims' was appointed for the first term, as "Governor of a Muslim majority State"?

Apparently in consultation with you, Dr. Farooq Abdullah, on February 15, 1990, issued a written statement to the press in Urdu in which he *inter alia,* said, "The Governor, in the personification of 'Hallaqu' and 'Changez Khan', is bent upon converting the valley into a vast graveyard. On account of continuous curfew since January 20, it is difficult to say how many hundreds of people have become victim of the bullets of the army and paramilitary forces, and in this general slaughter how many hundreds of houses have been destroyed. At this moment, when Kashmiris are witnessing their beloved country being converted into a vast graveyard. I appeal to the national and international upholders of humanity to intervene in Kashmir and have an international inquiry made into the general slaughter of Kashmiris at the hands of army and paramilitary forces".

Here is your 'patriot' calling Kashmir "Aziz Wattan", suggesting a separate country. Here is your 'national leader' asking for an international inquiry into the general slaughter of the Kashmiris by the Indian Army and paramilitary forces. Here is your 'responsible friend' speaking about the continuous curfew for 25 days in the valley and his consequent inability to find out many 'hundreds of innocent and unarmed Kashmiris' had been massacred and how many hundreds of Kashmiri houses razed to the ground, although he knew perfectly well that there had been a number of days when there was no day-curfew, partially or wholly, and the authorities had brought out the list of casualties, about 40 upto February 16, and were daily asking the public to provide with the additional names, if they had any, so that correction in the official list could be made. Here is an erstwhile Chief Minister who did not care to explain how 'innocent and unarmed' people were ruthlessly shooting down IAF officers, BSF jawans, senior officers of the Television and Telecommunications Department and young men in the streets; and how, while inciting people through lengthy and fiery statements, he did not find a single word to condemn such brutal murders.

Is the nation not entitled to know why you have not disowned such unfortunate behaviour on the part of Dr. Farooq Abdullah? And how do you account for his recent statement as published in *The Times of India* of February 7, 1991 : 'I directed my partymen to lie low, go across the border, get training in arms handling; do anything but not get caught by Jagmohan'?

Stabbing me in the back at personal level, perhaps, did not matter. But by keeping the pot boiling, you your proteges prolonged the agony of Kashmir and caused many more deaths and much more destruction. The politics of unscrupulousness was brought to its lowest depth.

ROOTS. You once said, 'I do not read history; I make history'. Apparently, you do not know that those who happen to make history without reading it, usually make bad history. They cannot understand the undercurrents and the fundamental forces that really shape the course of events and determine the ultimate destiny of a nation.

In the absence of historical perspective, you and the like of you never perceived the roots and tendrils which gave rise to the current crop of separatism and subversion in Kashmir. Poisonous seeds were persistently planted in the Kashmir psyche. And these were liberally fertilised. Those of you whose obligation it was to stop these plantations and their fertilisation, were not aware of even the elementary lesson of history; to compromise with the evil was only to rear greater evil; to ignore the inconvenient reality was only to compound it; to bow before the bully was only to invite the butcher the next day.

I could cite scores of cases to support my contention. Here I would restrict myself to only two examples.

Softness and Surrender. On October 2 1988, Mahatma Gandhi's birthday his statue was to be installed in the new High Court complex at Srinagar. The function had been announced. The Chief Justice of India, R.S. Pathak, was to do the formal installation. But a few Muslim lawyers objected. They threatened to cause disturbance at the time of the function. The Chief Minister gave in, almost willingly, to the bullying tactics. The function was cancelled.

What are the implications of what happened? A secular Kashmir, part of a secular India, could not have, even in its highest seat of justice, a statue of the Father of the Nation, of a sage, who laid down his life for communal harmony. Who was the person spearheading the move against the installation? It was none other than Mohd. Shafi Bhat, an advocate of the J&K High Court and an active number of the National Conference, who was later on given party ticket for Srinagar Lok Sabha seat in the elections held in November 1989 and with whom you kept warm company during your visit to Srinagar on March 7, 1990, to create as many difficulties as possible for Governor's administration.

At that time there was National Conference (F) Congress (I) Ministry in office. Such was its lack of adherence to principles, such was the character of Congressmen who formed part of the Ministry and such was its disposition to cling to power that not even a little finger was raised when the function was cancelled.

The bully's appetite could not have been whetted better. Intimidation could not have secured better results. The troublemakers could not have perceived a more casual and non-committed adversary. Was it not natural for them to nurture higher ambitions and think that more spectacular results could be achieved by deploying a more aggressive and threatening strategy? Only a naive would believe that in the context of the

Kashmir situation, softness and surrender on basic principles would not act as an invitation to terrorism and militancy.

The Union Government enacted the Religious Institutions (Prevention of Misuse) Act, 1988. It was made applicable to all the States of the Union except J&K. Because of Article 370, concurrence of the State Government was needed for extension of this law to the State. But the same was not given. Why? Because J&K is different what an argument for having a law which aimed at eradication of misuse of religious premises for political purposes.

Nowhere was this law needed more than in the State of J&K. Nowhere were religious places misused more than here. Nowhere were seeds of fanaticism and fundamentalism sown every Friday more assiduoulsy than from the pulpits of the mosques here. Nowhere was it preached more regularly than here that Indian democracy was un-Islamic, Indian secularism was un-Islamic and Indian socialism was un-Islamic. And yet, neither the State Government which was ruled by two supposedly secular parties, nor the Union Government took the matter seriously. What intrigued the most was that the law which was considered good for 100 million Muslims in other parts of India, was not considered good for 40 lakh Muslims of Kashmir.

What was the use of the nationalist forces ruling the country when they would not act in national interest at all, when they remained mental slaves of the politics of communalism; when they were inclined to place reliance on words and not on deeds; when they did not lead, but succumbed; when they encouraged, and not defeated, separatist elements; when, instead of building a new society strong in human and spiritual values, they did everything, wittingly or unwittingly, to repair, renovate and strengthen the old decaying and smelly sitadel of obscurantism; and when they invariably gave precedence to expediency over the basic goals and principles of our Constitution? What could be the result of all this? Did it require any unusual insight to understand where such ferocious forces would take us?

I leave it to the well-wishers of the nation to consider, without any political or personal bias, a basic question. How was it that Dr. Farooq was calling me Hallaqu and Changez Khan, and you were travelling all the way to Srinagar to 'expose' me as anti-Article 370, anti-Kashmiri and anti-Muslim and, at the same time, Miss Benazir Bhutto was vowing to tear me to pieces — 'Jagmohan ko Bhag-Bhag Mohan Kar Denge'?

There are many other facets of Kashmir's truth which lie buried underneath the heaps of disinformation and also of superficiality and shallowness. These days I am busy in an attempt to remove some of these heaps. One day, I hope, the country will acquire the true perspective of the problem. The Kashmiri masses would also realise that I was their greatest well-wisher. I wanted to save them permanently from the exploitative oligarches and also from the machinations of religious 'Czars' and forces of obscurantism.

You have already committed the sin of letting down the Bharat Mata in Kashmir. Now do not add to it another sin of letting down the other Mata also. There is, after all, some power above. Conscious of her. She may condone your negligence. But she would not condone your sin of blaming an innocent person for what were your own faults, particularly when he had been persistently reminding you of your obligations.

So far as I am concerned, I am content with my gloomy pride of having done the correct thing in Kashmir. True, I seemingly and, perhaps, temporarily, lost the goodwill of some of the locals. But I was not seeking a certificate from anyone. I had gone for the second term to do a national duty.

The country's polity and administration have assumed such a character that it has become incapable of solving from its roots, any serious problem. Elections have virtually lost all meaning. And these would continue to be meaningless until and unless Indian democracy and its constitutional structure acquires a healthy cultural base, a pure soul and soil, from which the seed of justice, truth and selfless service could sprout and blossom into a Great Tree providing shade and shelter from

Kanyakumari to Kashmir. Currently, the inner light is gone, and we are being led virtually by blind men with lanterns in their hands. We stumble from one crisis to another. As a poet says :

> It has happened
> and it goes on happening
> and it will happen again.

With best wishes,

Yours sincerely,

(Sd/-)
JAGMOHAN

54

Trade Agreement between the Government of India and the Government of the Islamic Republic of Pakistan

Islamabad, 23 January 1975

The Government of INDIA

AND

The Government of PAKISTAN,

Desiring to develop, extend and strengthen the commercial relations between the two countries on the basis of equality and mutual benefit,

Have Agreed as follows :

Article 1

The two Governments shall, subject to the laws, regulations and procedures in force in their respective countries from time to time, take all appropriate measures to facilitate, strengthen and diversify trade between the two countries.

Article 2

In order to advance the objectives of Article 1 of this Agreement, the two Governments shall also encourage relevant enterprises and organizations of their respective countries to explore the scope for long-term contracts and, where appropriate, to conclude such contracts.

Article 3

The two Governments undertake to grant import/export

licences in accordance with their respective laws and regulations relating to import/export and foreign exchange. To begin with, and unless otherwise agreed, trade will be conducted on Government-to-Government basis or through Government controlled Trade Corporations of the two countries.

Article 4

The two Governments shall accord to each other in their trade regulations the most favoured nation treatment in accordance with the provisions and decisions of the GATT.

Article 5

The two Governments agree to cooperate effectively with each other to prevent infringement and circumvention of the laws, rules and regulations of either country in regard to matters relating to foreign exchange and foreign trade.

Article 6

In order to advance the objectives of this Agreement each Government shall, subject to the laws and regulations in force in its country encourage and facilitate the holding within its territory of trade fairs and exhibitions by enterprises and organizations of the other country.

Article 7

All payments and charges in connection with trade between the two countries shall be effected in freely convertible currency in accordance with the foreign exchange regulations in force from time to time in each country.

Article 8

The goods exported from Pakistan and India under this Agreement will be of Pakistan and Indian origin and for consumption in India and Pakistan respectively. The said goods shall not be re-exported to third counties.

Article 9

For the purpose of promoting the aims of this Agreement a Committee of representatives to be designated by the respective Governments shall be established.

The committee shall meet at least once a year, or as often as may be mutually agreed upon alternatively in India and Pakistan.

The Committee shall :

(a) review the implementation of the provisions of this Agreement;

(b) examine and recommend measures for the solution of problems which may arise in the implementation of this Agreement or in the course of the development of trade between the two countries;

(c) consider proposals made by either of the Governments, within the framework of this Agreement, aimed at further expansion and diversification of trade between the two countries.

Article 10

This Agreement shall come into force on the date of signature and shall be valid for a period of one year. Thereafter, it shall automatically be extended for two years unless, within a minimum period of three months prior to the expiration of the initial period validity of one year, either Government gives to the other a written notice of its intention to terminate the Agreement.

Done at Islamabad on Twenty-third day of January 1975 in two originals in English, both texts being equally authentic.

For the Government of India	For the Government of Pakistan
(Sd/-)	(Sd/-)
Y.T. SHAH	EJAZ AHMED NAIK
Secretary to the Government of India,	Secretary to the Government of Pakistan,
Ministry of Commerce,	Ministry of Commerce,
Leader of the Indian Delegation	Leader of the Pakistan Delegation

Dated : 23-01-1975

MEMORANDUM OF UNDERSTANDING

Islamabad, 23 January 1975

1. For the purpose of giving effect to the provisions of Article 7 of the Trade Agreement and ensuring expeditious settlement of trade transactions under contracts concluded hereafter and other transactions incidental thereto, the two Governments' recognise the need of commercial banks in India and Pakistan entering into suitable agency arrangements, subject to laws and regulations in force in the respective countries from time to time. These arrangements will be applicable only to trade transactions concluded after the 23rd January, 1975. Exports from India to Pakistan will be covered by irrevocable documentary letters of credit opened by a bank in Pakistan with a bank in India and expressed in convertible currency. Similarly, exports from Pakistan to India will be covered by irrevocable documentary letters of credit opened by a bank in India with a bank in Pakistan and expressed in convertible currency.

In order to avoid multiplicity of banks handling transactions in initial stages on either side, such transactions may for the present be confined to the State Bank of India in India and the National Bank of Pakistan in-Pakistan. Suitable agency arrangements may be entered into between these two banks for this purpose. As trade between the two countries gathers momentum, arrangements may be reviewed at a later date with a view to including other banks in the financing of trade between India and Pakistan.

2. In accordance with clause 4 of the Trade Protocol of 39th November, 1974, the delegations from the concerned Organizations are scheduled to meet at the end of January, 1975 to explore the possibilities of trade in cotton. The delegations of the Government controlled corporations of the two countries will meet in March or April, 1975 in New Delhi to explore the possibilities of trade in other commodities such as, engineering goods, jute manufactures, tea, coal, iron and steel products, rice bidi leaves and railway track materials etc., which

have been indicated as available for export. Further meetings of the representatives of the concerned organizations will be held as and when necessary.

This Memorandum of Understanding will constitute an integral part of the Trade Agreement signed on this date.

Done at Islamabad on 23rd January 1975 in two originals, both of which are equally authentic.

(Sd/-)	(Sd/-)
Y.T. SHAH	EJAZ AHMED NAIK
Secretary to the Government of India,	Secretary to the Government of Pakistan,
Ministry of Commerce,	Ministry of Commerce,
Leader of the Indian Delegation	Leader of the Pakistan Delegation

Dated : 23-01-1975

55

Protocol between the Government of India and the Government of the Islamic Republic of Pakistan regarding Shipping Services

New Delhi, 15 January 1975

Recalling the provisions of the Simla Agreement of 1972 to progressively restore and normalise relations between the two countries, and

Recalling further the Protocol on Resumption of Trade between India and Pakistan signed at New Delhi on the 30th November 1974, and

Resolving to restore direct shipping services between the two countries. The Delegations of India and Pakistan, which met in New Delhi from the 11th to 15th January 1975,

Have agreed as follows :

1. Necessary steps will be taken by both the countries to restore direct shipping services by the 15th February 1975 on the principles of sovereign equality, and mutual benefit.

2. Such services will cover the carriage of cargo between the two countries.

3. Such carriage will only be by the vessels of the mercantile marine sailing under the flag of either country in accordance with its laws and regulations.

4. All cargo between the ports of the two countries shall be carried on the principle of equality in matters relating to cargo liftings and freight earnings on an annual basis.

5. Vessels of either country will load in the ports of one country only such cargo as is destined for the other country.

6. For coordination of all questions connected with the operation of direct shipping services between both the countries, the Government of India hereby nominate the Director General of Shipping, Bombay on their part and the Government of Pakistan likewise nominate the Director General of Ports and Shipping, Karachi, on their part.

7. The authorities referred to in Article (6) will nominate the shipping companies of their respective countries to determine by mutual discussion the details of operation of the services. For this purpose, the representatives of the Shipping Companies shall meet, as early as possible, on a mutually convenient date.

8. The vessels of either country, their crew, and cargoes shall be admitted to the territorial water and the ports of the other country and shall be accorded the most favoured nation treatment relating to their entry, stay, loading/unloading of cargo, leaving of the ports, and all necessary facilities for safe maritime navigation.

9. The provisions of Article (8) shall be subject to Article (5) and such restrictions as are or may be imposed, from time to, time, by the laws of either country.

10. Either country shall adopt, within the limits of their laws and port regulations, all appropriate measures to facilitate and expedite maritime traffic, to prevent delays to vessels and to expedite the carrying out of customs and other formalities, applicable at the ports.

11. All ship documents including those relating to nationality, registration, tonnage and survey issued or recognised by one country shall be recognised by the other country.

12. Either country shall recognise the seamen's identity documents issued by the appropriate authorities of the other country.

13. Holder of Seaman's identity documents specified in Article (12) shall, during the stay of the vessel in the ports of the

other country, be permitted to land on temporary shore leave without visa, on his obtaining a Landing Permit valid for a period not exceeding 24 hours, provided he deposits his Continuous Discharge Certificate with the Immigration Authorities and provided further that the crew list has been submitted to the concerned authorities in accordance with the laws and regulations in force in the port. The said person shall be subject to customs control. His entry and stay in port shall be governed by the, provisions of the India-Pakistan Visa Agreement of the 14th September 1974, and the laws and regulations in force in that port :

14. When a member of the crew disembarks in the port of the other country due to illness, he shall be permitted to enter a hospital. He shall also be permitted to rejoin ship or be repatriated if a member of the crew is left behind for reasons such as "missing the ship", or his transfer from the ship, he shall be permitted to rejoin ship or be repatriated.

15. The captain of the vessel staying in the port of the other country or a person authorised by him shall be permitted and assisted to contact or visit the Consular official representing the interest of the other country.

16. If a vessel of either country be involved in maritime peril or encounters any other danger off the coast or in the ports of the other country, the vessel, the cargo, the crew and the passengers shall receive the same assistance which is accorded to a national vessel, its cargo, crew and passengers. This will be subject to the respective laws and international obligations of the two countries.

17. The cargo, ship stores, machinery spares etc., of the damaged vessel which have to be off loaded, shall not be subject to customs duties and taxes provided the same are taken out of the country within a reasonable period.

18. All payments and expenses relating to shipping services between the two countries shall be effected in freely convertible currency in accordance with the foreign exchange regulations in force from time to time in each country.

19. The representatives of the two authorities referred to in Article (5) above shall meet, as necessary, to discuss and resolve all outstanding problems. If they are unable to settle any question concerning the interpretation or application of this Protocol, such questions shall be referred to the respective Governments for settlement.

20. To facilitate urgent consultations in matters relating to implementation of this Protocol and any arrangements made there under, visas shall be granted immediately, on request, to four nationals of either country nominated by the respective authorities referred to in Article (6), for travel to the other country. Names and full particulars of the nationals so nominated shall be exchanged as soon as possible and Consular authorities representing the interest of both the countries informed accordingly.

21. Both the governments shall take necessary steps to rescind with effect from the 1st February, 1975, the existing restrictions on the entry of merchant vessels of their countries to each other's ports.

22. The working of this Protocol shall be reviewed by the two Governments after the lapse of one year and thereafter as may be mutually agreed upon.

23. This Protocol will come into force on the date of signing.

(Sd/-)	(Sd/-)
M.R. AMAKRISHNAYYA	K.T. KIDWAI
Secretary to the Government of India, Ministry of Shipping and Transport and Leader of the Indian Delegation	Secretary to the Government of Pakistan, Ministry of Communications and Leader of the Pakistan Delegation

Dated : 15-01-1975

56

Protocol between the Government of India and the Government of the Islamic Republic of Pakistan on Resumption of Trade

New Delhi, 30 November 1974

Recalling the provisions of the Simla Agreement of 1972 to progressively restore and normalise relations between the two countries,

Reaffirming the desire of their respective Governments for resumption of trade and cooperation in economic and other agreed fields,

Resolving to explore possibilities of establishing channels of trade on a mutually beneficial basis,

Realising the significant opportunities arising out of economic growth in the two countries, and

Desiring to develop and extend the commercial relations between their two countries on the basis of equality and mutual benefit.

The Delegations of India and Pakistan which met in New Delhi from 26 to 30 November 1974,

Have agreed as follows :

1. Necessary steps will be taken by both countries to lift the embargo on trade between the two countries with effect from 7th December 1974.

2. Trade will be conducted on the basis of free convertible

currency in accordance with the foreign exchange regulations in force from time to time in each country.

3. Trade between the two countries will be on the basis of the most-favoured-nation treatment in accordance with the provisions and decisions of the GATT.

4. To begin with, and unless otherwise agreed, trade will be conducted on Government-to-Government basis or through Government Controlled Trade Corporations of the two countries, for which purposes representatives of the concerned organisations will meet from time to time.

In this connection, the immediate possibilities of commencing trade in the following commodities was noted :

Cotton
Engineering goods
Jute manufactures
Iron Ore
Railway equipment
Rice
Tea

5. Keeping in view the importance of immediate restoration of direct shipping services between the two countries for facilitating the movement of goods and trade, it was agreed that experts of the two countries should meet in December 1974 to work out details in this regard. Likewise, discussions will be arranged at a mutually convenient time for the restoration of the rail links to serve mutual trade :

6. A Trade Agreement will be concluded between India and Pakistan in the near future for which purpose a delegation from India will visit Pakistan in the first week of January 1975. This Protocol will come into force on the date of signing.

(Sd/-)	(Sd/-)
Y.T. SHAH	EJAZ AHMAD NAIK
Commerce Secretary,	Commerce Secretary,
Government of India	Government of Pakistan

Dated : 30-11-1974

57

Kashmir Accord, 13 November 1974

Agreed conclusions which led to Sheikh Mohammad Abdullah's accord with Mrs. Indira Gandhi, Prime Minister, and his subsequent assumption of office as Chief Minister in February 1975 :

1. The State of Jammu and Kashmir which is a constituent unit of the Union of India, shall, in its relation with the Union, continue to be governed by Article 370 of the Constitution of India.

2. The residuary powers of legislation shall remain with the State; however, Parliament will continue to have power to make laws relating to the prevention of activities directed towards disclaiming, questioning or disrupting the sovereignty and territorial integrity of India or bringing about secession of a part of the territory of India from the Union or causing insult to the Indian National Flag, the Indian National Anthem and the Constitution.

3. Where any provision of the Constitution of India had been applied to the State of Jammu and Kashmir with adaptations and modifications, such adaptations and modifications can be altered or repealed by an order of the President under Article 370, each individual proposal in this behalf being considered on its merits; but provisions of the Constitution of India already applied to the State of Jammu and Kashmir without adaptation or modification are unalterable.

4. With a view to assuring freedom to the State of Jammu and Kashmir to have its own legislation on matters like welfare measures cultural matters, social security, personal law and procedural laws, in a manner suited to the special conditions in the State, it is agreed that the State Government can review the laws made by Parliament or extended to the State after 1953 on any matter relatable to the Concurrent List and may decide which of them, in its opinion, needs amendment or repeal. Thereafter, appropriate steps may be taken under Article 254 of the Constitution of India. The grant of President's assent to such legislation would be sympathetically considered. The same approach would be adopted in regard to laws to be made by Parliament in future under the proviso to clause 2 of the Article. The State Government shall be consulted regarding the application of any such law to the State and the views of the State Government shall receive the fullest consideration

5. As an arrangement reciprocal to what has been provided under Article 368, a suitable modification of that Article as applied to the State should be made by Presidential order to the effect that no law made by the Legislature of the State of Jammu and Kashmir, seeking to make any change in or in the effect of any provision of Constitution of the State of Jammu and Kashmir relating to any of he under mentioned matters, shall take effect unless the Bill, having been reserved for the consideration of the President, receives his assent; the matters are :

(a) the appointment, powers, functions, duties, privileges and immunities of the Governor and

(b) the following matters relating to Elections namely the superintendence, direction and control of Elections by the Election Commission of India, eligibility for inclusion in the electoral rolls without discrimination, adult suffrage and composition of the legislative Council, being matters specified in sections 138, 139 140 and 50 of the Constitution of the State of Jammu and Kashmir.

6. No agreement was possible on the question of nomenclature of the Governor and the Chief Minister and the matter is, therefore, remitted to the Principals.

(Sd/-)	(Sd/-)
MIRZA MOHAMMAD AFZAL BEG	G. PARTHASARATHI

Dated : 13-11-1974.

58

Agreement between the Government of India and the Government of the Islamic Republic of Pakistan on Telecommunication

Islamabad, 14 September 1974

In accordance with the decision contained in para 3 of the Simla Agreement

The Government of INDIA

AND

The Government of PAKISTAN,

Desiring to restore and establish telecommunication service between the two countries,

Have agreed as follows :

ARTICLE I

ESTABLISHMENT OF TELECOMMUNICATION SERVICES

1. From a date to be mutually agreed upon, continuously operated telecommunications services shall be established over a direct land route between India and Pakistan.

2. Except to the extent indicated hereinafter, the telecommunications services shall be governed by the "Telegraph Regulations (Geneva-1973)", the "Telephone Regulations (Geneva-1973)" and the "International Telecommunication Convention (Malaga- Terremolines-1973)".

3. The technical and operational aspects of the Telegraph and Telephone Services shall be decided by mutual consent of

the telecommunications administrations of the Government of India and the Government of Pakistan. These shall be finalised by mutual discussions within one month.

ARTICLE II

PUBLIC TELEGRAM SERVICE

1. The classes of telegrams accepted between India and Pakistan shall be as listed in the Annexure I attached to this Agreement. Besides all classes of obligatory telegrams, as defined in Article 4 of the Telegraph Regulations (Geneva-1973) Urgent Private, Urgent Press and Ordinary Press Telegrams will be accepted. Private and Press Telegrams shall be accepted in plain language.

2. Press telegrams will be accepted only from authorised and duly registered representatives of newspapers, periodical publications, News Agencies or bureau and press services of diplomatic missions.

3. The International Telegraph Offices will be open for International Service all the 24 hours of the day. Delivery of all ordinary telegrams in India will be during 0600 to 2200 hours (Indian Standard Time) only. The delivery in Pakistan will be during 0600 to 2200 hours (Pakistan Standard Time).

4. The overall accounting rate per word shall be made up of the sum of the terminal and transit rates as applicable and shown in Annexure II to this Agreement.

5. There shall be no Transfer Account Service between India and Pakistan.

ARTICLE III

TELEPHONE SERVICES

1. For the purpose of this Service, India shall be divided into the following accounting Zones :

Zone I — Comprising all the States contiguous to Pakistan, the State of Uttar Pradesh and the Union Territory of Delhi.

Zone II — Comprising the rest of India except the city of Bombay.

Zone III — The City of Bombay (comprising the entire multi-exchange area).

2. Classes of Calls.

The following classes of calls as defined in the CCITT Recommendations (Geneva 1978) shall be accepted.

— Distress (emergency) calls

— Government calls.

— Service calls.

— Private calls.

3. Facilities offered to users.

Only the Station calls and the Personal calls will be accepted :

4. Operating Methods.

All calls will be completed on a manual basis via the nominated International Telephone Exchanges.

5. Accounting Rate.

(i) Terminal Calls :

In respect of calls between exchanges in Zone I of India and exchanges in Pakistan, the overall accounting rate shall be of 10 Gold Francs for the first three minutes duration or less. For each additional minute or part thereof it shall be on pro rata basis. The overall accounting rate shall be shared equally between the two countries.

(ii) In respect of calls between exchanges in Zone II and Zone III of India and exchanges in Pakistan, the overall accounting rate shall be 20 Gold Francs for the first three minutes duration or less. For each additional minute it shall be on pro rata basis. This shall be shared between India and Pakistan in the ratio 3 (India) : 1 (Pakistan) for Zone II. As regards the City of Bombay the ratio will be 2 (India) : 1 (Pakistan).

(iii) Transit Calls :

(a) For calls transited via India, the Indian share for the first three minutes or less shall be 15 Gold Francs. For every additional minute or part thereof, it shall be on a prorata basis.

(b) For calls transited via Pakistan, the Pakistan share for the first three minutes or less shall be 5 Gold Francs. For every additional minute or part thereof, it shall be on a pro rata basis.

ARTICLE IV

TELEX SERVICES

1. For the purpose of this Service, India shall be divided into the following accounting Zones :

Zone I — Comprising telex exchanges in all the States contiguous to Pakistan, the State of Uttar Pradesh and the Union Territory of Delhi.

Zone II — Comprising telex exchanges in the rest of India except the City of Bombay.

Zone III — The telex exchange in the City of Bombay.

2. Classes of Calls

Following classes of telex calls shall be accepted :

(a) Safety of Life Telex Calls (SVH),

(b) Government Telex Calls,

(c) Service Telex Calls,

(d) Ordinary Private Telex Calls,

(e) Requests for information.

3. Operating Methods :

All calls will be completed on a manual basis via the nominated International Telex Exchanges.

4. Accounting Rate.

(i) Terminal Calls :

In respect of calls between exchanges in Zone I of India and exchanges in Pakistan, the overall accounting rate shall be 8 Gold Francs for the first three minutes duration or less. For each additional minute it shall be on a pro rata basis; This shall be shared equally between the two countries.

(II) In respect of calls between exchange in Zone II and Zone III of India and exchanges in Pakistan, the overall accounting rate shall be 16 Gold Francs for the first three minutes duration or less. For each additional minute it shall be on prorata basis. This shall be shared between India and Pakistan in the ratio 3 (India) : 1 (Pakistan). As regards the city of Bombay the ratio will be 2 (India) : 1 (Pakistan).

(iii) Transit Calls :

(a) For calls transited via India, the Indian share for the first three minutes or less shall be 12 Gold Francs. For every additional minute or part thereof, it shall be on a prorata basis.

(b) For calls transited via Pakistan, the Pakistan share for the first three minutes or less shall be 4 Gold Francs. For every additional minute or part thereof, it shall be on a prorata basis.

ARTICLE V

ACCOUNTING PROCEDURE FOR TELECOMMUNICATIONS

1. The Government of India and the Government of Pakistan shall establish a monthly account showing all the amounts owed and forward it to the other Government concerned. The accounts shall be in the Forms as mutually agreed upon by the two sides.

2. The accounts shall be sent as promptly as possible but in any case before the end of the third month following that to which they relate.

3. In principle, an account shall be considered as accepted without the need for specific notification of acceptance to the Government which sent it.

4. Nevertheless, both the Governments shall have right to query the date in question during the period of two months after the receipt of the account, but only to the extent necessary to bring the differences within limits specified in para 6 below.

5. However, to avoid repetition of errors which are too small to entail a revision of the account, either of the Governments may draw the attention of the other Government which has prepared the monthly account, to obvious errors and

the latter Government must take action on this information as soon as practicable to avoid similar errors occurring in the future.

6. A revision which has begun shall be stopped following the exchange of observations between the two Administrations as soon as the difference is brought down to a sum not exceeding the maximum specified below : The limits apply to each of the three services separately.

For Telegram Services :

Amount of the account of creditor	Maximum difference
(a) less than 2500 Gold Francs	(a) 25 Gold Francs
(b) from 2500 to 100,000 Gold Francs.	(b) 1% of the sum of the creditor's account
(c) more than l00,000	(c) 1% of the first 100,000 Gold Francs Gold Francs and 0.5 % of the remainder of the creditor's account

(ii) For Telephone and Telex Services :

Amount of the account	Difference Exceeding
(a) less than 10,000 Gold Francs	(a) 100 Gold Francs
(b) 10,000 Gold Francs to 300,000 Gold Francs	(b) 1% of the sum of the account,
(c) More than 300,000 Gold Francs	(c) 3,000 Gold Francs

ARTICLE VI

PAYMENTS OF BALANCE OF ACCOUNTS

1. A quarterly settlement statement showing the balance from the monthly accounts for the period to which it relates shall be prepared as quickly as possible by the creditor

Administration and be sent in duplicate to the debtor Administration which, after verification, shall return one of the copies endorsed with its acceptance.

2. The payment of the balance due on account shall not be delayed pending settlement of any query on that account. Adjustments which are later agreed shall be included in the subsequent account.

3. Payment shall be affected as promptly as possible but in no case later than six weeks after the day on which the quarterly settlement statement is received by the debtor Administration. Beyond this period the creditor Administration shall have the right to charge interest at the rate of 6 percent per annum; reckoned from the day following the date of expiration of the said period.

4. The balance of telecommunications accounts, shall be drawn up in Gold Francs.

5. The payment of balance of telecommunication accounts shall be made in United States of America Dollars. The methods of conversion into such currency shall be as follows :

The amount of the payment in US Dollars shall be equivalent in value to the balance of the account. The amount which is equivalent in value to the balance of the account shall be determined by the relationship in effect on the day before payment between the value of the Gold Franc and the gold par value of the US dollars approved by the International Monetary Fund. In case a central rate of the US dollar has been established under the International Monetary Fund Executive Board decision subsequent to the approval given by the International Monetary Fund to the gold par value, the gold value of the central rate shall be used in determining the equivalent value.

6. The amounts due to India shall be credited by bank transfer to the account of the Indian Posts and Telegraphs Department in the State Bank of India, New York Branch. The amounts due to Pakistan shall be credited by bank transfer to the account of Pakistan Telegraph and Telephone Department in the National Bank of Pakistan, New York Branch.

7. The payment charges imposed in the debtor country (taxes, clearing charges, commission, etc.) shall be borne by the debtor. The charges imposed in the creditor country, including payment charges imposed by banks, shall be borne by the creditor.

8. If, between the time the remittance (cheque, etc.) is effected and the time the creditor receives it, a variation occurs in the equivalent value of the US dollar and if the difference resulting from such variation exceeds 5% of the amount due as calculated following such variation, the total difference shall be shared equally between debtor and creditor.

9. If there should be a radical change in the International Monetary System, which invalidates or makes inappropriate one or more of the foregoing paragraphs, India and Pakistan shall be free to adopt, by a separate mutual agreement, different procedure for the payment of balances of account pending a revision to Appendix to the Telegraph Regulations (Geneva-1973) and Appendix II to the Telephone Regulations (Geneva-1973).

ARTICLE VII

SETTLEMENT OF DIFFERENCES AND DISPUTES

1. A committee of Technical experts of both countries shall meet twice a year to discuss and resolve to the maximum extent possible all outstanding problems relating to the operational matters and the settlement of accounts.

2. Any question which arises between the parties concerning the interpretation of application of this Agreement or the existence of any fact which, if established, might constitute breach of this Agreement shall first be examined by the above-mentioned Committee of the Technical Experts which will endeavour to resolve the difference by Agreement.

3. If the Committee of Experts is unable to reach agreement on any question then difference will be deemed to have arisen which shall be resolved through bilateral discussions between the two Governments.

ARTICLE VIII

PAYMENT OF PAST DUES

It was agreed that payment of outstanding amounts relating to Telecommunication dues will be discussed and settled by the representatives of the two Governments at an early date.

ARTICLE IX

MODIFICATION AND DURATION OF AGREEMENT

1. This Agreement may be modified from time to time by mutual consent of the two Governments.

2. This Agreement may be suspended by either side if outstanding balances of accounts occurring under this Agreement remain unpaid for a period of one year.

3. This Agreement is valid for two years from the date of its signing by the two Governments unless it is reviewed and extended by mutual agreement, between the two Governments before the expiry date.

4. IN WITNESS WHEREOF the undersigned duly authorised for that purpose have signed this Agreement in the two originals on Saturday the 14th September 1974, at Islamabad.

For the Government of India	For the Government of Pakistan
(Sd/-)	(Sd/-)
KEWAL SINGH AGHA	SHAHI
Foreign Secretary,	Foreign Secretary,
Government of India	Government of Pakistan

Dated : 14-09-1974

ANNEXURE I

CLASSIFICATION AND CLASS FOR TELEGRAMS BETWEEN INDIA AND PAKISTAN

SECTION A

Obligatory Telegrams

1. Telegram relating to the safety of life	1. SVH
2. (a) Government Telegrams (b) Telegrams relative to the application of the United Nations Charter	2. (a) XFS with paid service indication "ET AT "PRIORITY for Government Telegrams with priority and "ETAT" or Government without priority. (b) XPS with paid service indications "ETAT" PRIORITY NATIONS for "ETAT NATIONS" for the telegrams with and without priority respectively.
3. Telegram concerning persons protected in time of war by the Geneva Convention of l2th August, 1949	3. RCT
4. Ordinary private telegrams	4. XF
5. Telegraph service correspondence	5. RST, FST: XT (Urgent) T
6. Meteorological Telegrams	6. OBS

SECTION B

Optional Telegrams and Special Services

1. Urgent private telegrams	1. XXF with paid service indication "Urgent"
2. Urgent press" telegrams	2. XZ with paid service indication "Urgent Press
3. Ordinary Press	3. Z with paid service indication "Press"
4. Telephone	4. TFx (XZ telephone number) (paid service indication) TLXx (XZ telex number) (paid service indication)
5. Telex delivery	

NOTE

(1) Minimum charges for all classes of telegrams shall be for 7 words, except in case of Press Telegrams for which the minimum charges will be for 14 words.

(2) RTP (Receiver to pay) Meteorological Telograms bearing press or other bearing messages shall not be allowed.

ANNEXURE II

	Terminal Charge (Per Word) for each country	Transit Charge (Per Word) for each country
Ordinary Telegrams Government Telegrams Telegrams relating to the applications of the United Nations Charter Paid Service Advices Urgent Press Telegrams	27 Gold Centimes	27 Gold Centimes
Ordinary Press Telegrams Urgent Telegrams Meteorological Telegrams	9 Gold Centimes 54 Gold Centimes 14 Gold Centimes	9 Gold Centimes 54 Gold Centimes 14 Gold Centimes
Urgent Telegrams concerning persons protected in times of War by the Geneva Convention of l2th August, 1949	27 Gold Centimes	27 Gold Centimes
Ordinary Telegram concerning persons protected in times of war by the Geneva Convention of l2th August, 1949.	7 Gold Centimes	7 Gold Centimes

59

Agreement between the Government of India and the Government of the Islamic Republic of Pakistan relating to the Exchange of Postal Articles

Islamabad, 14 September 1974

In accordance with the decisions contained in Para 3 of the Simla Agreement and in pursuance of Article 8 of the Constitution of the Universal Postal Union

The Government of INDIA

AND

The Government of PAKISTAN,

Desiring to restore and establish a Postal Service between the two countries,

Have agreed as follows :

ARTICLE I

SCOPE OF THE AGREEMENT

1. The provisions of this Agreement shall apply to letter-post items, insured letters and boxes and parcels originating in either country and intended for delivery in the other.

2. The exchange of letter-post items, insured letters and boxes and postal parcels between India and Pakistan shall be governed by the provisions of the Convention and Agreements of the Universal Postal Union to which both the countries are signatories, except to the extent such provisions are modified in

the subsequent Articles. The term "the Convention and Agreement of the Universal Postal Union" used in this Agreement shall be taken to include the Convention of the Universal Postal Union, 1969, with its Final Protocol and Detailed Regulations and the Postal Parcels Agreement, 1969, with its Final Protocol and Detailed Regulations.

3. The facilities for registration and insurance shall be available in respect of letter-post items posted in either country for delivery in the other, on payment of fees in accordance with the provisions of the Convention and Agreement of the Universal Postal Union.

4. The facility of Express Delivery Service shall not be available in respect of letter-post items and parcels posted in either country for delivery in the other.

ARTICLE II

CLASSES OF POSTAL ARTICLES AND CONDITIONS FOR THEIR TRANSMISSION

1. The term "letter-post items" applies to letters, letter-cards (or aerogrammes), postcards, printed papers (including registered newspapers), literature for the blind and small packets.

2. The weight limits and dimensions of the letter-post items shall conform to those laid down in the Universal Postal Union Convention and its Detailed Regulations.

3. Insured letters shall not contain articles subject to customs duty.

4. Insured boxes shall not contain (a) documents having the character of current and personal correspondence; and (b) bank notes, currency notes or securities of any kind payable to bearer.

5. Insured items shall be subject to customs and import and export and exchange control regulations in force from time to time in each country.

6. The insured value may not exceed the actual value of the contents of the item, subject to a maximum of 1250 Gold

Francs, but it shall be permissible to insure only part of that value.

ARTICLE III

RATES

1. The postage rates, air surcharges and postal fees applicable to letter — post items and parcels in either country for delivery in the other shall be in accordance with the provisions of the Convention and Agreement of the Universal Postal Union.

2. Subject to the provisions of Convention and Agreement of the Universal Postal Union, changes in rates and fees shall, whenever necessary, be made by each Postal Administration, under intimation to the other.

ARTICLE IV

SPECIAL AND SUPPLEMENTARY CHARGES

1. All special and supplementary charges applicable to letter-post items and parcels posted in either country for delivery in the other shall be in accordance with the provisions of the Convention and Agreement of the Universal Postal Union.

2. When an enquiry or request for information is, at the request of the interested Party, to be transmitted by air, it will give rise to the collection of the respective air surcharge, or double this surcharge, if the reply is also to be transmitted by air. In both cases, the amount of surcharge will be retained in full by the Administration which collects it. If the use of telegraph is requested, the cost of the telegram will also be collected.

ARTICLE V

PARCELS

The following special provisions shall apply to postal parcels posted in either country for delivery in the other :

1. Maximum weight of a parcel shall be 10 Kgs.

2. The maximum insurance limit of a Parcel shall be 1250 Gold Francs.

3. Parcels shall be subject to Customs and Import and Export Exchange Control Regulations in force from time to time in the country of origin and destination.

ARTICLE VI

AIR MAIL

The provisions concerning airmail correspondence as laid down in the Universal Postal Union Convention shall be applicable in the case of airmail correspondence posted in either country for delivery in the other, subject to the following special provisions :

1. The surcharge on all items of airmail shall be in addition to the surface postage;

2. Each Administration shall be entitled to fix the rates of air surcharges on various items of airmail under intimation to the other, subject to the provisions of the Convention and Agreements of the Universal Postal Union.

ARTICLE VII

AIR PARCELS

The exchange of air parcels shall be covered by the same special provisions as laid down in Article V. Each Administration shall be at liberty to fix a separate air surcharge in addition to the surface parcel, postage rates or an air surcharge-cum-parcel postage taking into account the cost of air conveyance. Air parcels which cannot be delivered to the addressees for any reason whatsoever shall be returned to the country of origin only by the surface route.

ARTICLE VIII

SETTLEMENT OF ACCOUNTS

1. The manner of preparation, acceptance and settlement of postal accounts between India and Pakistan shall be governed by the provisions of the Universal Postal Union Convention and the Universal Postal Union Agreement, except as modified by this Agreement.

2. The net payment of balances of postal accounts shall be

made in United States of America Dollars. The method of conversion into such currency shall be as follows :

The amount of the payment in US Dollars shall be equivalent in value to the balance of the account. The amount which is equivalent in value to the balance of the account shall be determined by the relationship in effect on the day before payment between the value of the gold francs and the gold, par value of the US Dollars approved by the International Monetary Fund. In case a central rate of the US Dollar has been established under the International Monetary Fund Executive Board decision subsequent to the approval given in the International Monetary Fund to the Gold par value, the gold value of that central rate shall be used in determining the equivalent value.

3. The amounts due to India shall be credited by bank transfer to the account of the Post and Telegraph Department in the State Bank of India, New York Branch.

4. The amounts due to Pakistan shall be credited by bank transfer to the account of Government of Pakistan in the National Bank of Pakistan, New York Branch.

5. Payment shall be made as quickly as possible and at the latest within four months from the date of receipt of the general or special liquidation accounts, accounts or statements drawn up by common consent, notification, requests for payments on account, etc., indicating the amounts of balances to be settled, after that period the amounts due shall be chargeable with interest at the rate of 5% per annum.

6. If, between the time the remittance (cheque etc.) is effected and the time the creditor receives it, a variation occurs in the equivalent value of the US Dollar and if the difference resulting from such variation exceeds 5% of the amount due as calculated following such variation, the total difference shall be shared equally between debtor and creditor.

7. If there should be a radical change in the International Monetary system, which invalidates or makes inappropriate one or more of the foregoing paragraphs, India and Pakistan

may, by a separate mutual agreement, adopt a new procedure for the payment of balances of accounts.

ARTICLE IX

SETTLEMENT OF OUTSTANDING DUES

It was agreed that payment of outstanding amounts relating to postal dues will be discussed and settled by the representatives of the two Governments at an early date.

ARTICLE X

SETTLEMENT OF DIFFERENCES AND DISPUTES

1. A Committee of Technical Experts of both the countries shall meet twice a year to discuss and resolve to the maximum extent possible all outstanding problems relating to the operational matters and the settlement of accounts.

2. Any question which arises between the Parties concerning the interpretation of application of this Agreement or the existence of any fact which, if established, might constitute breach of this Agreement, shall first be examined by the above mentioned Committee of the Technical Experts which will endeavour to resolve the differences by agreement.

3. If the Committee of Technical Experts is unable to reach agreement on any question then a difference will be deemed to have arisen which shall be resolved through bilateral discussions between the two Governments.

ARTICLE XI

ENTRY INTO FORCE, MODIFICATION AND DURATION

1. This Agreement shall come into force from the date to be mutually agreed upon.

2. The Technical and Operational aspects of the Postal Service shall be decided by mutual agreement of the Postal Administration of the two countries.

3. This Agreement may be modified from time to time by mutual consent of the two Governments.

4. The provisions in the Agreement relating to Air Mail

Service shall come into force only after the establishment of the air links between the two countries.

5. Exchange of mail by sea shall come into force only after the establishment of shipping services between the two countries.

6. This Agreement may be suspended by either side if balances of accounts accruing under this Agreement remain unpaid for a period of two years.

7. This Agreement is valid for five years from the date of endorsement, subject to the provision that it can be terminated by either Government after giving a notice of one year of its intention to do so.

In witness whereof, the undersigned, duly authorised for that purpose, have signed this Agreement in two originals, on Saturday, the 14th September 1974, at Islamabad.

(Sd/-)

KEWAL SINGH
Foreign Secretary,
Ministry of External Affairs,
Government of India

(Sd/-)

AGHA SHAHI
Foreign Secretary,
Ministry of Foreign Affairs,
Government of Pakistan

Dated : 14-09-1974

60

Protocol Constituting an Agreement between the Government of India and the Government of the Islamic Republic of Pakistan on Visit to Religious Shrines

Islamabad, 14 September 1974

The Government of INDIA

AND

The Government of PAKISTAN,

Taking note of the sentiments and devotion of the various communities in the two countries for the historic and sacred shrines in the other

Have agreed on the following principles for facilitating visits to such shrines :

(i) Such visits from one country to the other shall be allowed without discrimination as to religion or sect. The list of shrines to be visited will be finalised shortly through correspondence. The agreed list may be enlarged from time to time by mutual agreement.

(ii) Upto 20 parties may be allowed to visit from one country to the other every year. This number may be revised from time to time.

(iii) Every effort should continue to be made to ensure that places of religious worship mentioned in the agreed list are properly maintained and their sanctity preserved.

(iv) Such visitors will be given Visitor Category visas.

(Sd/-)	(Sd/-)
KEWAL SINGH	AGHA SHAHI
Foreign Secretary,	Foreign Secretary,
Ministry of External Affairs,	Ministry of Foreign Affairs,
Government of India	Government of Pakistan

Dated : 14-09-1974

61

Agreement between the Government of India and the Government of the Islamic Republic of Pakistan regarding Visa

Islamabad, 14 September 1974

Thc Government of INDIA

AND

The Government of PAKISTAN

In pursuance of the provisions in the Simla Agreement of July 1972 regarding the extension of travel facilities to nationals of either country desiring to visit the other

Have agreed as follows :

1. Nationals of either country visiting the other shall possess a valid passport and a visa for the purpose.

2. The visas will be of the following categories :

3. (a) **Diplomatic Visa**

(i) A diplomatic visa valid for multiple entries will be issued to the Heads of the Diplomatic and Consular Missions, members of the Mission holding diplomatic or consular rank, their wives and children, and regular Diplomatic Couriers. The period of its validity will ordinarily be one year.

(ii) A diplomatic visa valid for single entry will be given to high ranking dignitaries. It will also be given to high ranking officials visiting on official business or to attend international conferences and to the members of their families accompanying them. This visa will ordinarily be valid for one month.

(b) **Non-Diplomatic Visa**

A non-diplomatic visa valid for multiple entries will be issued to non-diplomatic members of the Diplomatic or Consular Mission, their wives and children and the personal servants of members of the Mission holding Diplomatic or Consular ranks. The period of its validity will ordinarily be one year. It will be valid for stay at the place of assignment which will be specified and shall also be valid for journeys performed while accompanying a holder of a diplomatic visa.

(c) **Official Visa**

An official visa valid for single entry will be issued to officials not entitled to diplomatic or non-diplomatic visa of either country visiting the other on official business including participation in international conferences. This visa will ordinarily be valid for one month and for specified places.

(d) **Visitor Visa**

(i) A visitor visa will be issued to persons visiting the other country to meet relatives or friends, for business or any other legitimate purpose. This visa shall be for single entry and valid for a period not exceeding three months. However, the visa may be issued for a longer period not exceeding one year if owing to the nature of work or business a prolonged stay is necessary.

(ii) Places to be visited shall be specified in the visa.

(e) **Transit Visa**

Transit visa valid for stay in the city/port of entry for 72 hours will be issued to persons travelling by air or sea and proceeding to another country through Pakistan/India. No visa will be required for a passenger directly transiting through an airport/seaport, but his stay shall be confined to the area in the airport/seaport set apart for international transit passengers.

GENERAL PROVISIONS

3. If a visa is not availed of within three months of the date of its issue, it shall stand cancelled. The period of validity of a visa for stay shall count from the date of entry.

4. **Check Posts**

The following checkposts are hereby designated for entry/

exit for the nationals of either country going to/coming from the other country : These checkposts shall be specified on the visas :

(a) **By Air.** Karachi/Lahore/Islamabad (Pakistan) and Bombay/Delhi/Amritsar (India).

(b) **By Sea.** Karachi (Pakistan) and Bombay (India).

(c) **By Land.** Wagha/Attari and Khokhrapar/Munabao border checkposts.

5. **Registration**

Holders of visitor and transit visas shall be required to register themselves at the checkposts of entry and shall, within 24 hours of their reaching in the specified place of stay, report their arrival in writing to the prescribed authority or the nearest police station. They shall also make a similar report 24 hours prior to their intended departure from the place of stay.

6. **Seaman**

A seaman visiting a port as a member of the crew of a ship need not hold a passport or a visa. He may be issued a Landing Permit valid for the port of entry for a period not exceeding 24 hours, provided he deposits his Continuous Discharge Certificate (nullie) with the Immigration Authorities.

7. **Fee**

A fee of Rupees five Pakistani/Indian will be payable for the issuance or extension of visitor or transit visas.

8. This Agreement supersedes all previous Agreements on the subject.

Signed at Islamabad on September 14, 1974.

For the Government of India	For the Government of Pakistan
(Sd/-)	(Sd/-)
KEWAL SINGH	AGHA SHAHI
Foreign Secretary,	Foreign Secretary,
Government of India	Government of Pakistan

Dated : 14-09-1974

62

Agreement between the Government of India and the Government of the Islamic Republic of Pakistan on Release and Repatriation of Persons detained in either Country Prior to the Conflict of 1971

New Delhi, 9 April 1974

The Minister of External Affairs, Government of India, and the Minister of State for Defence and Foreign Affairs, Government of Pakistan, examined the question of the nationals of either country detained in the other prior to the conflict of 1971. They agreed that this was a humanitarian question which should be settled quickly with a view to alleviating the suffering of the hundreds of individuals involved and their families.

2. With this objective in view, the Government of India and the Government of Pakistan

Have Agreed as follows :

(i) All nationals of either country detained in the other prior to the conflict of 1971 shall be released and repatriated, irrespective of the charges on which they are detained, with the maximum possible despatch but in no case later than 14th August, 1974. After that date, neither country shall continue to detain any national of the other who was arrested prior to the conflict of 1971.

(ii) The process of release and repatriation shall commence without waiting for the compilation of complete lists of such detainees. The detainees so far visited by the representatives of the Swiss Missions, shall be repatriated forthwith. The remaining detainees shall similarly be released and repatriated after they are located by the representatives of the Swiss Mission in either country :

(iii) The two Governments shall give extensive publicity to this Agreement in the Press and over the Radio and bring it to the attention of the Governments of their States/Provinces and of the authorities in charge of all jails, prisons and detention centres for immediate compliance.

(iv) Each Government shall provide all necessary facilities to the delegation of the International Committee of the Red Cross to trace those of the pre-war detainees who are still reported to be missing after 14th August 1974.

(v) If a detainee claims to be the national of the country in which he is detained, his case shall be investigated and decided by mutual agreement between the two governments.

(vi) Pending their release and repatriation all detainees shall be treated with humanity and consideration.

3. This Agreement shall enter into force on signature.

Signed in duplicate at New Delhi on 9th April 1974.

For the Government of India

(Sd/-)

SWARAN SINGH
Minister of External Affairs,
Government of India

For the Government of Pakistan

(Sd/-)

AZIZ AHMED
Minister of State for Defence
and Foreign Affairs,
Government of Pakistan

Dated : 9-04-1974

63

Agreement between the Government of India and the Government of the Islamic Republic of Pakistan regarding Repatriation of Persons

New Delhi, 28 August 1973

Desirous of solving the humanitarian problems resulting from the conflict of 1971 and thus enabling the vast majority of human beings referred to in the Joint Indo-Bangladesh Declaration to go to their respective countries, India and Pakistan have reached the following agreement :

(i) The immediate implementation of the solution of these humanitarian problems is without prejudice to the respective positions of the Parties concerned relating to the case of 195 prisoners of war referred to in clauses (vi) and (vii) of this paragraph;

(ii) Subject to clause (i) repatriation of all Pakistani prisoners of war and civilian internees will commence from the utmost despatch as soon as logistic arrangements are completed and from a date to be settled by mutual agreement;

(iii) Simultaneously, the repatriation of all Bengalees in Pakistan, and all Pakistanis in Bangladesh referred to in clause (v) below, to their respective countries will commence;

(iv) In the matter of repatriation of all categories of persons the principle of simultaneity will be observed throughout as far as possible;

(v) Without prejudice to the respective positions of Bangladesh and Pakistan on the question of non-Bangalees, who are stated to have "opted for repatriation to Pakistan", the Government of Pakistan guided by considerations of humanity, agrees, initially, to receive a substantial number of such non-Bangalees from Bangladesh. It is further agreed that the Prime Ministers of Bangladesh and Pakistan or their designated representatives will thereafter meet to decide what additional number of persons, who may wish to migrate to Pakistan, may be permitted to do so. Bangladesh has made it clear that it will participate in such a meeting only on the basis of sovereign equality;

(vi) Bangladesh agrees that no trials of the 195 prisoners of war shall take place during the entire period of repatriation and that pending the settlement envisaged in clause (vii) below these prisoners of war shall remain in India;

(vii) On completion of repatriation of Pakistan prisoners of war and civilian internees in India; Bangalees in Pakistan and Pakistanis in Bangladesh referred to in clause (v) above, or earlier, if they so agree, Bangladesh, India and Pakistan will discuss and settle the question of 195 prisoners of war. Bangladesh has made it clear that it can participate in such a meeting only on the basis of sovereign equality.

The Special representatives are confident that the completion of repatriation provided for in this Agreement would make a signal contribution to the promotion of reconciliation in the sub-continent and create an atmosphere favorable to a constructive outcome of the meeting of the three countries;

(viii) The time schedule for the completion of repatriation of the Pakistani prisoners of war and civilian internees from India, the Bangalees from Pakistan and the Pakistanis referred to in clause (v) above from Bangladesh, will be worked out by India in consultation with Bangladesh and Pakistan, as the case may be. The Government of India will make the logistic arrangements for the Pakistani prisoners of war and civilian internees who are to be repatriated to Pakistan. The Government of Pakistan will make logistic arrangements within its territory upto agreed points of exit for the repatriation of Bangladesh nationals to Bangladesh. The Government of Bangladesh will make necessary arrangements for the transport of these persons from such agreed points of exit to Bangladesh. The Government of Bangladesh will make logistic arrangements within its territory upto agreed points of exit for the movement of the Pakistanis referred to in clause (v) above who will go to Pakistan. The Government of Pakistan will make necessary arrangements for the transport of these persons from such agreed points of exit to Pakistan. In making logistic arrangements the Governments concerned may seek the assistance of international humanitarian organisations and others;

(ix) For the purpose of facilitating the repatriation provided for in this Agreement, the representatives of the Swiss Federal Government and any international humanitarian organisation entrusted with this task shall have unrestricted access at all times to Bangalees in Pakistan and to Pakistanis in Bangladesh referred to in clause (v) above. The Government of Bangladesh and the Government of Pakistan will provide all assistance and facilities to such representatives in this regard including facilities for adequate publicity for the benefit of the persons entitled to repatriation under this Agreement;

(x) All persons to be repatriated in accordance with this Agreement will be treated with humanity and consideration.

The Government of India and the Government of Pakistan have concurred in this Agreement. The Special Representative of the Prime Minister of India, having consulted the Government of Bangladesh has also conveyed the concurrence of Bangladesh Government in this Agreement.

Done in New Delhi on August 28, 1973 in three originals, all of which are equally authentic.

(Sd/-)
P.N. HAKSAR
Special Representative
of the Prime Minister of India

(Sd/-)
AZIZ AHMED
Minister of State for Defence
and Foreign Affairs,
Government of Pakistan

Dated : 28-08-1973

64

Prime Minister Indira Gandhi's Speech on the Simla Agreement in the Rajya Sabha on 2 August 1973

This is an issue on which the entire world seems to be United. There has been tremendous enthusiasm for this Agreement and for the new spirit that they see awakened on our sub-continent. Where is the enthusiasm less? I wonder if my honourable friends have taken the trouble to examine this. Nobody has been quiet. But whose appreciation or enthusiasm has been muted? It is those People whose enthusiasm has been muted whenever there has been any question of the interest or strength of INDIA — I would even say that it is those people who have been actively against our interest. These are the voices in the world today which are not so strong and enthusiastic in favour of this Agreement. Would it be wrong if we say, as some honourable friends have said that this party is echoing those outside voices? I have no hesitation in repeating that what the Jana Sangh wants in India is what the military regime in Pakistan had wanted in Pakistan. History has shown that this policy has failed. This is the picture, a picture of confrontation. When I spoke of toys, I did not mean that land was a toy. I was speaking about the conception or the attitude of demanding a tooth for a tooth and eye for an eye. That is not a mature attitude nor an attitude which in today's world can be advantageous to our country.

Neither is the spirit of bargaining, which another honourable friend has advised. We are not out to bargain. We are a mature people who have only one aim before us and that is how to make our country strong. And by strength we do not mean merely military strength. I think that is a small part of a country's strength. When we talk of strength, we mean the strength of the people. And that can come only when the people have understanding, when they have maturity and when the affairs of the nation are handled with a certain amount of sagacity and foresight. Nobody has made the claim for the Simla Agreement that all problems are solved. In fact I would say that this is simply not possible at any time anywhere in the world. Problems will always remain. Our endeavour is to take each step so as to be in a better position to face the new problems that must arise. With the Simla Agreement India is in a better position to face the new problems that must arise. With the Simla Agreement India is in a better position to face the future. In fact I would say that the Simla Agreement is in pursuance of the domestic and the international policy which India has followed all these years. Since Independence and even before Independence this is what the Congress Party has believed in. It believed even then in friendship with all countries. I believed even then in the peace in the world and co-operative endeavour to end the poverty and the misery of the underprivileged of the world. At a time when we had no strength in our hands or in our voices we had no wealth, no armaments or any thing, even at that time, we stood solidly by all those who were equally oppressed. We did not make the excuse that we had our own struggle and never could help the people of Africa or that we could not pay attention to what was happening in Asia. On the contrary we stated this even though we were poor, we were weak, but whatever we had the strength of our voice our moral support or whatever we can give more than moral support, that we would be at the disposal of all those who were in similar situations. Whatever our relations with China today, India was the first and the only country which sent a medical team to China at that time. And in what conditions did this team live? I saw some of the members when they left and I saw them on their return. I could not recognise them when they came back. They looked more like skeletons. This was because of lack of food and lack of sleep. They could have refused to stay in such conditions and said, “We cannot work.” But they had gone to do a job and they did it. This was the spirit. This was the spirit of our policies and it is in this spirit that we act today also.

We see that countries which has opposed us and which had abused us are one by lone coming round to our policy. They may not use the word ‘non-alignment’. But what does ‘nonalignment’ mean? It means that regardless of the political systems of our country and regardless of the attitude of a country, you can build bridges with that country. Between no two countries was there greater enmity than the United States of America and China. In fact, if there is a certain amount of tension between us and the United States it was on this ground, namely our friendship with China and the Soviet Union. What do we find now? We are left behind and they are more *bhai-bhai* than anybody else. The best food is the Chinese food and the best medical treatment is Acupuncture. In the United States and many parts of Europe many think that the best is Chinese. Soon after a journey to the Soviet Union was arranged and there were some more embracings and hand shakes. What for? If any vindication or proof is necessary I do not think it is necessary — this shows ours is the right policy.

We stand for particular policies. Today a great change is taking place all over the world. More and more people are accepting certain realities. May be the US Administration, in spite of its new found friendship with some countries, is not changing. But we cannot ignore the fact that the young people of America are giving deeper thought to these matters. So the world is changing. We have been told by some Hon’ble Members that there have been her agreement with Pakistan. What has happened to them. And in spite of previous talks about peace, have there not been wars? There have been wars. We cannot deny this. But we cannot deny also that today the situation in India has changed. Today there is more political cohesion and greater unity amongst the people. In every way the country is stronger and I think that our people have better understanding of the problems of the country and are willing to sacrifice, to fight and to face the challenges of the future. There is a great change in Pakistan. It may be that the Pakistanis did not want that change. But the change is there regardless of whether they desire it or not. They cannot ignore that change. When we look at the situation, we cannot also ignore that this change has taken place. Even President Bhutto himself has admitted that he was the father of the policy of confrontation with India. He himself now acknowledges that the situation has changed today and that the need of the times is peace. So things have changed. Some opposition members have taken me and Sardar Swaran Singh to task, because we have not categorically asserted that we know that there will be no war, that we know that President Bhutto is a different man. I don't do so. I am not used to making such categorical statements. I can only describe our assessment of the situation and I can also say with some assurance that so far I have not often been wrong in my assessment. So what I say is my assessment of the situation.

Some of the questions which are being put today, "How do you know that this will not happen?" "Peace will not be peace", etc. These some questions were posed at the time of Bangladesh also. It was said very categorically, "You say the refugees will return. But we know that they will not return and we know that you will not able to send them back". They did not think that Bangladesh could be freed. But, all those events did happen, this is obvious to all. A hundred and one events are taking place every day which are equally true, equally relevant, which are not so tangible to the opposition or even to some of us. Nevertheless, these things are happening. There are vast forces at work in India, in Pakistan and all over the world. The question before us is this : do we encourage these good forces or do we put a spoke in its wheel? To my mind, this is a straight forward question before us. It is possible that one makes the best effort possible and yet one falls. But is that a reason to say that we should not make that effort? So we have made an effort and I believe that we have succeeded, insofar as we can, in the first step. I do not know whether at the second step we can go very much further. But I know that a beginning has been made from which it will be difficult for anybody to go back. If something untoward does happen, as I have said in the other House and at other places, if there is war, well, we are ready. Then we cannot say, "No. We have accepted peace and, therefore, we are not ready for this attack". But we will do everything possible to see that peace succeeds and succeeds with honour. Why? Because-I have said this many times peace is an ideal and we do believe in ideals. But, peace is also a necessity.

I have always believed and I do believe even today that India's major enemy is not Pakistan, it is not even the Big Powers which are interested in their spheres of influence. India's greatest enemy is the economic backwardness of the country. It is the poverty of the country. If we did not have that heavy handicap, we could have done many things in the world. But, we have the handicap and nobody is going to help us to overcome it except we ourselves and we cannot overcome it unless we have peace. Therefore, peace is essential for our country and I believe that it is essential for Pakistan. I also believe that tension between the three countries of the subcontinent, will always be a weakening factor and one which may be exploited by outside forces. So, the second question before us is this : do we want interference by outside forces or do we want to settle our affairs ourselves, however, difficult they may be? We have believed that we must settle differences amongst ourselves, however, complex they may be and a beginning in that direction has also been made.

I am sorry, I have diverted from my point about Asian unity. I have spoken about Asia. I should like the countries of Asia to be united. But, unity for what purpose? You cannot have unity by giving up your ideals, values or your basic principles. In India, we follow a certain policy. Why? Not because we do not like America and so if America does something, we must we perverse and criticise America. Not at all. Personally I am not against America or any other country. But we disapprove of what US Administration is doing in Vietnam. We believe that this US action is not only against the interests of the people of

Vietnam, it is against the interests of every country in Asia and every country in the world. But there are countries in Asia which are supporting this American policy. What can we do? We want to be friends with them. But we can't have that close friendship with them as we can with countries which agree with our policy.

Just a few months back, Hon'ble members opposite were very anxious that we should be friends with Taiwan. I do not know whether their enthusiasm is as great today. The enthusiasm of the Western countries in this matter is not only waning, it has completely collapsed. The situation is developing as we had always thought it would be one day. We could not prophesy that it would happen in 1970, 1971 or 1972. But we know that it would happen.

We want the countries of Asia to stand together — not against Africa or Latin America. But when we can look after our own home first, only then can we be effective in a large circle. From that point of view, what happens in Asia is our more immediate concern. But we are equally interested in the peaceful development and progress of the under-privileged and developing countries of Africa and Latin America. But we can play a greater role in Asia, and therefore, we must at least try to solve the quarrels and tensions of Asia as soon as we can.

Hon'ble Members, I hope, will forgive me if I digress a little. If you look back into history, you will see that every country started with small units, gradually increasing. India is one country. We know that each of our States has some problems with neighbouring States. Now, they can quarrel and they can go to war as did the old rajas on all kinds of small and big matters or they can settle these matters peacefully. One State may suffer a little or another may suffer a little. But in the process we evolve something by which we can all become much stronger. And it is this that makes a nation. Fortunately, in our country we have that spirit in the States now. A number of long-standing problems of the States are being gradually solved, because each realises that by not coming to an agreement both suffer equally and the whole country suffers.

So we have to look at problems of friendship with Pakistan from that angle only 'Can we get something from Pakistan? Can Pakistan take something from us?' But, 'can we create an atmosphere and a situation in which we can together face the far greater dangers outside that threaten us?'

The other point raised was : How was it that at first no agreement could be reached and then suddenly at the end there was agreement? Now, nothing happens so suddenly. There is preparation for whatever happens. You can say that war was won on a particular day. But we did not arrive at it suddenly; we were working towards that end all the time. The battle is on before the war : the preparation is there. When you are having talks, you proceed gradually. Immediate decision does not come because naturally during the talks you make certain points and so on. But the preparation is there all the time, with every meeting you are moving. The agreement was signed at a certain time, well, that was because of circumstances. A dinner had been arranged, it was a formal dinner; it could not be postponed. A press conference had been arranged; that could not be postponed. Obviously, the final thing had to wait until after all this was over. If we could have said, "Let us postpone these and finish the business", well, that business could perhaps have been completed by six o'clock. It need not have waited for so long. These are all small points.

It is not my intention to compare this agreement with the Tashkent one because as I have said, the situation, the circumstances in both the countries, the attitudes of the people, all are entirely different. But since my Hon'ble friend opposite has quoted President Bhutto at such length, I shall also refer to a remark. President Bhutto has said that he had not accepted the Tashkent Agreement. He did not accept it while he was in Tashkent. He went back and told his country he had not accepted it and, according to him, his country also did not accept. Well, whether it was so or not I do not know. He has said this. But the Simla Agreement he has accepted and other parties in Pakistan have accepted it. Whether we like him or not, he has also got elected with a fairly big majority. His party has the majority there but even in places where he has not, other parties have accepted the agreement. President Bhutto is trying, and I think trying with success to get the people of Pakistan to accept it. Just as there are some voices in India against it, there are voices in Pakistan against it. So, this is also a big difference between the two agreements.

Now, I do not want to go into the business of the United Nations. Quite honestly, I am not bothered whether they go to the United Nations or whether they do not go to the United Nations. I am sure of ourselves, I am sure of whatever delegation we send there. If Pakistan goes to the United Nations we can meet them there. I have no fear of their getting away with anything at the United Nations. If they want to go to war, as I said, we do not want to go to war, as I said, we should like to do everything possible not to have war. But if they attack us, we are prepared far that also, I am not, afraid of that. I have full confidence in our armies; I have full confidence in our people. These are all false bogeys or red herrings to divert us from our real path.

Mention was made of opportunity. This was the very first opportunity we have had of making a new beginning towards peace and we have grasped that opportunity. If we had let this opportunity pass, I do not think it would have come our way again at least in this generation. So we have not let any opportunity go.

From the beginning we have taken a number of initiatives and we do not intend to let the initiative out of our hands. As in this country and or so abroad also our tactics have not been the tactics of confrontation even with the Jana Sangh much as they would like to provoke us. Occasionally, some of our members do get provoked but I do not think that this gains us anything and I have never supported this sort of thing. My way of handling situations is entirely different here or anywhere. It is to work for a situation which is conductive to certain thinking and action. Now, the Jana Sangh was very vocal against socialism; we do not hear that now. The Jana Sangh was very vocal against non-alignment, we do not hear that now. And not only the Jana Sangh, you will not hear such remarks from almost anybody in public now. A situation is created, a public opinion is created in which such remarks are not acceptable. It is in our hands to create a situation where on a larger screen, even in international affairs, certain things do not happen. I cannot prophesy that all will go as we want but we do have a certain strength, a certain initiative in our hands and if we can use it for good purpose that is a much better than to aggravate the atmosphere of confrontation.

What is the test of a people's loyalty? The test is that every time there was an invasion of Kashmir the people of Kashmir stood solidly by India. Does this not show that they are with us. To doubt their loyalty and sincerity is not good. I should like to express my deep appreciation of the past that in spite of religion being evoked — and we know that when religion is injected into any argument, people sometimes tend to lose their rationality, the people of Kashmir have been solidly with us in every crisis and I have no doubt that they will remain so. I am not afraid of my speeches.

There was some talk about our relations with our smaller neighbours. We want to have good relations with all our neighbours and we have done everything possible to convince them of our friendship for them, of our concern for them and of our desire to help them but whether the sort of jingoistic and chauvinistic speeches which are sometimes made in the House or outside, it is for the Hon'ble members themselves to consider, will inspire confidence in these small countries. If the feeling is created that we are out to get what we can in a chauvinistic manner, will these countries be confident of their safety, I am just posing the question.

So the basic issue before us is, what sort of world do we want? Are we concerned with the world or are we concerned only with India and we think that India can develop isolated from the world? The Jana Sangh, although born much later then our party, lives somewhat in the past and, if I may say so, they look further back, into the more remote past. We live in the present and we look to the future. It is only by looking towards the future and endeavouring to shape the future that the present can be made livable. And to make it livable we must have peace. We must have a constructive and creative attitude. The Simla Agreement, with all its faults, is a good step.

65

Simla Agreement

2 July 1972

The Simla Agreement signed by Prime Minister Indira Gandhi and President Zulfikar Ali Bhutto of Pakistan on 2nd July 1972 was much more than a peace treaty seeking to reverse the consequences of the 1971 war (*i.e.*, to bring about withdrawals of troops and an exchange of PoWs). It was a comprehensive blue print for good neighbourly relations between India and Pakistan. Under the Simla Agreement both countries undertook to abjure conflict and confrontation which had marred relations in the past, and to work towards the establishment of durable peace, friendship and co-operation.

The Simla Agreement contains a set of guiding principles, mutually agreed to by India and Pakistan, which both sides would adhere to while managing relations with each other. These emphasize : respect for each other's territorial integrity and sovereignty; non-interference in each other's internal affairs; respect for each other's unity, political independence; sovereign equality; and abjuring hostile propaganda. The following principles of the Agreement are, however, particularly noteworthy :

- A mutual commitment to the peaceful resolution of all issues through direct bilateral approaches.
- To build the foundations of a co-operative relationship with special focus on people to people contacts.
- To uphold the inviolability of the Line of Control in

Jammu and Kashmir, which is a most important CBM between India and Pakistan, and a key to durable peace.

India has faithfully observed the Simla Agreement in the conduct of its relations with Pakistan.

SIMLA AGREEMENT

Agreement on Bilateral Relations Between the Government of India and the Government of Pakistan.

1. The Government of India and the Government of Pakistan are resolved that the two countries put an end to the conflict and confrontation that have hitherto marred their relations and work for the promotion of a friendly and harmonious relationship and the establishment of durable peace in the sub-continent so that both countries may henceforth devote their resources and energies to the pressing talk of advancing the welfare of their people.

In order to achieve this objective, the Government of India and the Government of Pakistan have agreed as follows :

(i) That the principles and purposes of the Charter of the United Nations shall govern the relations between the two countries;

(ii) That the two countries are resolved to settle their differences by peaceful means through bilateral negotiations or by any other peaceful means mutually agreed upon between them. Pending the final settlement of any of the problems between the two countries, neither side shall unilaterally alter the situation and both shall prevent the organization, assistance or encouragement of any acts detrimental to the maintenance of peaceful and harmonious relations;

(iii) That the pre-requisite for reconciliation, good neighbourliness and durable peace between them is a commitment by both the countries to peaceful co-existence, respect for each other's territorial integrity and sovereignty and non-interference in each other's internal affairs, on the basis of equality and mutual benefit;

(iv) That the basic issues and causes of conflict which have bedevilled the relations between the two countries for the last 25 years shall be resolved by peaceful means;

(v) That they shall always respect each other's national unity, territorial integrity, political independence and sovereign equality;

(vi) That in accordance with the Charter of the United Nations they will refrain from the threat or use of force against the territorial integrity or political independence of each other.

2. Both Governments will take all steps within their power to prevent hostile propaganda directed against each other. Both countries will encourage the dissemination of such information as would promote the development of friendly relations between them.

3. In order progressively to restore and normalize relations between the two countries step by step, it was agreed that :

(i) Steps shall be taken to resume communications, postal, telegraphic, sea, land including border posts and air links including overflights.

(ii) Appropriate steps shall be taken to promote travel facilities for the nationals of the other country.

(iii) Trade and co-operation in economic and other agreed fields will be resumed as far as possible.

(iv) Exchange in the fields of science and culture will be promoted.

In this connection delegations from the two countries will meet from time to time to work out the necessary details.

4. In order to initiate the process of the establishment of durable peace, both the Governments agree that :

(i) Indian and Pakistani forces shall be withdrawn to their side of the international border.

(ii) In Jammu and Kashmir, the line of control resulting from the cease-fire of December 17, 1971 shall be respected by both sides without prejudice to the recognized position of either side. Neither side shall seek to alter it unilaterally, irrespective of mutual differences and legal interpretations. Both sides further undertake to refrain from the threat or the use of force in violation of this Line.

(iii) The withdrawals shall commence upon entry into force of this Agreement and shall be completed within a period of 30 days thereof.

5. This Agreement will be subject to ratification by both countries in accordance with their respective constitutional procedures, and will come into force with effect from the date on which the Instruments of Ratification are exchanged.

6. Both Governments agree that their respective Heads will meet again at a mutually convenient time in the future and that, in the meanwhile, the representatives of the two sides will meet to discuss further the modalities and arrangements for the establishment of durable peace and normalization of relations, including the questions of repatriation of prisoners of war and civilian internees, a final settlement of Jammu and Kashmir and the resumption of diplomatic relations.

(Sd/-)
INDIRA GANDHI
Prime Minister,
Republic of India

(Sd/-)
ZULFIKAR ALI BHUTTO
President,
Islamic Republic of Pakistan

Dated : 2-07-1972

66

Simla Agreement — Statement to the Press by H.E. Mr. Niaz A. Naik, Foreign Secretary of Pakistan

The Indian Foreign Secretary, H.E. Mr. M. Rasgotra, and I had most useful talks during the last two days in an atmosphere marked by mutual goodwill and cordiality. We have exchanged views on a number of international issues of common interest to both. As was expected much of our time was devoted to bilateral matters. We greatly value the spirit of such discussions which facilitate better understanding of each other's perceptions. On many international issues our views are same. We have been profoundly impressed by Mr. Rasgotra's deep understanding and by his lucid exposition of views of his Government. We took the opportunity to review recent developments in regard to the situation in Afghanistan and especially against the background of recent Geneva indirect discussions aimed at political settlement in Afghanistan. As you are aware, both Pakistan and India adhere to the declaration of the Non-aligned Foreign Ministers meeting of February, 1981 and the Havana Declaration of June, 1982 which discussed the tragic situation in Lebanon resulting from the Israeli aggression, un-ending agony of the people of West Beirut and the travail of the Palestinias pitted against the overwhelming Israeli armed might and brutality has evoked profound feelings of outrage. More effective restrictions need to be imposed on the Israeli policy of aggression and expansionism.

In regard to the Iran-Iraq war, we shared the wish that this protracted conflict between the two neighbouring Non-aligned countries would end and thus spare the people of the two developing countries further loss of life and property.

We expressed our disappointment over the lack of progress in the North-South Dialogue and shared the imperative need to launch urgently the Global Negotiations on International Co-operation.

In regard to the bilateral matters, an exchange of views took place against the background of the discussions between the Foreign Secretaries of the two countries last January. We gave our draft of the Non-aggression Pact to India on 1st June. Towards the end of the same month, India sent us a draft agreement on the establishment of a Joint Commission. Now Mr. Rasgotra has given us the proposed draft. Treaty of Peace, Friendship and Co-operation between India and Pakistan and elaborate and multifaceted proposal which will require study.

We look forward for further exchanges of views. The Foreign Secretary of India has extended an invitation to me to visit India which I have accepted with pleasure. The Government of Pakistan desires good-neighbourly relations with India and we believe that its objective can be achieved on a step-by-step-basis.

67

Resolution 307 (1971) adopted by the Security Council at its 1616th Meeting, on 21 December 1971

The Security Council,

Having discussed the grave situation in the sub-continent, which remains a threat to international peace and security.

Noting General Assembly Resolution 2793 (XXVI) of 7 December 1971,

Noting the reply of the Government of Pakistan on 9 December, 1971,

Noting the reply of the Government of India on 12 December 1971,

Having heard the statements of the Deputy Prime Minister of Pakistan and the Foreign Minister of India,

Noting further the statement made at the 1616th meeting of the Security Council by the Foreign Minister of India containing a unilateral declaration of a cease-fire in the Western theater,

Noting Pakistan's agreement to the cease-fire in the Western theater with effect from 17, December 1971,

Noting that consequently a cease-fire and a cessation of hostilities prevail,

1. *Demands* that a durable cease-fire and cessation of all hostilities in all areas of conflict be strictly observed and remain in effect until withdrawals take place, as soon as practicable, of all armed forces to their

respective territories and to positions which fully respect the cease-fire line in Jammu and Kashmir supervised by the United Nations Military Observer Group in India and Pakistan;

2. *Calls upon* all Member States to refrain from any action which may aggravate the situation in the sub-continent or endanger international peace;

3. *Calls upon* all those concerned to take all measures necessary to preserve human life and for the observance of the Geneva conventions of 1949 and to apply in full their provisions as regards the protection of the wounded and sick, prisoners of war and civilian population;

4. *Calls for* international assistance in the relief of suffering and the rehabilitation of refugees and their return in safety and dignity to their homes, and for full co-operation with the Secretary-General to that effect;

5. *Authorizes* the Secretary-General to appoint if necessary a special representative to lend his good offices for the solution of humanitarian problems;

6. *Requests* the Secretary-General to keep the Council informed without delay on developments relating to the implementation of the present resolution;

7. *Decides* to remain seized of the matter and to keep it under active consideration.

The Security Council voted on this Resolution on 21-12-1971 with the following result :

In favour : 13 votes.

Against : None.

Abstaining : 2 (Poland and USSR).

68

Instrument of Surrender by the Eastern Command, Lt. General A.A.K. Niazi in front of General Officer Commanding in Chief of Indian and Bangladesh Forces in the Eastern Theatre, Lt. General Jagjit Singh Aurora

Dacca, 16 December 1971

The Pakistan Eastern Command agree to surrender all Pakistan Armed Forces in Bangladesh to Lieutenant General Jagjit Singh Aurora, General Officer Commanding-in-chief of the Indian and Bangladesh forces in the Eastern theatre. This surrender includes all Pakistan land, air and naval forces as also all Para-military forces and civil armed forces. These forces will lay down their arms and surrender at the places where they are currently located to the nearest regular troops under the command of Lieutenant general Jagjit Singh Aurora.

The Pakistan eastern command shall come under the order of Lieutenant General Jagjit Singh Aurora as soon as this instrument has been signed. Disobedience of orders will be regarded as a breach of the surrender terms and will be dealt with in accordance with the accepted laws and usages of war. The decision of Lieutenant-General Jagjit Singh Aurora will be final. Should any doubt arise as to the meaning or interpretation of the surrender terms.

Lieutenant General-Jagjit-Singh-Aurora gives a solemn assurance that personnel who surrender shall be treated with dignity and respect that soldiers are entitled to in accordance with the provisions of the Geneva Convention and guarantees the safety and well being of all Pakistan military and Para-military forces who surrender. Protection will be provided to foreign nationals, ethnic minorities and personnel of West Pakistan origin by the forces under the command of Lieutenant General Jagjit Singh Aurora.

(Sd/-)

JAGJIT SINGH AURORA
Lieutenant General,
General Officer
Commanding-in-Chief,
Eastern Command,
(India)

(Sd/-)

AMIR ABDULLAH KHAN NIAZI
Lieutenant General,
Martial law Administrator,
Zone B And Commander,
Eastern Command,
(Pakistan)

Dated : 16-12-1971

69

Question considered by the Security Council at its 1606th, 1607th and 1608th Meetings on 4, 5 and 6 December 1971

The General Assembly,

Noting the reports of the Secretary-General of 3 and 4, December 1971 and the letter from the President of the Security council transmitting the text of Council Resolution 303 (1971) of 6, December 1971,

Gravely concerned that hostilities have broken out between India and Pakistan which constitute an immediate threat to international peace and security,

Recognizing the need to deal appropriately at a subsequent stage, within the framework of the Charter of the United Nations, with the issues which have given rise to the hostilities,

Convinced that an early political solution would be necessary for the restoration of conditions of normalcy in the area of conflict and for the return of the refugees to their homes,

Mindful of the provisions of the Charter, in particular of Article 2, paragraph 4,

Recalling the Declaration on the Strengthening of International Security, particularly paragraphs 4, 5 and 6.

Recognizing further the need to take immediate measures to bring about an immediate cessation of hostilities between India and Pakistan and effect a withdrawal of their armed forces to their own side of the India-Pakistan borders,

Mindful of the purposes and principles of the Charter and of the General Assembly's responsibilities under the relevant provisions of the Charter and of Assembly resolution 377 A (V) of 3 November 1950,

1. *Calls upon* the Governments of India and Pakistan to take forthwith all measures for an immediate cease-fire and withdrawal of their armed forces on the territory of the other to their own side of the India-Pakistan borders;
2. *Urges* that efforts be intensified in order to bring about, speedily and in accordance with the purposes and principles of the Charter of the United Nations, conditions necessary for the voluntary return of the East Pakistan refugees to their homes;
3. *Calls for* the full co-operation of all States with Secretary-General for rendering assistance to and relieving the distress of those refugees;
4. *Urges* that every effort be made to safeguard the lives and well-being of the civilian population in the area of conflict;
5. *Requests* the Secretary-General to keep the General Assembly and the Security Council promptly and currently informed on the implementation of the present resolution;
6. *Decides* to follow the question closely and to meet again should the situation so demand;
7. *Calls* upon the Security Council to take appropriate action in the light of the present resolution.

70

Agreement between the Government of India and the Government of Pakistan on Withdrawal of Troops

New Delhi, 22 January 1966

INTRODUCTION

This Agreement is in four parts :

Part I — Procedure concerning the immediate disengagement of troops and reduction of tension;

Part II — Procedure concerning the withdrawal of troops from the occupied areas;

Part III — Procedure concerning reduction of tension in the Eastern Sector;

Part IV — General Points.

PART I

DISENGAGEMENT OF TROOPS AND REDUCTION OF TENSION

PHASE 1

Both forces will withdraw 1,000 yards from the Line of Actual Control in sectors as specified below :

(a) Rajasthan/Sind

(b) Amritsar/Lahore

(c) Jammu/Sialkot

(d) Akhnur/Chhamb (from River Chenab NW 8061 To Mawa Wali Khad NW 7770)

In all other sectors including sectors divided by the 1949 Cease Fire Line, troops will continue to hold their respective picquets as by so doing they will be automatically separated from each other. The only exception to this will be where, in hilly terrain, opposing forces are at present considered to be too close to each other, each side will withdraw to a distance to be mutually agreed upon by the local commanders not below the rank of Brigadier.

[Note : In the Amritsar-Lahore sector, this 1000 yards withdrawal will be modified so that Pakistani troops who are actually on the West bank of the BRB Canal and Indian troops who are on the East bank of the BRB Canal facing each other will withdraw all armed personnel off the embankment to a distance of 200 yards on each side. Unarmed personnel may, however, live, move and work in this area. The same principle will apply in Sulaimanki-Fazilka Sector, Hussainiwala Sector and Khem Karan Sector]. After the withdrawal in this phase no new defences of any kind will be prepared in occupied territory.

There will be no movement of armed military, para-military or police personnel, either armed or unarmed within the demilitarised zone and no civilian personnel will be permitted within it by either side.

The period for completion of this phase will be five days.

PHASE II

In this phase both sides will remove and nullify all defences which will include the :

(a) lifting of mines and

(b) dismantling of all other defence works, less permanent defence structures constructed of steel and cement.

The period for completing this phase will be twenty-one days which will commence immediately after the five-day period mentioned in para 5.

Working parties for this purpose will be found by unarmed military personnel in uniform. No civilian or civil labour will be used for these tasks.

While every effort will be made to dismantle all defence works within the specified period, where owing to weather and other Conditions it is not possible to complete this, the uncleared area so left will be clearly marked and a sketch of these given to the other side.

There will be no firing of weapons or use of explosives within 10,000 meters of the Line of Actual Control. Where explosives have to be used to dismantle defence works, this will only be done under supervision as specified later and after due intimation to the other side.

The present Agreement affecting restriction on flights of aircraft will continue to apply.

To ensure that the action agreed to in PART I above is being implemented in letter and in spirit, the good offices of UNMOGIP and UNIPOM will be utilised. In the event of a disagreement, their decision will be final and binding on both sides.

PART II

WITHDRAWAL OF TROOPS FROM OCCUPIED AREAS

After the dismantling of defences has taken place, all troops, para-military forces and armed police who are now on the other side of the international border and Cease Fire Line, will be withdrawn. This withdrawal will be completed by 25th February 1966. If in any particular sector or part of a sector, the dismantling of defences has been completed earlier than the last date specified, withdrawal may be sectorwise if mutually agreed to.

During this withdrawal, there will be no follow up by civilians, armed military, para-military or police personnel until 25 February 1966. Only unarmed military personnel at a strength mutually agreed upon at the sector level may move into these unoccupied areas for normal police duties.

After troops of both sides have crossed into their own territory, the procedure which was being followed by Pakistan and India before 5 August, 1965, for the security of the international border and the Cease Fire Line, will apply.

Attention is drawn to Ground Rules 1961 for West Pakistan/ Punjab, Rajasthan and Gujarat (India).

It is essential that under all circumstances troops must move out of occupied areas by 25 February, 1966, even if the dismantling of defence and lifting of mines have not been completed.

For immediate settlement of any points of dispute that may arise, sector commanders not below the rank of Major General will be designated by name and appointment both by India and Pakistan who will meet to settle the differences. Telephone or R/T communication will be established between these designated sector commanders and will be permanently manned.

Any matter on which there is disagreement will be referred to the C-in-C, Pakistan Army, and COA's, India, for their joint decision. If the issue is still not resolved by them the good offices of Major General T. Marambio will be utilised and his decision will be final and binding on both sides.

PART III

REDUCTION OF TENSION IN THE EASTERN SECTOR

The limit of withdrawal in the Eastern Sector will be left to local commanders not below the rank of Major General to mutually decide where necessary, in consultation with the civil authorities concerned. Both sides will arrive at a working agreement as soon as possible.

Border Security Forces consisting of armed para-military units, police or any other irregular forces of both sides will not open fire across the border under any circumstances.

Any encroachment across the border will be dealt with through apprehension of personnel concerned and thereafter handing them over to civil authorities.

In any case where firing takes place across the border it will be investigated on the spot by a joint team consisting of border personnel from both sides within 24 hours of occurrence. Brigade Commanders/ DIGs responsible for this investigation will be designated by name and appointment sector wise for West Bengal, Assam and Tripura by India and for the adjoining areas of East Pakistan by Pakistan.

Liaison between commanders and telephone communications at various levels will be established as given in para 12 and 13 of the Ground Rules for Indo-East Pakistan border.

To ensure that the above Agreement is fully implemented, quarterly meetings will take place between Army and Police authorities of India and Pakistan, alternately in India and Pakistan, to assess the extent to which the Agreement is working in practice.

These are a supplement to the Ground Rules formulated by the Military Sub-Committee of the Indian and Pakistani delegations on 20 October, 1959.

PART IV

GENERAL POINTS

In order to resolve any problems that may arise in the implementation of this Agreement and to further maintain friendly relations between the two countries, the C-in-C Pakistan and the COA India will meet from time to time. The meetings will be held alternately in India and Pakistan and will be initiated by the respective Governments concerned.

Ground rules to implement this withdrawal Agreement in the Western Sector will be formulated by Lt. General Bakhtiar Rana Pakistan, and Lt. General Harbaksh Singh-India, under the Chairmanship of Major General T. Marambio as early as possible.

The Agreement comes into effect as from 0600 hours IST/ 0630 hours WPT 25 January 1966.

(Sd/-)	(Sd/-)
The Chief of Army Staff,	Commander-in-Chief,
India	Pakistan Army

Dated : 22-01-1966

71

Tashkent Declaration of 1966

10 January 1966

The Prime Minister of India and the President of Pakistan having met at Tashkent and having discussed the existing relations between India and Pakistan, hereby declare their firm resolve to restore normal and peaceful relations between their countries and to promote understanding and friendly relations between their people. They consider the attainment of these objectives of vital importance for the welfare of the 600 million people of India and Pakistan.

I

The Prime Minister of India and the President of Pakistan agree that both sides will exert all efforts to create good neighbourly relations between India and Pakistan in accordance with the United Nations Charter. They reaffirm their obligation under the Charter not to have recourse to force and to settle their disputes through peaceful means. They considered that the interests of peace in their region and particularly in the Indo-Pakistan sub-continent and, indeed, the interests of the peoples of India and Pakistan were not served by the continuance of tension between the two countries. It was against this background that Jammu and Kashmir was discussed, and each of the sides set forth its respective position.

II

The Prime Minister of India and the President of Pakistan

have agreed that all armed personnel of the two countries shall be withdrawn not later than 25, February 1966 to the positions they held prior to 5, August 1965, and both sides shall observe the cease-fire terms on the cease-fire line.

III

The Prime Minister of India and the President of Pakistan have agreed that relations between India and Pakistan shall be based on the principle of non-interference in the internal affairs of each other.

IV

The Prime Minister of India and the President of Pakistan have agreed that both sides will discourage any propaganda directed against the other country, and will encourage propaganda which promotes the development of friendly relations between the two countries.

V

The Prime Minister of India and the President of Pakistan have agreed that the High Commissioner of India to Pakistan and the High Commissioner of Pakistan to India will return to their posts and that the normal functioning of diplomatic missions of both countries will be restored. Both Governments shall observe the Vienna Convention of 1961 on Diplomatic Intercourse.

VI

The Prime Minister of India and the President of Pakistan have agreed to consider measures towards the restoration of economic and trade relations, communications, as well as cultural exchanges between India and Pakistan, and to take measures to implement the existing agreement between India and Pakistan.

VII

The Prime Minister of India and the President of Pakistan

have agreed that they give instructions to their respective authorities to carry out the repatriation of the prisoners of war.

VIII

The Prime Minister of India and the President of Pakistan have agreed that both the sides will continue the discussion of questions relating to the problems of refugees and evictions/ illegal immigrations. They also agreed that both sides will create conditions which will prevent the exodus of people. They further agreed to discuss the return of the property and assets taken over by either side in connection with the conflict.

IX

The Prime Minister of India and the President of Pakistan have agreed that the sides will continue meetings both at the highest and at other levels on matters of direct concern to both countries. Both sides have recognized the need to set up joint Indian-Pakistani bodies, which will report to their Governments in order to decide what further steps should be taken.

The Prime Minister of India and the President of Pakistan record their feelings of deep appreciation and gratitude to the leaders of the Soviet Union, the Soviet Government and personally to the Chairman of the Council of the Ministers of USSR for their constructive, friendly and noble part in bringing about the present meeting, which has resulted in mutually satisfactory results. They also express to the Government and friendly people of Uzbekistan their sincere thankfulness for their overwhelming reception and generous hospitality.

We invite the Chairman of the Council of Ministers of USSR to witness this Declaration.

(Sd/-)
LAL BAHADUR
Prime Minister of India

(Sd/-)
M.A. KHAN, FM.
President of Pakistan

Dated : 10-01-1966.

A

THE TEXT OF A RADIO BROADCAST GIVEN BY THE MINISTER OF EXTERNAL AFFAIRS, SARDAR SWARAN SINGH, ON JANUARY 15, 1966 ON THE TASHKENT DECLARATION

I speak to you as one who was privileged to be associated with our late Prime Minister Shri Lal Bahadur Shastri in Tashkent during his mission of peace. The week that we spent in Tashkent was unforgettable. They were days of meetings, negotiations and sincere efforts to reach understanding and meeting of minds. The Prime Minister and his colleagues worked as a team, determined to see the establishment of peace and goodwill between India and Pakistan. We were all proud to week under his inspiring leadership. After strenuous efforts in which Chairman Kosygin played a most notable good offices role, President Ayub Khan and Prime Minister Shastri were able to reach agreement on a declaration which was signed in Tashkent on the 10th of January.

In the Tashkent Declaration India and Pakistan have chosen to turn away from mutual conflict and have resolved to base their relations on peace, friendship and good neighbourliness.

Remarkable Achievement

This in itself is a remarkable achievement which reverses the trends of the past 17 years and marks a new era in the relations between the two countries. The central point of the whole Declaration is the renunciation of force by both sides for the settlement of their disputes. For many years in the past, India had emphasized the importance of a no-war declaration by both countries, to the effect that all differences and disputes between them should be settled peacefully without resort to arms. Unfortunately no agreement could be reached on such a declaration between India and Pakistan all these years. It is a tribute to the statemanship and sincerity of purpose of the President of Pakistan and of Prime Minister Shastri that at last both countries have agreed not to have recourse to force and to settle their disputes through peaceful means.

It has always been our view that it is only in an atmosphere of freedom from tension and of goodwill created by such a declaration that both sides could reach solutions to the problems between them.

Renunciation of Force

Article I of the Tashkent Declaration seeks to embody the agreement regarding renunciation of force. The crucial sentence therein reads "they reaffirm their obligation under the Charter not to have recourse to force and to settle their disputes through peaceful means". The greater part of the discussion in Tashkent centred round this basic question. Prime Minister Shastri made it clear that the main issue was whether or not the two countries wanted to settle their disputes peacefully. He insisted on a clear affirmation that there shall be no resort to force. The Pakistan position was that any declaration would be valueless unless there was a political settlement or a self-executing machinery for the settlement of the Kashmir question was set up. Eventually, after a great deal of discussions there was agreement that the Declaration should specifically mention agreement on non-use of force as a means of settling any disputes between the two countries. This has been done by a categorical reaffirmation of the obligation which both countries have, as members of the United Nations, to refrain in their mutual relationship from the threat or use of force.

Withdrawal of Armed Personnel

Article II of the Declaration provides for the withdrawal of all armed personnel of the two countries not later than February 25, 1966 to the pre-August 5 positions, as required in UN Resolutions. Prime Minister Shastri gave the fullest consideration to all aspects of the question of withdrawals before agreeing to this clause. He very carefully examined his letter of September 14 to the U.N. Secretary-General in which he had stated "that when consequent upon the cease-fire becoming effective further details are considered, we shall not agree to any disposition which will leave the door open to further infiltrations or prevent us from dealing with infiltrations that have taken place". The late Prime Minister and the entire Indian delegation felt that the conditions laid down by the Prime Minister had been completely met by Pakistan's agreement not only to withdraw all armed personnel, but also to respect, after withdrawals, the cease-fire terms on the cease-fire line and the undertaking of non-interference in each other's internal affairs.

Prime Minister Shastri had made it clear, on more than one occasion, that if the question of Kashmir was raised by President Ayub, he would have to reiterate India's viewpoint and this is exactly what he did as Article I of the Declaration indicates. The important point is that though the viewpoints of both countries of Kashmir continue to be irreconcilable, both sides have nevertheless, agreed not to take, recourse to arms over this or any other question.

Joint Indo-Pakistan Bodies

There are provisions in the Declaration which refer to normalisation of relations and discussion of various other problems. It is hoped that for a consideration of these, joint Indo-Pakistani bodies will be constituted. Meetings at Ministerial and Heads of Government level are also contemplated. All these are very salutary provisions. It is only in these ways that we can tackle the various outstanding problems between the two countries.

Spirit of Peace and Goodwill

More important than the words of the Declaration is the spirit underlying it. We are confident that the Tashkent Declaration, signed by the two Heads of Government and witnessed by the Chairman of the council of Ministers of the U.S.S.R., embodies the spirit of peace and goodwill on which future relations between the two countries can be based to the lasting benefit of their people. It is our intention to implement the declaration faithfully. We already initiated the steps for the normalisation of relations between the two countries. Our High Commissioner to Pakistan is returning to his post. The Pakistan High Commissioner has already arrived in Delhi. The three Chiefs of Services from both countries are going to meet shortly. The direct contacts between Defence Chiefs will not only facilitate withdrawals, but also consider measures to ensure tranquillity on the Indo-Pakistan borders in the East and the West, as well as across the cease-fire line.

The Tashkent Declaration is a tribute to the vision and statesmanship of the President of Pakistan and the Prime Minister of India. Equally, one cannot but recognise the tremendous contribution which was made by Mr. Kosygin who not only sponsored the idea of the conference, but also, at all stages and particularly when difficulties arose, acted as a messenger of peace and helped to resolve all obstacles. He did not propose much less impose, any particular solutions. Yet without his good offices, the Tashkent Declaration could not have taken shape.

Tashkent Declaration A Triumph of Peace

The Tashkent Declaration is a declaration of peace and goodwill between India and Pakistan. It has been hailed all over the world as a great act of statesmanship and as a significant contribution to world peace. Dozens of messages of congratulations have been received from Heads of Government and States all over the world. The Tashkent Declaration implemented sincerely and earnestly, will make an immeasurable contribution to the happiness of millions of people in the subcontinent and to peace in Asia and the world. Both India and Pakistan can use their resources for economic development and for betterment of the standards of living of their people. The dangerous tensions which have characterised the relations between the two countries will be eliminated. Both countries will be able to conserve their resources for peaceful economic development. Their security will be strengthened by the assurance of peace flowing from the Declaration.

Virtual agreement on the text of the Tashkent Declaration was reached at midnight of the 9th January. The next day, Prime Minister Shastri felt greatly relaxed and entertained President Ayub at a quiet lunch a couple of hours before the Declaration was actually signed. No one who saw him that afternoon looking hale and hearty feeling obviously happy at the triumph of peace and goodwill, would have had any inkling of the impending tragedy.

The Tashkent Declaration is a monument to Prime Minister Shastri's wisdom, statesmanship and love of peace. This Declaration is his last gift to our nation. He wanted us to work for peace as steadfastly and courageously as we had fought to preserve our honour and integrity. It is up to us to live up to his expectations, All of us, in whatever walk of life and wherever we are, at the Centre or in the States, in towns or in villages, should dedicate ourselves to working for the basic objectives of peace and amity between India and Pakistan embodied in the Tashkent Declaration.

(*Source* : Foreign Affairs Record).

B

STATEMENT OF PAKISTAN PRESIDENT AYUB KHAN ON TASHKENT DECLARATION (14, JANUARY 1966)

On the 4th of this month I went to Tashkent to meet the Indian Prime Minister. I must explain to you the background of this historic meeting.

When our two armies clashed in Azad Kashmir and the situation took a serious turn, the Soviet Prime Minister invited the leaders of the two countries to Tashkent to provide us opportunity to settle our differences in a peaceful and an honourable manner.

We received the Soviet invitation on 4 September. Two days later, India launched an Attack on our sacred territory. What followed is known to all of you. The entire nation rose like one man and came through this ordeal in a gloriously successful manner. The heroic deeds of our armed forces as well as the civilian population will for ever be cherished in our history.

We have always held the view that countries must settle their differences on the basis of peace and justice.

We want peace for the whole world and as a member of the United Nations, we have accepted the obligations to settle differences not by force but in a peaceful manner and through mutual understanding.

As for our differences with India, we have always made it clear that the basic cause of this conflict was the dispute about Jammu and Kashmir and there is a Security Council resolution on this issue. According to this historic resolution, the people of Jammu and Kashmir have the right to decide whether they want to accede to Pakistan or to India. India is a party to this agreement and has pledged to the United Nations that it would give to the people of the State their right to freely choose their own future.

For the last eighteen years, we have been constantly endeavouring to persuade India to fulfill its commitment. Unfortunately, India did nothing to honour it with the result that the people of Jammu and Kashmir rose in an open revolt. When the Indian forces launched repeated attacks on the Azad Kashmir territory, the Pakistan Army had no option but to take action in support of the people of Jammu and Kashmir. The resulting armed conflict between the two countries amply demonstrated to the world that there would be no peace between India and Pakistan unless the Kashmir dispute was settled.

The Security Council resolution of 20 September provided for a cease-fire and the withdrawal of armed forces. It also provided that after the withdrawal of forces the Security Council would take steps to resolve the basic issue of Jammu and Kashmir. The resolution expressed the hope that till the completion of the withdrawal, the two countries should try to settle the dispute between themselves.

My meeting with the late Mr. Lai Bahadur Shastri in Tashkent was a step in this direction. The Government of the USSR and their Prime Minister made at all out effort for the success of these talks. We were received with great enthusiasm by the Russian people and their leaders who observed impartiality throughout these negotiations. We are grateful to them for all this.

The Indian Prime Minister wanted us to sign a no-war pact

but we made it clear to him that we would never be a signatory to such a pact unless the Jammu and Kashmir dispute was settled honourably and equitably. We, however, offered to reaffirm our obligation under the U.N. Charter. This obligation means that nations will not resort to force unless they have explored all avenues of peaceful settlement. We also impressed upon the Indian Prime Minister that the future of the people of the two countries depended on peace in the subcontinent and that this peace could not be lasting unless the Kashmir dispute was amicably settled. If this dispute was not settled both the countries would continue with war-like preparations and their resources, instead of being dedicated to the welfare of their people, would be diverted to the purpose of war.

Personally, I had a feeling that Indian Prime Minister was agreeable to what I said but he wanted that we should first normalise our relations and then grapple with the basic issue. We explained our respective points of view to each other but unfortunately we reached no conclusions. As for Pakistan, we stuck to our belief that the basic cause was the dispute concerning Jammu and Kashmir and unless this was settled there could be no peace between India and Pakistan. Pakistan was not prepared to consider Jammu and Kashmir as part of India or that it was their internal affair. The people of Jammu and Kashmir had a right to decide their own future and we will continue to support their inalienable right.

I would invite you to consider the various provisions of the Tashkent Declaration against this background. The Declaration has in no way detracted from or damaged our national viewpoint on Kashmir. Their right to choose their future remains inviolate.

I hope that this Declaration will open new avenues for the settlement of the Kashmir issue. First, we will take up this matter with the Indian representatives and then, after the withdrawal of forces, the Security Council also will be in a position to deal with it. Moreover, the interest shown by the Soviet Government in the settlement of the dispute will also facilitate the task.

I appeal to you to show the same sense of purpose and discipline in achieving peace as you did in achieving victory during the last war. The sacrifices made during that period are indelibly marked on our hearts and I assure you that no sacrifice will go in vain.

Whatever steps your Government has taken or is taking they ate for your good. We have been given assurances that sincere efforts will be made to settle the Indo-Pakistan dispute in a just and equitable manner. It is, therefore, necessary that we should take the fullest advantage of this effort. It can only be translated into action if we on our part fully implement the Tashkent Declaration. I am sure, the nation will help the Government make a success of this effort for peace. If God forbid, for some reason or other, this effort does not bear fruit, it will not mean that we will ever be oblivious of our national interests or fail to safeguard the country's defence. In any case, we have to build up our defence effort.

The Tashkent Declaration has been hailed in many parts of the country but there are those as well who are not satisfied with it. I am fully aware of their misgivings and honour the sentiments which give rise to them. It is obvious that if the Kashmir dispute had been honourably settled at the Tashkent meeting you would have welcomed it : but complicated issues are not easy to solve and the Government has to adopt various means to solve it, according to circumstances.

There may be some amongst us who will take advantage of your feelings and will try to mislead you. They are not more patriotic perhaps than you and me and are in fact after their own selfish gain. You should be aware of their machinations. You should remain firm in your faith and steadfast in your discipline. The ordeal is not yet over. Let us bow out heads to the Almighty and pray for the strengthening of our will and determination.

Pakistan Paindabad.

C

STATEMENT OF SHRI SWARAN SINGH IN THE LOK SABHA ON TASHKENT AGREEMENT, FEBRUARY 21, 1996

The question of withdrawals of armed personnel from Haji Pir, Tithwal and Kargil has come up for comments; it has also been criticised by certain Hon'ble members. The question of infiltrators has also been mentioned. As a matter of fact, these two points are interconnected, and I would like to say something on these two points together. We have first to see the objective that we had before us when the Indian armed forces moved to Kargil, to Tithwal and to Haji Pir. It is very important, because we were facing aggression, and this massive aggression originated in the form of a large number of armed personnel crossing over to that part of Jammu and Kashmir which is in the actual possession and control, administrative and the rest, of the Government of India.

When we took up this matter with the Pakistan Government and pointed out to them the serious situation created by these armed infiltrators coming across into Indian territory, the Government of Pakistan did not accept and responsibility. It then became necessary for us to take defensive measures to check infiltration, because the responsibility in this respect was not accepted by the Government of Pakistan. It was in that context that the Indian armed forces moved into these two passes Tithwal and Haii Pir; and we moved into Kargil because our line of communication to the Ladakh area was under constant threat by the snipping and other provocative acts which were indulged in by the Pakistan forces. These were the objectives before us when we moved to these passes.

We have now to see whether, when we agreed to withdraw, our objective had not been realised, whether the reason for which we moved to these passes still persisted at the time we agreed to this withdrawal. We gave very careful consideration to the various aspects. This was a very serious matter, and we attached a very great deal of importance to it; it was necessary for us to give the most careful consideration to the implications of the step that we were taking in agreeing to the withdrawal from these areas.

As I said when I initiated this debate, three conditions, were agreed to by Pakistan. Firstly, both countries agreed that the use of force would be abjured in the settlement of any dispute; secondly, that cease-fire terms on the cease-fire line would be adhered to and respected by the two Parties, and thirdly, that there would be non-interference in each other's internal affairs. Even one of these considerations or conditions is enough to correct the mischief that can be created by the movement of infiltrators.

Sending armed infiltrators, for instance, is obviously use of force, and if both parties agree that force will not be used for the enforcement of any claim or the settlement of any dispute, obviously they cannot say that they will send these infiltrators in the exercise of their right to enforce a claim or to settle a dispute. It is quite another thing, a separate issue to which I will come, as to whether they will respect this or not, but my point is : is the sending of infiltrators protected or can it be resorted to by any loophole that is there in the agreement? My contention is that we should keep these two things separate, the interpretation of the agreements, and then other party's intentions or the question whether they will respect the terms of the agreement or not. At this stage, I am on this question whether the agreement itself covers armed infiltrators or whether, notwithstanding the terms of this agreement, and even if they are adhered to, they can make out a case that they can send infiltrators.

Pakistan has at no stage said that they have got the right to send infiltrators. All along they have denied having sent infiltrators, and even now they do not say that they have the right to send infiltrators. That is an important point.

One of the first conditions of the agreement is not to use force, and sending armed infiltrators is use of force. That is what I am trying to contend. It is quite clear that even Pakistan has not said that they are entitled to send infiltrators or to use force even if Kashmir is not an internal matter of India. We do not accept Pakistan's contention that Jammu and Kashmir is not an integral part of India, and any interference by sending infiltrators even by whipping up agitations there trying to support those who are not accepting the right of the local government there, is very much interference. We do not accept their interpretation of Jammu and Kashmir not being an internal problem or an internal responsibility of the Government of India.

The second point that has been mentioned is that they do not accept Jammu and Kashmir as the internal problem of India, and, therefore, there may be a loophole for sending infiltrators. My reply to this is two-fold. Firstly, it is our interpretation, it is our very firm stand, that Jammu and Kashmir is an integral part of India, and that its sovereignty is not negotiable. In these circumstances, any unilateral interpretation is not acceptable.

We do not accept this interpretation that they have got the right to interfere in this. So far as the question of armed infiltrators is concerned, whatever may be their position with regard to Jammu and Kashmir, even if they are keeping up a dispute on that issue, which we do not accept — we clearly say that there is no dispute — even then I contend that the clause relating to non-use of force covers this completely and any step that they take to interfere with the established administration on our side of the cease-fire line is a clear violation of the Tashkent declaration. It is, therefore, something about which we need not have any doubt in our minds. Prof. Hem Barua says : if it is an internal matter then why was it discussed? It is very clear in the Tashkent deceleration and it is not left in doubt. I would recall that Prime Minister Shastri had on more than one occasions made the position clear in this House : "I am not going to discuss Kashmir."

He had also said : if the other party says that it wants to discuss Kashmir or they want to raise some point, all that I have to do is to state clearly that Jammu and Kashmir is an integral part of India; that is the position to which he said India would steadfastly adhere. In this context, at the meetings in Tashkent between our late Prime Minister and President Ayub Khan, it is a fact that President Ayub did raise the question of Kashmir.

Our late Prime Minister made a clear and categorical statement that Jammu and Kashmir is an integral part of India and that is the position to which he strongly adhered; we are not going to alter that position. As to what President Ayub said, or their Foreign Minister said, it is well-known; they say from time to time that the people of that area should be permitted to express their desire about their future but in reply to that we categorically reject any such claims and reiterate our stand on Jammu and Kashmir, it is not discussing the question of Kashmir, it is only a reiteration of the position, and that fact, Mr. Speaker, is clearly enunciated in the declaration. The declaration says that the two sides reiterated their Position. Prof. Hem Barua is hurling the declaration at us. We went through every word of it. Shri Dwivedy raised a point that the position and manners in which this sentence is used perhaps might cast same cloud on our assertion. That is not at all correct. Article 1 says that the Prime Minister of India and the President of Pakistan agree that both sides will exert all efforts to create good neighbourliness between India and Pakistan in accordance with UN charter. That is unexceptionable. They reaffirm their obligation under the charter not to have recourse to force but to settle their disputes through peaceful means. I would very strongly urge that this is a very clear and categorical reaffirmation of the obligation not to use force, this should not be lightly dismissed; it is a clear affirmation of their obligation. They considered that the interests of peace in the region, particularly in the Indo-Pakistan sub-continent and indeed the interests of the people of India and Pakistan were not served by the continuance of tension between the two countries. They also said that our attitude should be to develop good neighbourly relations, to discontinue tension. It was in this context and against this background that Jammu and Kashmir was discussed and each side set forth its respective position. I have already said what our Position was: namely, that it is an integral part of India. The other party said that they have got their own claim. They agreed to disagree on this issue. To bring about good neighbourly relations, it was said there were other matters which should be attended to and the rest of the declaration proceeds to mention some of the other matters. The mention of this background against which Jammu and Kashmir was discussed is a point which bring out our clear statement and position on Jammu and Kashmir. I would also like to mention that in the course of my talks with the Foreign Minister of Pakistan and his colleagues, talks during which on our side my colleague Shir Chavan and other members of the delegation were present, I reiterated our position and our stand on Jammu and Kashmir in unmistakable terms.

There are a large number of others. The Indian position on Jammu and Kashmir was not whittled down in the slightest; we reiterated in clear and unmistakable terms our stand, and Pakistan is in doubt about our stand.

No newspaper, no critic or supporter of the Tashkent declaration from Pakistan has ever asserted that India has deviated from its stand on Jammu and Kashmir. On an issue on which even Pakistan does not claim that we have changed our stand on Jammu and Kashmir, it is not wise or in our national interest to continue to agitate these points and unnecessarily to create doubts even when the other party is in no doubt.

I do not want to go into the whole history of how this wave of infiltration started and how we took preventive action by moving into some of the passes and how vigorously our security forces took very stern and effective measures to deal with the infiltrators who were operating in Jammu and Kashmir territory. . . . (*Interruptions.*)

The infiltrators who had crossed over were being dealt with and our security forces and our police made a very thorough job of it. If ultimately we were able to control the situation it was due to the effective steps that were taken by the security forces. I would also like to add that the government of Jammu and

Kashmir and, if I may add, the people there, acted very strongly and they fully co-operated with these steps taken by the authorities in dealing with the infiltrators. It was this support given to us, the lack of the response which mistakenly Pakistan thought they would get from the people, which was mainly responsible for thwarting the designs of the infiltrators.

We are grateful to the people who gave information to the local authorities. We had a large number of non-officials who traced the movement of these people and supplied information to the authorities which ultimately led to the mopping up operations and in providing the necessary security to the areas and to the targets which unfortunately had been aimed at by the infiltrators.

I would also like to add that after the cease-fire operations, although Pakistan did continue to keep this posture that they had never sent these infiltrators, and continued to disown their responsibility, we have definite information that they called upon these people, who had been sent across, to return to that area. We had definite information on that score, and a large bulk of the people actually crossed over into the other territory. (*Interruption*). Our security forces also have been stepping up their efforts, which continued after the cease-fire, because our Prime Minister had made it absolutely clear that any cease-fire agreement that it arrived at or any cease-fire arrangement that is accepted does not mean that our efforts to deal with the infiltrators or to deal with them effectively would anyway be influenced by the cease-fire. We made the position clear that this is an internal, law and order matter, and we had to function effectively. It was the combined effect of these two things, the continuous by our security and armed forces, the civilians and the civilian government — all this combined effort put so much pressure on them and they found, particularly after the cease-fire, that there was no point in their staying on. A large number were actually thrown out and pushed back into the other territory. We have definite information about the order which was available with us when they sent across these infiltrators, through a variety of sources, that after the cease-fire, particularly —

Out of the total number of infiltrators, who were in thousands, a good bulk has been thrown back. A large number of them were killed : some of them were also arrested. The number that might be left there might be very, very small. It is very difficult for me to give any number, but it cannot be more than a few odds and ends, say, half a dozen or 10 people in one remote area or the other. I have not got the census or the list. If we knew the exact number, we would get hold of them or kill them or shoot them, those who come here without any authority. But the point is, the Pakistan Government, naturally from the very beginning, had taken the attitude that they are not concerned with these, that they have not sent them; we have information that they had done so and they had sent across these people. We had information that they were receiving messages and we intercepted some of those messages, and it was on that basis that we kept the country and this House fully informed about their activity; that they were sent across and they were supported. We had also information — we had definite information — that they were withdrawn after the ceasefire. So, this was a combined effect of the two-pronged operation, pressure by us, by our security forces, and also their attitude that they wanted to withdraw.

In a matter like this, we have to see the results and need not insist on a public statement that they have withdrawn. I am sure that even on this statement of mine they might say, "No; we never sent anyone; we have not withdrawn anyone". They may say, as in their earlier statement that "We have not sent any man even in the initial stages". So, we have to look to the situation on the ground and view it realitically, and realise that in future, these conditions we accepted; that non-use of force is accepted; non-interference in one's internal affairs is accepted; and that observance of the cease-fire terms on the cease-fire line is accepted, for after that sending in armed personnel across the cease-fire line is a clear violation of the cease-fire terms and the cease-fire line. So, in actual fact also, based upon this agreement that they have entered upon, we were fully satisfied that the question of infiltrators is not likely to arise hereafter, and it is covered by the agreement. It was thereafter that we agreed in respect of Haji Pir and Tithwal the passage through which we had moved in order to check further infiltration.

We are clear that if the terms of the agreement are adhered to, then, the question of sending infiltrators does not arise. It is a very pertinent question and a practical question, that they do not adhere to the obligations that they have undertaken, then what is our guarantee? It is a very pertinent question. But the answer to this is the same as with all the other agreements that have been entered into between two countries. In a matter like this, if we start with this attitude that any agreement that is entered into is not likely to be adhered to that they will find some excuses to go back upon the agreement, then, the reply is that we know how to deal with the situation, Then a new situation develops altogether. The agreement is clear. If they do not adhere to it, if they go behind the agreement and do not faithfully carry out their obligations under it but surreptitiously take resort to something else, then it is a clear violation of the agreement; then a situation arises, and we will take the sternest measure to meet the situation, and of that we have never made any secret. I would beg of this House to see that the agreement is very clear, and that the ultimate protection in this case is provided by the agreement and by their adherence to this agreement. If the agreement is not adhered to, what follows depends upon our capacity to deal with the situation. Many of our foreign friends, sympathetic friends, have many times mentioned to us that a country of 45 crores or 48 crores people hardly needs to go to the international community to say that this is a nuisance by the infiltrators. But there should be some solemn agreement on their part that they will never send infiltrators. They have admitted their responsibility; though not in these clear words, if the terms are adhered to, it is covered. If they do not observe these terms then it is a situation where our strength and our capacity to deal with them will be the real guarantee. That is something which we have not to lose sight of.

Sending infiltrators is a clear interference in our internal affairs. Even if they unilaterally do not accept it, it cannot be an explanation of the declaration terms. Thirdly, this is a contravention of the cease-fire terms. Sending in armed personnel across the cease-fire line is contravention of the cease-fire terms.

D

THE MINISTER OF EXTERNAL AFFAIRS, SARDAR SWARAN SINGH'S STATEMENT IN THE GENERAL ASSEMBLY OF THE UNITED NATIONS ON SEPTEMBER 29, 1966

Mr. President, I am conscious that the hour is late and we all have other pressing engagements. I should, therefore, be as brief as possible.

The Foreign Minister of Pakistan has today referred to India in abusive but familiar terms. Like other representatives of Pakistan who have exploited, indeed misused, this august forum, he has offered to the distinguished delegates assembled here a mixture of half truths and fantasies. What is painful is that in the process of hurting abuse against India, the Foreign Minister of Pakistan has completely ignored that provision of the Tashkent Declaration which stated the specific agreement of the two sides that they will "discourage any propaganda directed against the other country and will encourage propaganda which promotes the development of friendly relations between the two countries." Among other things, India has been branded an aggressor and India has been compared to South Africa. The fact of India's defensive action in September last year has been presented by the Foreign Minister of Pakistan to this Assembly as aggression. The fact of Pakistan's aggression on the Indian State of Jammu and Kashmir twice within the last 19 years has been conveniently ignored and kept back from this Assembly. Now, Mr. President, I Prefer to be constructive; I prefer not to violate the Tashkent Declaration. As far as the record is concerned, the same charges had been made time and again and refuted by the delegation of India on every occasion. I am not going to take the time of this Assembly by once again covering the whole ground. There are two points, however, which need to be brought to the attention of this Assembly.

First, it is amazing that the Foreign Minister of Pakistan has taken exception to reiteration by the leaders of India of the Indian stand that the State of Jammu and Kashmir is a constituent State of India. This position of India has been stated by the Indian delegation on innumerable occasions both in this Assembly as well as in the Security Council. While participating in the general debate last year I myself stated and I quote "it is, therefore, necessary for me to make my government's position clear beyond any shadow of doubt. Legally, constitutionally, morally and on the basis of the will of the people, the State of Jammu and Kashmir is an integral part of the Indian Union. This is the position on which India takes its stand and will continue to do so. The people of Jammu and Kashmir, together with their fellow citizens in other parts of India, are the architects of the largest democratic state in the world, a state rooted in popular will expressed through freely chosen institutions and periodic general elections, based on adult franchise. There is no better way of giving reality to the freedom of a people". The fact that India is prepared to discuss all differences with Pakistan in accordance with the letter and spirit of Tashkent Declaration and to settle those differences by peaceful means in a spirit of good-neighbourly relations does not mean and cannot mean that India must give up its stand in regard to the status of the Indian State of Jammu and Kashmir. If each side were to insist on preconditions, would we not be entitled to say to Pakistan that it must first not only give up its point of view on Kashmir but also, as a prior condition for talks, vacate two fifths of Indian territory in Jammu Kashmir that it illegally occupied and still occupies? Mr. President, in our reading of the letter of the Tashkent Declaration and in our appreciation of its spirit, what is required to be done by the leaders of the two countries is that they must settle all their differences without conditioning lenient of one dispute on the settlement of another. It is time to recall that at the time of signing the Tashkent Declaration, "each of the sides set forth its respective position" on Jammu and Kashmir and this fact is mentioned in article I of the Declaration. Recognizing this absence of reconciliation of the respective view points on Jammu and Kashmir, India and Pakistan agreed to take several steps mentioned in article II to IX of the Tashkent Declaration. Article IX has special significance in the present context. It states : "The Prime Minister of India and the President of Pakistan have agreed that the sides will continue meetings both at the highest and at other levels on matters of direct concern to both countries. Both sides have recognized the need to set up joint Indian-Pakistani bodies which will report to their Governments in order to decide what further steps should be taken". The present effort of Pakistan to refuse to implement this article and to make it contingent on what Pakistan chooses to describe as "meaningful talks" on Jammu and Kashmir is contrary to the provisions of the Tashkent Declaration.

The second point which I wish to clarify, Mr. President, relates to the ministerial meeting between India and Pakistan in March of this year. The Foreign Minister of Pakistan has made reference to the communique issued after that meeting. The operative part of the communique is that the two parties will meet again and discuss all their differences. In spite of India's best efforts to start these talks, the intransigence of Pakistan has not made it possible for a further meeting as contemplated in the communique issued after the Rawalpindi talks in March this year. The Foreign Minister of Pakistan did not, perhaps he could not, refer to the substance of the discussion held in March. This is so perhaps because he was not present at the talks. Since I led the delegation of India to that ministerial meeting, I can speak with some authority and assurance in regard to the attitude taken by India then — an attitude which remains the same today. It is that, regardless of differences between the two countries indeed because of those very differences, the most important provision of the Tashkent Declaration, that is restoration of normal relations between the two countries must be brought about by all possible means. As we in India see it, Mr. President, the way to the settlement of all differences is not to put conditions towards the conclusion of agreement on all problems at one and the same time. What Pakistan desired in March this year was that even though the two countries might arrive at an agreement on a specific issue between the two countries that agreement could not be implemented as long as there was no settlement of the question of Kashmir. Now, Mr. President, the Tashkent Declaration has been registered with the United Nations. Its copies are available to all delegations, and I invite all those who are interested, to study the document. There is no basis in that Declaration to support the thesis of Pakistan that restoration of normal relations between the two countries, in other words, settlement of differences between the two countries could not come about unless there was first an agreement on the question of Kashmir.

Mr. President, as recently as last month, we have offered to Pakistan to hold discussion on all outstanding issues between the two countries without any preconditions. To our deep regret, and I believe to the deep regret of this Assembly, Pakistan has once again rejected our offer. Today, the Foreign Minister of Pakistan has come to this Assembly and complained that India is not prepared to implement the Tashkent Declaration. Mr. President, on behalf of India, I would like to reiterate that India continues to adhere to the Tashkent Declaration in letter and in spirit and is ever ready to start talks for settling all the differences between India and Pakistan by peaceful means in a spirit of good neighbourly relations and with a view to reverse the deteriorating trend of the relationship between the two countries. I make this offer here and now to the Foreign Minister of Pakistan. Let us sit down and discuss ways and means of implementing all the provisions of the Tashkent Declaration.

Mr. President, before I conclude I would like to quote from a statement made by the Prime Minister of India, to the Afro-Asian group here on April 1, 1966. She said and I quote "It is Mr. President, on behalf of India, I would like to the two countries. I make this offer here and is it not enough that there should be peaceful co-existence among the great powers of the world; we should also set an example and co-exist peacefully among ourselves. The essentials for peaceful co-existence are the determination not to use force and not to intervene in each other's affairs and the desire to settle all disputes by peaceful means. It is in this spirit that India, less than three months ago, signed the Tashkent Declaration with Pakistan in which the two countries reaffirmed their obligations under the Charter, not to use force but to settle their disputes through peaceful means. The Tashkent Declaration provides India and Pakistan with a new framework in which to restore normal and peaceful relations between the two countries and to promote understanding, and friendly relations between the two people. The underlying concept of the Declaration was the deep conviction that peaceful relations between India and Pakistan are vital for the maintenance of their political independence and the achievement of their economic and social development. If all the provisions of the Declaration are implemented faithfully in letter and spirit, an atmosphere will be created in which all differences between the two countries can be settled peacefully. Political problems with emotional overtones — and there are strong emotions on both sides in this problem — cannot be solved unless the people of both countries appreciate the vital necessity of peaceful and friendly relations between them".

After the Minister of External Affairs, Sardar Swaran Singh, had replied to the Pakistan Foreign Minister's earlier statement in the General Assembly on September 29, the Pakistan Foreign Minister again took the floor to make a brief statement. Replying to this statement; Sardar Swaran Singh said :

I must apologise for asking for the floor. I thought that I had said in very categorical terms that India is prepared to enter into discussions without any preconditions and that in such discussion each side will be fully justified in raising any point. I said also that India would be prepared to discuss any matter raised by the Pakistan delegation, just as the latter should be prepared to discuss any matter raised by India.

The fact that the Foreign Minister of Pakistan could anticipate what I would say and therefore, came with a prepared text to reply to it only show that we are going through this exercise, knowing each other's point of view and trying to meet it by statements and counter statements.

I do not wish to delay the Assembly by taking any more time. I make this appeal to the Foreign Minister of Pakistan. Let us begin talks in right earnest, and not just continue to exchange diplomatic notes or statements and counter-statements on the floor of the General Assembly. There is no substitute for direct talks and no substitute for trying to understand each other's point of view. Let us devote ourselves to improving the relations between our two countries. It is only by adopting that attitude that the people of India and the people of Pakistan can live in peace and friendship and good-neighbourly relations, an objective which is very dear to us and, I hope, dear also to Pakistan.

E

STATEMENT OF THE FOREIGN MINISTER OF PAKISTAN DATED 1, AUGUST 1968

My attention has been drawn to a recent press report stating that the Indian Prime Minister had declared that India was not obligated under the Tashkent Declaration to settle the Kashmir dispute with Pakistan.

The world knows that the Tashkent meeting was arranged at the wise initiative of Mr. Kosygin as a follow through to the UN Security Council resolution of 20 September 1965 which had brought an end to the armed conflict between the two countries over Jammu and Kashmir. It is not secret that the Kashmir dispute formed the hard core of talks in Taskent. In fact, Article IX of the declaration provided a machinery for settling disputes existing between the two countries. Kashmir is the basic and the most important dispute. Therefore, it follows that contrary to the impression which Mrs. Gandhi has sought to create, India is very much obligated to settle the Kashmir dispute in terms of the Tashkent Declaration.

I am not surprised at India's attempt to deny the existence of its commitment under a solemn agreement, On one excuse or the other, India has not fulfilled its pledge to hold a plebiscite in Jammu and Kashmir and it continues to deprive the people of the State 'of the exercise of their right of self-determination. Not to mention the Taskent Declaration, what has India done to fulfil its pledge to hold a plebiscite in Jammu and Kashmir or to meet the obligations under the UNCIP resolution of 13, August 1948 and 5, January 1949?

India's latest attempt to wriggle out of its commitment merely highlights its equivocal attitude and make-believe posture towards negotiations with Pakistan on Kashmir and other unresolved issues between the two countries. At one time India claimed that it is prepared for discussions with Pakistan on all subjects including Kashmir, at any time, at any level and at any place. Yet, the Indian Prime Minister says that "India has nothing to negotiate with Pakistan on Kashmir". The highly organised propaganda machine in New Delhi goes on repeating professions of India's good-will towards Pakistan. Yet India is not prepared to have meaningful talks with Pakistan on the Kashmir dispute which has twice led the two countries to war.

Whatsoever the Indian leaders may say, the Kashmir issue has not been foreclosed. Nor will this dispute disappear by India's unilateral repudiation of international agreements. Statesmanship demands that India should face the reality of the situation and join hands with Pakistan in an earnest effort to find a just and equitable solution of the bitterness and blood between our two countries. Pakistan will always be ready to co-operate with India in this effort which could lead to the establishment of genuine peace and amity in the subcontinent.

72

Tashkent Summit — Prime Minister Lal Bahadur Shastri's speech at the Opening Session

The Prime Minister of India, Shri Lal Bahadur Shastri, and President Ayub Khan of Pakistan met at Tashkent (USSR) from January 4 to January 10, 1966, and discussed the relations existing between the two countries.

Speaking at the opening session of the Tashkent Meeting on January 4, Prime Minister Shastri said :

First of all, I want to convey to you, Chairman Kosygin, the feelings of sincere appreciation with which my people, my Government and I hailed your bold initiative which has brought me and President Ayub Khan of Pakistan together in this historic Asian city. It is with great pleasure that I express on my behalf and on behalf of my delegation our gratitude for the hospitality which has been lavished upon us and the care and attention which has been bestowed upon us. The great welcome which the people of Tashkent gave us was indeed very moving.

Positive Response

Our response to your invitation for a meeting in Tashkent was immediate and positive. The objective of peace which inspired you is indeed a noble one. Peace is vital for both India and Pakistan and indeed for the world as a whole. It should be our endeavour to try to open a new chapter in Indo-Pakistan relationship. I would not like to go into past history. I feel, and I am sure President Ayub Khan also feels, that the conflict which took place between our two countries was most unfortunate.

Our objective at this meeting should be not recrimination over the past, but a new look towards the future.

I know that there are many unresolved differences between our two countries. Even between countries with the best of relationship, there are differences and even disputes. The question which we have both to face is whether we should think of force as a method of solving them, or whether we should decide and declare that force will never be used. If other countries, even those with vast resources and much deeper differences, can avoid an armed conflict and live together on the basis of peaceful co-existence, should not countries like India and Pakistan whose main problem is the economic betterment of their people, give up the idea of solving any problems by recourse to arms?

Respect For Territorial Integrity

The only justification for the use of force in international relations is to repel aggression. Our assurance to each other not to use force would mean, therefore, that each agrees to respect the territorial integrity of the other. We have always said, and I say it today also, that we unreservedly accept Pakistan's sovereignty and territorial integrity. Equally, we have to preserve our own territorial integrity and sovereignty. Respect for each other's sovereignty is essential for peace and good relations.

Once this has been clearly accepted, the whole character of Indo-Pakistan relationship could be transformed to the benefit of the people of both countries. Let me say quite clearly and very sincerely that we wish Pakistan's progress and prosperity. We have ourselves been striving to better the lives of our people. We are convinced that prosperity would come sooner to the sub-continent, if there was better relationship between India and Pakistan.

Peaceful Co-Existence

The foundation of such relationship should be, as I have said, the acceptance of the policy of peaceful co-existence. In pursuance of this, action will have to be taken on several fronts. For instance, the atmosphere of cold war has to be removed. If through propaganda, in the press or by radio, a feeling of animosity or distrust is generated and sustained between the two countries, whatever we, as Heads of the two Governments might say, there will always exist the danger of a conflict. Our aim should be to improve the totality of the relationship between the two countries. Our trade has been shrinking. It should grow instead. Many rivets flow between India and Pakistan. Instead of being a source of controversy, they could, through co-operative endeavour, enrich both our countries. There are many other area of economic co-operation which, given goodwill and understanding, can be developed to our mutual advantage.

In saying all this, I am not trying to suggest that we could or should shut our eyes to the many points of difference that exist between the two countries. I do not want to enumerate them, What I do say, however, is that all these problems must be resolved through talks and negotiations and not by resort to force. An armed conflict creates more problems than it solves. It is an impediment to understanding and agreement. On the other hand, in an atmosphere of peace, we can make real progress towards solving the differences between us.

Renunciation of Force

It would be a notable achievement if at this meeting which Chairman Kosygin has convened, an agreement could emerge for renouncing the use of force for settling our differences. This should pave the way for the kind of good neighbourly relations which both countries need and would also make the solution of many of our problems much easier. We could and should, of course, discuss other matters as well, but even if we differ on some of them and cannot see our way to an immediate agreement, we should still not forsake the path of peace.

Not War But Peace

A heavy responsibility lies on our shoulders. The sub-continent has a population of 600 million — one-fifth of the human race. If India and Pakistan have to progress and prosper, they must learn to live in peace. If there is constant conflict and hostility, our people would suffer even greater hardships. Instead of fighting each other, let us start fighting poverty, disease and ignorance. The problems, the hopes and the aspirations of the common people of both the countries are the same. They want no conflict and war, but peace and progress. They need, not arms and ammunition, but food, clothing and shelter. If we are to fulfil this obligation to our people, we should, in this meeting, try to achieve something specific and positive.

This is a momentous meeting. The eyes of the world are upon us. Let it not be said that the President of Pakistan and the Prime Minister of India met and failed to reach an agreement. Let us show by our actions that we are capable of seeing our own problems in the wider context of world events.

73

Resolution 215 (1965) adopted by the Security Council at its 1251st Meeting on 5 November 1965

The Security Council,

Regretting the delay in the full achievement of a complete and effective cease-fire and a prompt withdrawal of armed personnel to the positions held by them before 5, August 1965, as called for in its resolution 209 (1965) of 4 September, 210 (1965) of 6 September, 211 (1965) of 20 September and 214 (1965) of 27 September 1965,

1. *Reaffirms* its resolution 211 (1965) of 20 September 1965 in all its parts;
2. *Requests* the Governments of India and Pakistan to co-operate towards a full implementation of paragraph 1 of resolution 211 (1965); calls upon them to instruct their armed personnel to co-operate with the United Nations and cease all military activity; and insists that there be an end to violations of the Cease-Fire,
3. *Demands* the prompt and unconditional execution of the proposal already agreed to in principle by the Governments of India and Pakistan that their representatives meet with a suitable representative of the Secretary-General, to be appointed without delay after consultation with both parties, for the purpose of formulating and agreed plan and schedule for the withdrawals by both parties; urges that such a meeting

shall take place as soon as possible and that such a plan contain a time-limit on its implementation; and requests the Secretary-General to report on the progress achieved in this respect within three weeks of the adoption of the present resolution;

4. *Requests* the Secretary-General to submit for its consideration as soon as possible a report on compliance with the present resolution.

*The Security Council voted on this Resolution on 5-11-1965 with the following result :

In favor : Bolivia, China, France, **Ivory Coast, **Malaysia, **Netherlands, U.K., U.S.A., and **Uruguay

Against : None.

Abstaining : **Jordan, and U.S.S.R.

**Non-Permanent Members of the Security Council.

74

Acceptance of Cease-Fire Proposals of the Security Council by the Government of India and the Government of Pakistan

New Delhi, 16 September 1965 and
Rawalpindi, 22 September 1965

Letter dated 17 September 1965 from the Permanent Representative of India addressed to the President of the Security Council

I have the honour to request you to circulate as a Security Council document the enclosed statement of the Prime Minister of India which he made in Parliament on 16 September 1965 :

Please accept, etc.

(Sd/-)

G. PARTHASARATHI,

Ambassador, Extraordinary and Plenipotentiary.

PRIME MINISTER SHASTRI'S STATEMENT IN PARLIAMENT

New Delhi, 16 September 1965

Prime Minister Shastri made the following statement in the Parliament in New Delhi on 16 September 1965 :

As Members are aware, the Secretary General of the United Nations, U Thant arrived in New Delhi on 12 September 1965 and after staying here for three days he left yesterday for New York. We welcomed him amongst ourselves not only as a high dignitary but also as representative of the World Organization on which lies the heavy responsibility of preserving international peace. The Secretary General and I had free and frank discussions. He met the Foreign Minister and also saw the Defence Minister.

During the discussions the Secretary-General drew attention to the grave implications of the present conflict, specially in relation to the welfare of the 600 million people belonging to India and Pakistan. He referred to the Security Council resolution of 4 and 6 September and appealed that cease-fire should be ordered immediately by both countries.

I gave factual narration of events as they had taken place and pointed out that the present conflict was not of our seeking. It was started by Pakistan when thousands of armed infiltrators invaded our State of Jammu and Kashmir commencing from 5 August 1965 with the objective of destroying or capturing vital positions such as airports, police stations and bridges and ultimately of seizing power forcibly from the State Government at Srinagar. Finding that its initial invasion had largely failed, Pakistan had launched on 1 September 1965, massive armed attack not only across the Cease-Fire Line but across the international frontier as well. Pakistan had thus not only started the conflict but had further escalated it in such manner as to leave India with no choice except to take counter-measures in self defence.

I explained all this to the Secretary General and told him that the present conflict had been forced upon us by Pakistani aggression. We were determined however to preserve fully and completely the sovereignty and territorial integrity of our country of which the State of Jammu and Kashmir formed an integral part; nor could we accept a situation in which Pakistan may continue its armed aggression on India time and again.

The Secretary General was particularly anxious that as first step we should agree to cease-fire and to cessation of hostilities.

I told him that cease-fire in regard to fighting between troops was understandable but the question of raiders would still remain on our hands. I pointed out that we would have to continue to deal effectively with these raiders, many of whom were still at large in the State of Jammu and Kashmir, unless of course Pakistan undertook to withdraw them from our territory.

We went into the pros and cons of cease-fire in some detail. Subsequently I received a letter from the Secretary General in which his appeal for cease-fire was reiterated. A copy of this letter has been placed on the Table of the House. After full consideration of all aspects, we sent a reply of which also a copy is laid on the Table of the House. As Honourable Members would see from a perusal of this letter, we raised no objection to the Secretary General's proposal for cease-fire. However, in regard to certain matters of vital importance to India we made our stand perfectly clear. For instance, as already stated, we would have to deal with the raiders who were still sporadically attacking public property or harassing people in the State of Jammu and Kashmir. Also, we could not possibly revert to a situation in which we may find ourselves once again unable to prevent infiltrations or to deal effectively with those who had already come in. In regard to the political aspect of the question, we made it clear that we were fully determined to maintain the sovereignty and territorial integrity of India of which the State of Jammu and Kashmir was an integral part. From this resolve we could never be deflected no matter what the pressure or threat. These were not conditions attached to our acceptance of cease-fire but were meant to be clear and unequivocal reiteration of our stand in regard to those vital matters.

Late in the evening on 1 September I received a further letter from the Secretary General saying that he could not give any undertaking to which I sent reply yesterday morning pointing out that as a matter of fact we had not asked him to give any undertaking to us. Our acceptance of the cease-fire proposal thus complied fully with the appeal of the Secretary General. Copies of these letters also have been tabled.

The Secretary General told me prior to his departure from New Delhi that if by the evening of 15 September 1965 Pakistan did not give a reply agreeing to ceasefire, we should take it that agreement on this question had not been possible. Since no such acceptance was received by the stipulated time, an announcement was made that our Defence forces will have to continue operations with unabated vigour. Although the Secretary General's present effort to bring about stoppage of hostilities in order to pave the way for peace has not been fruitful through no lack of cooperation from us, he intends, as he has announced publicly, to pursue his efforts further and just before leaving Delhi he sent me a further letter, copy of which is being placed on the Table of the House. We will send a considered reply as soon as possible.

As Members would see, we have made every effort to cxtend all co-operation to the United Nations in its efforts to restore peace and we accepted the Secretary General's proposal for immediate cease-fire. Pakistan on the other hand has given no such acceptance. In fact, indications are that she is intent upon continuing fight unless her own plan involving withdrawal of armed forces of India and Pakistan from the entire State of Jammu and Kashmir, induction of United Nations Force and plebiscite within three months there after is agreed to. Let me state on the floor of this House that not one of these conditions is acceptable to India. It is obvious now that Pakistan launched aggression on India by 5 August, 1965, with a view to making an attempt to revive the settled issue of the State of Jammu and Kashmir. She wants to force a decision by naked aggression. This we cannot possibly allow. We have no alternative therefore but to carry on our struggle. We fully realize that the present armed conflict between India and Pakistan will cause untold hardships and misery to people in both countries. However, I am confident that our countrymen would cheerfully undergo those hardships but they would not allow the aggressor to endanger our freedom or to annex our territories.

I have seen some press reports of Ayub Khan's press conference of yesterday. Among other things he is reported to have observed that good sense required that India and Pakistan live together in peace. If this is a new and sincere thought I would greatly welcome it however belated it might be. But if past experience is any guide, these remarks would appear to be part of propaganda to beguile the world. Previously also Ayub Khan has talked of the virtue of peace and has followed it up by unprovoked aggressions on India in Kutch and subsequently in Kashmir. Ayub Khan has, I trust, by now seen the result of Pakistan's policy of hate and hostility against India.

As circumstances exist today the nation has to be continuously alert and be ready for any sacrifice to preserve our freedom and integrity. I am greatly beholden to Parliament, to all political parties and indeed to the entire nation for their united stand against the aggressor. I want also to express once again the gratitude of the nation to the valiant Armed Forces who have already demonstrated that they are capable not only of defending our frontiers but also of delivering crushing blows to the invader. Their deeds of heroism will make a glorious chapter in the annals of India. This Parliament and the whole country is proud of them. I am confident we will continue to meet this challenge with the same determination and courage.

Letter dated 22nd September 1965 from the Permanent Representative of Pakistan addressed to the Secretary General.

I have the honour to transmit the following message from the President of Pakistan which I have received from Rawalpindi at 2.00 EDT (1100 Rawalpindi time) today.

"Pakistan considers the Security Council resolution No. 211 of 20th September as unsatisfactory. However, in the interest of international peace, and in order to enable the Security Council to evolve a self-executing procedure which will lead to an honourable settlement of the root cause of the present conflict, namely, the Jammu and Kashmir dispute, I have issued the following orders to the Pakistan Armed forces :

(1) They will stop fighting as from 1205 hours West Pakistan time today.

(2) As from that time they will not fire on enemy forces unless fired upon;

(3) provided the Indian Government issues similar orders to its Armed Forces."

Please accept, etc.

(Sd/-)

SYED AMJAD ALI
Permanent Representative of Pakistan to the United Nations.

75

Agreement between the Government of India and the Government of Pakistan relating to Cease-Fire and the Restoration of the *status quo* as on 1 January 1965 in the Gujarat/West Pakistan Border and Determination of the Border in that Area

New Delhi, 30 June 1965

Whereas both the Governments of India and Pakistan have agreed to a cease-fire and to restoration of the *status quo* as at 1st January 1965 in the area of the Gujarat/West Pakistan border, in the confidence that this will also contribute to a reduction of the present tension along the entire Indo-Pakistan border;

Whereas it is necessary that after the *status quo* has been established in the aforesaid Gujarat/West Pakistan border area, arrangements should be made for determination and demarcation of the border in that area;

Now therefore, the two Governments agree that the following action shall be taken in regard to the said area :

Article 1

There shall be an immediate cease-fire with effect from 0030 hrs GMT, 1 July, 1965.

Article 2

on the cease-fire :

(i) All troops on both sides will immediately begin to withdraw;

(ii) This process will be completed within seven days;

(iii) Indian police may then re-occupy the post at Chhad Bet in strength no greater than that employed at the post on 31 December 1964;

(iv) Indian and Pakistan police may patrol on the tracks on which they were patrolling prior to 1 January 1965, provided that their patrolling will not exceed in intensity that which they were doing prior to 1st January 1965 and during the monsoon period will not exceed in intensity that done during the monsoon period of 1964;

(v) If patrols of Indian and Pakistan police should come into contact they will not interfere with each other, and in particular will act in accordance with West Pakistan/India border ground rules agreed to in January 1960;

(vi) Officials of the two Governments will meet immediately after the cease-fire and from time to time thereafter as may prove desirable in order to consider whether any problems arise in the implementation of the provisions of paragraphs (iii) to (v) above and to agree on the settlement of any such problem.

Article 3

(i) In view of the fact that :

(A) India claims that there is no territorial dispute as there is a well established boundary running roughly along the northern edge of the Rann of Kutch as shown in the pre-partition maps, which needs to be demarcated on the ground;

(B) Pakistan claims that the border between India and Pakistan in the Rann of Kutch runs roughly along the 24th Parallel as is clear from several pre-partition and post-partition documents and therefore the dispute involves some 3,500 square miles of territory;

(C) At discussions in January 1960, it was agreed by Ministers of the two Governments that they would each collect further data, regarding, the Kutch-Sind boundary and that further discussions would be held later with a view to arriving at a settlement of this dispute; as soon as officials have finished the task referred to in Article 2(vi), which in any case will not be later than one month after the cease-fire, Ministers of the two Governments will meet in order to agree on the determination of the border in the light of their respective claims, and the arrangements for its demarcation. At this meeting and at any proceeding before the Tribunal referred to in Article 3(ii) and (iv) below, each Government will be free to present and develop their case in full.

(ii) In the event of no agreement between the Ministers of the two Governments on the determination of the border being reached within two months of the cease-fire, the two Governments shall, as contemplated in the joint communiqué of 24 October 1959, have recourse to the Tribunal referred to in (iii) below for determination of the border in the light of their respective claims and evidence produced before it and the decision of the Tribunal shall be final and binding on both parties.

(iii) For this purpose there will be constituted, within four months of the cease-fire, a Tribunal consisting of three persons, one of whom would be a national of either India or Pakistan. One member shall be nominated by each Government and the third member, who will be the Chairman, shall be jointly selected by the two Governments. In the event of the two Governments failing to agree on the selection of the Chairman within three months of the cease-fire they shall request the Secretary-General of the United Nations to nominate the Chairman.

(iv) The decision of the Tribunal referred to in (iii) above shall be binding on both Governments, and shall not be questioned on any ground whatsoever. Both Governments undertake to implement the Findings of the Tribunal in full as quickly as possible and shall refer to the Tribunal for decision of any difficulties which may arise between them in the implementation of these findings. For that purpose the Tribunal shall remain in being until its findings have been implemented in full.

In witness where of the undersigned have signed the present Agreement.

Done in duplicate at New Delhi, this thirtieth day of June 1965 in the English language.

For the Government of India	For the Government of Pakistan
(Sd/-)	(Sd/-)
M. AZIM HUSAIN	M. A. HUSAIN

Dated : 30-06-1965

76

Statement of the President of the Security Council (French Representative) made on the 18 May 1964, at the Eleventh Hundred and Seventeenth meeting of the Security Council. (Document No. S/PV. 1117, dated the 18 May 1964) Summarising the Conclusion of the Debate on Kashmir

I

(a) The members of the Council noted that this week's debate was a continuation of our discussions of February and March on the question of Jammu and Kashmir. They recalled that they had already, particularly during the debate in February, stated the views of their Governments on the basic facts of the problem, including the relevant United Nations resolutions, the question as to the juridical status of Jammu and Kashmir, and the principles of the Charter applicable to the case. They confirmed that the statements which they had made at that time were still valid;

(b) The members of the Council expressed their concern with respect to two great countries which have everything to gain from re-establishing good relations with each other and whose present disputes, particularly that cantering upon Jammu and Kashmir, should be settled amicably in the interest of world peace;

(c) The members of the Council expressed their feeling that recent developments were such as might lead to the adoption of more flexible positions to better mutual understanding, and, therefore, to a situation in which conversations between the parties concerned would have better prospects of leading to a settlement;

(d) The members of the Council expressed their conviction that everything should be done to consolidate those favorable factors and to avoid jeopardizing those prospects and that this required an attitude of conciliatory moderation on the part of the both parties and an attitude of caution, but also of vigilant attention, on the part of the United Nations;

(e) The members of the Council expressed the hope that both Parties would refrain from any act which might aggravate the situation and that they would take steps calculated to reestablish an atmosphere of moderation between the two countries and peace and harmony between the communities;

(f) The members of the Council expressed the hope that, in the light of our recent debates, the two countries concerned would resume their contacts in the near future with a view to settling their disputes, Particularly that cantering upon Jammu and Kashmir, by negotiation;

II

Several members of the Council expressed the view that the Secretary-General of the United Nations might possibly give useful assistance to the parties in order to facilitate the resumption of negotiations in the event of the latter encountering difficulties. Other members of the Council, however, expressed the view that the negotiations between India and Pakistan might be complicated by any outside intervention, and that even the principle of having recourse to the Secretary-General should be a matter for agreement between the parties.

III

The India-Pakistan question remains on the agenda of the Security Council.

77

Trade Agreement between the Government of India and the Government of Pakistan

Karachi, 1 September 1963

The Government of India and the Government of Pakistan,

With a view to developing, extending and consolidating trade and economic relations between the two countries,

Have resolved to enter into the following Agreement :

Article I

The two Governments recognising the needs and requirements of each other in the context of their developing economies undertake to explore all possibilities for expansion and promotion of trade between the two countries on the basis of mutual advantage.

Article II

Each Government shall accord to the commerce of the country of the other Government treatment no less favourable than that accorded to the commerce of any third country.

Article III

The provisions of Article II shall not apply to the grant or continuance of any :

(a) privileges which are or will be granted by either of the two Governments in order to facilitate frontier trade,

(b) preferences, advantages, privileges or immunities

accorded by either country to any third country prior to the 15th August 1947, or in replacement thereof and

(c) any advantages accorded in connection with Customs, Union, or Free Trade Zone of which either may become a member.

Article IV

With regard to commodities mentioned in Schedules 'A' and 'B' to this Agreement, the two Governments shall facilitate imports and exports to each others territories in accordance with their respective laws, regulations and procedures.

Article V

The Export and/or Import of goods not included in Schedules 'A' and 'B' will also be permitted in accordance with the laws, regulations and procedures in force in either country from time to time.

Article VI

The two Governments further agree to enter into such Special Arrangements, including arrangements relating to Border Trade, as may be considered by them to be necessary, from time to time, during the period of the validity of this Agreement to facilitate the movement of goods from one country to the other.

Article VII

The two Governments agree to accord subject to their respective laws and regulations, reasonable facilities for the holding of trade fairs and exhibitions and visits of businessmen and Trade Delegations sponsored by the Government concerned.

Article VIII

In order to facilitate the implementation of this Agreement, the two Governments shall consult each other as and when necessary and also review the working of the Agreement at least once a year.

Article IX

This Agreement shall come into force from the 1st of September 1963 and shall remain in force for a period of two years. The Agreement will be extended for a further period of one year unless either party gives to the other notice for its termination three months before the expiry of the said period of two years.

Done at Karachi this first day of September, 1963 A.D. in two original copies in English language, both of which are equally authentic,

(Sd/-)	(Sd/-)
S. VOHRA	E.A. NAIK
For the Government of India	For the Government of Pakistan

SCHEDULE 'A'

LIST OF ITEMS EXPORTABLE FROM INDIA

I. Animal and Marine Products

1. Leather Manufactures excluding boots and shoes
2. Finished leather
3. Animal casings.

II. Agricultural Products

1. Cigar and Cigarettes
2. Hemp other than manila, sisal and aloe
3. Palmyra fibre
4. Tapioca, Tapioca Flour (Manioc Meal) and products
5. Saga
6. Fresh fruits including bananas
7. Fruits products
8. Plywood (commercial and Tea-chests)
9. Cotton seed oil
10. Henna powder

11. Coir, Coir yarn and coir products
12. Tobacco (raw and manufactured)
13. Tamarind
14. Turmeric
15. Castor oil
16. Groundnut oil
17. Linseed oil
18. Salad oil
19. Cotton seed cake
20. Deoiled cake (Rice bran)
21. Vegetable oil
22. Essential oils
23. Beedi leaves,

III. Drugs, Pharmaceuticals, Chemicals and Allied Products

1. Calcined magnesite
2. Bichromates
3. Alumina ferric
4. Ferro manganese
5. Pigments, paints and varnishes
6. Printing inks other than black
7. Fountain pen ink
8. Myrohalan and ermact
9. Nux voinica alkaloids and preparations
10. Soaps, toiletries, hair oil and perfumes
11. Glycerine
12. Hydraulic brake fluid
13. Pharmaceuticals, drugs, medicines, vaccine, serums, etc. wholly indigenous.
14. Safety matches and fireworks
15. Crockery

16. Magnesium chloride
17. Ethyl Alcohol and Industrial Alcohol
18. Rubber products including bicycles tyres and tubes other than those types of tyres and tubes export of which is banned.
19. Asbestos products
20. Liquid Glucose
21. Benzene
22. Surgical cotton
23. Strychnine
24. Morphine
25. Bromides (Sodium and Potassium and Calcium)
26. Liquid Bromide
27. All antibiotics
28. All alkaloids
29. Synthetic drugs
30. Tetracyclins
31. Hamycin
32. Anti-Tubercular drugs (P.A.S. and Salts)
33. Anti-Dysentry drugs
34. Bleaching powder
36. Hydrochloric acid
36. Hydrogen peroxide
37. So dium, car nate
38. Liquid phlorine
39. Anti-Leprotic drugs (D.S.S. and Derivatives)
40. Amodiaquin
41. Vitamin A'
42. Vitamin C'
43. Ernetine
44. Sanfonine

45. Quinine
46. Brucine
47. Synthetic hormones
48. Aspirin
49. Calcium gluconate and other calcium salts
50. Ferro gluconate
51. Nikethamide
52. Insecticides, pesticides (formulatics only), Fungicides
53. Dyeing and tanning products
54. Dentiffics.

IV. Engineering Products

1. Aluminium and A.C.S. conductors
2. Insulators
3. Distribution Transformers
4. Transmission poles and towers
5. Air conditioners, water coolers and refrigerators
6. Public address equipment
7. Radio receivers
8. Batteries
9. Rubber and plastic insulated house wiring cables
10. Electric motors
11. Bicycles and bicycle parts
12. Oil expellers
13. Electricity House service meters
14. Agricultural implements (if tractor drawn)
15. Cotton and hair belting
16. Screws and hinges
17. Diesel engines (stationary)
18. Coated abrasives
19. Duplicators

20. Zip fasteners
21. Buckles
22. Eyelets
23. Vacuum bottles and flasks
24. Collapsible tubes
25. Ball bearings
26. Pumps (coupled with prime movers or not) (Centrifugal pumps)
27. Pumps driven by diesel engines and electric motors
28. Railway materials including rolling stock, etc.
29. Precision and scientific instruments; survey instruments
30. Machinery parts
31. Metal containers
32. Paper and pulp making machinery
33. Grey iron castings, forgings and cast iron pipes
34. Rolled steel products
35. Steel castings and forgings
36. Foundry castings for machine parts
37. Crown corks
38. Cutlery
39. Nuts, bolts, etc.
40. Sewing machines
41. Electric fans and parts
42. Safety Razor blades
43. Handtools and small tools
44. Ebonite sheets
45. Steel furniture
46. Tin plates containers
47. Household utensils of iron and steel, brass and aluminium

48. Kerosene stoves
49. Weighing machines
50. Split pulleys
51. Scientific instruments of all types
51 G1 buckets
53. Arc welding electrodes
54. Enamelled copper wire
55. Sandpaper
56. Locks and padlocks
57. Steel structural and fabrication and conduit pipes and fittings
58. Sugarcane crushing machinery
59. Pressure lamps and stoves
60. Milk steel pipes
61. Electric tools, appliances and accessories such as conduit pipes, switches, bells, holders, cut-outs, etc.
62. Rods and tubes
63. Fire extinguishers
64. Textile machinery
65. Cement machinery

V. Mining Products

1. Mica bricks
2. Micanite
3. Ground mica
5. Ilmenite
6. Magnesite
7. Iron ore
8. Manganese ore
9. Coal and coke
10. Limestone
11. Stone boulders and Pakur stones

VI. Plastics and Sports Goods

1. Spectacle frames
2. Fountain pens
3. Plastic and Moulded goods including umbrella handles
4. Linoleum
5. Leather cloth
6. Bangles
7. Sports goods
8. Decorative laminate.

VII. Cotton and Woollen, Textiles, such as

1. Cotton, silk, art silk, and rayon fabrics
2. Handloom fabrics
3. Cotton sewing thread
4. Durries
5. Furnishing fabrics
6. Garments

VIII. Food

1. Spices including pepper, provisions and oilman stores
2. Preserved fruits and vegetable products (Bottled and canned)
3. Processed food
4. Cane, Jaggery and Powder (Indian Gūr)

IX. Household and Building Materials

1. Window, door and other frames
2. G.T. Pipes and fittings
3. Household heating and electrical fittings and fixtures
4. Cooking ranges and heaters
5. Electric irons, toasters, kettles, etc.
6. Roofing tiles
7. Sanitary ware

8. Manhole covers and plates
9. Hurricane lanterns
10. Safes, strong boxes.
11. Roof fittings
12. Prefabricated building materials, sanitary and plumbing materials.

X. Others

1. Biscuits
2. Confectionery and chocolates
3. Potable spirits and beer
4. Red Earthen tiles
5. Agarbathies & Pencils
7. Carbon paper and typewriter ribbons
8. Books (Printed and others)
9. Brass artware and other handicrafts
10. Bees wax
11. Paraffin wax
12. Opium, raw
13. Exposed cinematographic films whether developed or not
14. Gramophone records
15. Clocks and watches
16. Umbrella and umbrella parts
17. Handicrafts and cottage industry products
18. Artificial dentures
19. Stationery articles
20. Ball-point pencils
21. Sandalwood chips
22. Cigarette paper
23. Cycle rims

24. Artistic silver, copper, brass and bidri products
25. printing inks
26. Guar gum
27. Ivory articles
28. Wood carvings
29. Earthenware
30. Filigiri work
31. Fancy jewellery
32. Basket ware
33. Shellac and seed lac
34. Forest produce including bamboos, canes and sun grass
35. Khari salt
36. Silbatta
37. Cutch and gambier
38. Myrobalan and Myrobalan products
39. Glass and glassware including tableware
40. Furs, raw or tanned, all sorts and manufactures thereof
41. Bile of Cow (oxgall)
42. Sheep casings
43. Animal hair (new)
44. Dried blood of animals
45. Gelatine and take glue
46. Cotton raw
47. Cotton waste soft [as at (i) to (xiii) below], cotton linters and yellow pickings :
    - (i) Bondas
    - (ii) Card Fly
    - (iii) Card strips
    - (iv) Comber fly

(v) Cylinder fly

(vi) Droppings willowed and un-willowed

(vii) Flat fly willowed and un-willowed

(viii) Cutter fly

(ix) Luckrine fly

(x) Oily

(xi) Rings weep

(xii) Rubbings

(xiii) Solid bondas

48. Hard cotton waste in cuts or pieces not exceeding three inches in length
49. Cotton seed and cotton seed oil cake
50. Cotton seed hull fibres
51. Cotton seed hull or husks
52. Cotton durries and carpets used for floor coverings
53. Cotton rope and niwar
54. Fishing ropes
55. Cotton fishing nets
56. Cotton rags
57. Cotton yarn
58. Cotton textiles, (grey or specialised goods)
59. Handloom cloth
60. Hosiery
61. Sewing thread
62. Readymade garments
63. Cotton wool absorbent
64. Kgrpok, Kapok seed and Kapok seed oil
65. Sunn hemp
66. Raw silk waste, unprocessed
67. Cumin seeds

68. Castor seed and castor seed cake
69. Oil seed cake, all sorts
70. Guar seed and its by-products
71. Essential oils
72. Shark liver oil
73. Methylated spirit
74. Power Alcohol
75. Molasses
    A. Dhanicha seeds
    B. Chuna Khari pearls
    C. Eggs and Poultry
    D. Books and Periodicals
76. Dried fish, fish meal and fish maws
77. Bones crushed, bonemeal and bone grit
78. Bone dust and bone sinews and similar articles
79. Horns and hooves, crushed and uncrushed including shavings
80. Honey and bees wax
81. Herbs, crude drugs, extracts and indigenous drugs and medicines
82. Artemissia
83. Ephedra and Ephedrine hydrochloride including crystals and extracts
84. Santonine
85. Drugs and Pharmaceuticals
86. Glycerine
87. Chemicals
88. Pyrethrum insecticides
89. Turpentine
90. Henna leaves and powder
91. Saltpetre

92. Rosin
93. Rock salt and sea salt
94. Chrome ore
95. Gypsum
96. Magnesium Silicate (Soap stone)
97. Sodium silicate
98. Lime and lime stone (from West Pakistan only)
99. Surgical instruments including parts and accessories thereof
100. Medical, dental and veterinary instruments and appliances, Hospital equipment
101. Surgical rubber goods
102. Scissors, all sorts
103. Cutlery
104. Household utensils
    A. Forest Produce
    B. Fresh Fruits
    C. Green spices
    D. Betel nuts
105. Aluminium, Brass, copper and other metallic wares, all sorts
106. Hardware all sorts
107. Machinery and spare parts
108. Mechanical tools
109. Electrical goods including fans, etc.
110. Musical instruments including parts and accessories thereof
111. Articles made of marble
112. Ivory goods
113. Brass and ivory inlaid wooden articles
114. Handicraft articles, all sorts

115. Embroidered goods, all sorts
116. Novelties and Curies other than those containing silver and gold
117. Gold and silver thread (real zari) and imitation articles made therefrom
118. Kashmir Artware
119. Pashmina cloth and manufactures thereof with or without silk and/or cotton embroidery work
120. Art fabrics
121. Toys, all sorts
122. Conch shell products
123. Ded shoes
124. Glass bangles
125. Hand bags
126. Peshawari Chappals with Zari and embroidery work
127. Canvas shoes with rubber soles
128. Tea
129. Rice
130. Biscuits and confectioneries
131. Canned and Bottled fruits, chutnies, pickles, jellies, curry powder and syrups
132. Canned fish, frozen fish and prawns and shrimps
133. Beer
134. Tobacco including Virginia type
    A. Betel leaves
    B. Fluorspar
    C. Nylon guts and mono filament
    D. Live Tortoise
135. Macaroni and vermicelli
136. Sports goods, all sorts, games, gymnastics and athletic , accessories and requisites thereof.
137. Guts for tennis rackets and strings for musical instruments

138. Rubber manufactures,
139. Rattan (cane) furniture and its other manufactures
140. Hurricane Lanterns
141. Pressure lamps, stoves and mantles
142. Sewing machines
143. Padlock
144. Sanitary ware
145. Ornamental tiles
146. Cement, Portland
147. Asbestos sheets
148. Toilet requisites and perfumery
149. Razor Blades
150. Spectacle Frames
151. Sun glasses
152. Imitation Jewellery
153. Fountain pens and pencils
154. Plastic manufactures
155. Buttons (Mother of pearl, horns, etc.) all sorts
156. Bicycles and parts
157. Cycle tyres and tubes
158. Paints and varnishes
159. Newsprint, paper and board, all sorts.
160. Gramophone records
161. Postage stamps
162. Chemical Fertilizers including Urea
163. Industrial alcohol
164. Fresh fish
165. Coal

Note : The export of goods included in this list will be subject to availability and in accordance with the laws and regulations and procedures in force in Pakistan from time to time.

PROTOCOL

PROTOCOL TO THE TRADE AGREEMENT BETWEEN THE GOVERNMENT OF INDIA AND THE GOVERNMENT OF PAKISTAN SIGNED ON THE 1ST SEPTEMBER 1963

In pursuance of Article VI of the Trade Agreement between the Government of India and Government of Pakistan, the two Governments have agreed to enter into, by means of this Protocol,

S.No	Commodities	Country of Exports	Country of Import and Quantities		Route	Remarks
			Pakistan			
1.	Coal	India	East 95QOO tons (per month)	West 20QOO tons (per month)	By all rail route	Provided supplies are not interrupted by muses beyond human control, such as shoes, accidents, floods, etc.
2.	Stones boulders including pakur stone	India	15,00 tones (per month) Pakistan (East)		By rail-cum sea route	To be considered by the Government of India if this quantity also could be supplied by all rail route.
3.	Raw jute and jute cuttings	Pakistan	India 40,000 tons (per year)			
4.	Raw cotton	Pakistan	India 10,000 tons (per year.)		By rail (Broad gauge)	The movement of boulders will be subject to details being settled between the Railways concerned
			India		By rail (Meter gauge)	Ditto.
			India			Quantities to be indicated by India to Pakistan by the end of September each year.

This Protocol is signed at Karachi on the first day of September 1963, in two original copies in English language, both of which are equally authentic.

(Sd/-) S. VOHRA
For the Government of India.

(Sd/-) E.A. NAIK
For the Government of Pakistan.

Dated : 1-09-1963

EXCHANGE OF LETTERS,

Karachi, 1 September 1963

My Dear Mr. Vohra,

During the course of the discussions between our two delegations regarding the conclusion of the new Trade Agreement signed to-day, it was agreed that the validity of the Trade Agreement between India and Pakistan, dated March 21, 1960 shall be deemed to have been extended to August 31, 1963.

I shall be grateful if you can kindly confirm that the above sets out correctly the understanding reached between us.

Yours sincerely,

(Sd/-)

E.A. NAIK

Mr. S. VOHRA
Leader of the Indian Trade Delegation, Karachi.

My Dear Mr. Naik,

I write to acknowledge the receipt of your letter of today's date which reads as follows

(Text Not Reproduced)

I confirm that the foregoing correctly sets out the understanding reached between us.

Yours sincerely,

(Sd/-)

S. VOHRA

Mr. E. A. NAIK,
Leader, Pakistan Trade Delegation, Karachi.

Karachi, 1 September 1963

My Dear Mr. Naik,

During the course of discussions between our two delegations regarding the review of the Trade Agreement' between the Government of Pakistan and the Government of India dated March 21, 1960 and regarding the conclusion of the new Trade Agreement between the two countries signed today, it was agreed as under :

(a) With reference to para 7 of Protocol No. 1 of the abovesaid Agreement dated March 21,1960, the amount outstanding in the "National Bank of Pakistan Clearing Account 'A'" maintained with the State Bank of India under the said Protocol No. I may be liquidated by import by India of the following commodities from Pakistan :

(i) Commodities mentioned in Group 'E' of Schedule I of Annexure I to the Protocol No. I mentioned above.

(ii) Urea.

(iii) Industrial Alcohol.

(iv) Such other commodities as may be mutually agreed upon.

(b) The "National Bank of Pakistan Clearing Account 'A'" with the State Bank of India will be continued beyond August 31, 1963 under the terms and conditions provided in Protocol No. 1 to the above-said Agreement, dated March 21, 1960 and the banking arrangements made between the National Bank of Pakistan and the State Bank of India in pursuance thereof, till such time as the entire amount outstanding is liquidated.

(c) It was agreed that the following commodities upto the quantity/value mentioned against each may be imported by India towards the liquidation of the said amount outstanding :

	Commodity	Quantity/Value
1.	Urea	30.000 tons
2.	Gypsum	Indian Rs 50,00,000
3.	Industrial alcohol	Indian Rs 12,00,000

The prices, specifications, quantities etc. of urea and Gypsum will be negotiated by the concerned Pakistan Industrial Development Corporation, on the one hand, and the State Trading Corporation of India and the Fertiliser Corporation of India, respectively, on the other, to the satisfaction of the Contracting Parties. Contracts will be entered likewise between the concerned manufacturers and the State Trading Corporation of India regarding export of Industrial Alcohol.

(d) It was agreed that subject to the rules and regulations for the time being in force, Pakistan will facilitate the export to India of the commodities as mentioned in paragraph 1(a) and 1(c) above.

2. I shall grateful if you would kindly confirm that the above sets out correctly the understanding reached.

Yours sincerely

(Sd/-)

S. VOHRA
Leader, Indian Trade Delegation

Mr. E.A. NAIK,
Leader, Pakistan Trade Delegation, Karachi.

Karachi. 1 September 1963

My Dear Mr. Vohra,

I write to acknowledge receipt of your letter of to-day's date which reads as follows :

(Text Not Reproduced)

2. I confirm that the above sets out correctly the understanding reached.

Yours sincerely,

(Sd/-)

E. A. NAIK, Leader, Pakistan Trade Delegation

Mr. S. VOHRA, Leader, Indian Trade Delegation, Karachi.

PROTOCOL I

PROTOCOL I TO THE TRADE AGREEMENT OF IST SEPTEMBER 1963 BETWEEN THE GOVERNMENTS OF INDIA AND PAKISTAN, RAWALPINDI, 17 JULY, 1964

In pursuance of Article VI of the Trade Agreement between the Government of India and the Government of the Islamic Republic of Pakistan signed on the 1st September 1963 the two Governments have agreed to enter into the following special Arrangement to facilitate, on a self-balancing basis, the exchange between the two countries of the commodities mentioned in the Schedule below, to the extent of the values mentioned against each subject to the conditions mentioned hereinafter :

Exports from Pakistan to India		Exports from India to Pakistan	
Joshi Rice		Coal	Rs. 200 lakhs
Kagni Rice	Rs. 365 lakhs	Biri leaves,	Rs. 40 lakhs
		Spices, (excluding chillies, ginger, cloves and turmeric)	Rs. 45 lakhs
		Lime stone,	Rs. 10 lakhs
		Umbrella fittings,	Rs. 12 lakhs
		Tone boulders,	Rs. 10 lakhs
		Crude Drugs,	Rs. 12 lakhs
		Railway equipment.	Rs. 36 lakhs
Total	Rs. 365 lakhs	Total	Rs. 365 lakhs

78

Sino-Pakistan Frontier Agreement, 1963

2 March 1963

Below is the text of the Sino-Pak Border agreement 1963 through which Pakistan illegally ceded 1/3rd of the territory of Jammu and Kashmir to China.

The Government of the People's Republic of China and the Government of Pakistan;

having agreed, with a view to ensuring the prevailing peace and tranquility on the border, to formally delimit and demarcate the boundary between China's Sinking and the contiguous areas the defence of which is under the actual control of Pakistan, in a spirit of fairness, reasonableness, mutual understanding and mutual accommodation, and on the basis of the ten principles as enunciated in the Bandung conference.

Being convinced that this would not only give full expression to the desire of the people of China and Pakistan for the development of good neighbourly and friendly relations, but also help safeguard Asian and world peace.

Have resolved for this purpose to conclude the present agreement and have appointed as their respective plenipotentiaries the following :

For the Government of the People's Republic of China, Chen Yi, Minister of Foreign Affairs.

For the Government of the Pakistan, Zulfikar Bhutto, Minister of External Affairs.

Who, having mutually examined their full powers and found them to be in good and due form have agreed upon following :

Article 1

In view of the fact that the boundary between China's Sinkiang and the contiguous areas the defence of which is under the actual control of Pakistan has never been formally delimited, two parties agree to delimit it on the basis of the traditional customary boundary line including features and in a spirit of equality, mutual benefit and friendly co-operation.

Article 2

In accordance with the principle expounded in Article 1 of the present agreement, the two parties have fixed as follows the alignment of the entire boundary line between China's Sinkiang and the contiguous areas the defence of which is under the actual control of Pakistan :

1. Commencing from its north western extremity at height 5,630 metres (a peak the reference coordinates of which are approximately longitude 74 degrees 34 minutes east and latitude 37 degrees 3 minutes north), the boundary line runs generally eastward and then South-eastward strictly along the main watershed between the tributaries of the Tashkurgan river of the Tarim river system on the one hand on the tributes of the Hunza river of the Indus river system on the other hand, passing through the Kilik Daban (Dawan), the Mintake Daban (pass), the Kharchanai Daban (named on the Chinese map only), the Mutsgila Daban (named on the Chinese map only) and the Parpik Pass (named on the Pakistan map only) and reaches the Khunjerab (Yutr Daban (Pass).

2. After passing through the Kunjerab (Yutr) Daban (pass) the boundary line runs generally southward along the above-mentioned main watershed upto a mountain-top south of the Daban (pass), where it leaves the main watershed to follow the crest of a spur lying generally in a south-easterly direction, which is the watershed between the Akjilga river (a nameless corresponding river on the Pakistan map) on the one hand, and the Taghumbash (Oprang) river and the Koliman Su (Orang

Jilga) on the other hand. According to the map of the Chinese side, the boundary line, after leaving the south-eastern extremity of the spur, runs along a small section of the middle line of the bed of the Koliman Su to reach its confluence with the Elechin river. According to the map of the Pakistan side, the boundary line, after leaving the south-eastern extremity of this spur, reaches the sharp bend of the Shaksgam of Muztagh river.

3. From the aforesaid point, the boundary lines runs up the Kelechin river (Shaksgam or Muztagh river) along the middle line of its bed its confluence (reference coordinates approximately longitude 76 degrees 2 minutes east and latitude 36 degrees 26 minutes north) with the Shorbulak Daria (Shimshal river or Braldu river).

4. From the confluence of the aforesaid two rivers, the boundary line, according to the map of the Chinese side, ascends the crest of a spur and runs along it to join the Karakoram range main watershed at a mountain-top (reference coordinates approximately longitude 75 degrees 54 minutes east and latitude 36 degrees 15 minutes north) which on this map is shown as belonging to the Shorgulak mountain. According to the map of the Pakistan side, the boundary line from the confluence of the above mentioned two river ascends the crest of a corresponding spur and runs along it, passing through height 6.520 meters (21,390 feet) till it joins the Karakoram range main watershed at a peak (reference coordinates approximately longitude 75 degrees 57 minutes east and latitude 36 degrees 3 minutes north).

5. Thence, the boundary line, running generally south-ward and then eastward strictly follows the Karakoram range main watershed which separates the Tarim river drainage system from the Indus river drainage system, passing through the east Mustagh pass (Muztagh pass), the top of the Chogri peak (K-2) the top of the broad peak, the top of the Gasherbrum mountain (8,068), the Indirakoli pass (names of the Chinese maps only) and the top of the Teramn Kankri peak, and reaches its south-eastern extremity at the Karakoram pass. Then alignment of the entire boundary line as described in section one of this article,

has been drawn on the one million scale map of the Pakistan side in English which are signed and attached to the present agreement. In view of the fact that the maps of the two sides are not fully identical in their representation of topographical features the two parties have agreed that the actual features on the ground shall prevail, so far as the location and alignment of the boundary described in section one is concerned, and that they will be determined as far as possible by joint survey on the ground.

Article 3

The two parties have agreed that :

(i) Wherever the boundary follows a river, the middle line of the river bed shall be the boundary line and that

(ii) Wherever the boundary passes through a deban (pass) the water-parting line thereof shall be the boundary line.

Article 4

One the two parties have agreed to set up, as soon as possible, a joint boundary demarcation commission. Each side will appoint a chairman, one or more members and a certain number of advisers and technical staff. The joint boundary demarcation commission is charged with the responsibility in accordance with the provisions of the present agreement, to hold concrete discussions on and carry out the following tasks jointly :

1. To conduct necessary surveys of the boundary area on the ground, as stated in Article 2 of the present agreement so as to set up boundary markers at places considered to be appropriate by the two parties and to delineate the boundary line of the jointly prepared accurate maps.

To draft a protocol setting forth in detail the alignment of the entire boundary line and the location of all the boundary markers and prepare and get printed detailed maps, to be attached to the protocol, with the boundary line and the location of the boundary markers shown on them.

2. The aforesaid protocol, upon being signed by representatives of the governments of the two countries, shall become an annex to the present agreement, and the detailed maps shall replace the maps attached to the present agreement. 3) Upon the conclusion of the above-mentioned protocol, the tasks of the joint boundary demarcation commission shall be terminated.

Article 5

The two parties have agreed that any dispute concerning the boundary which may arise after the delimitation of boundary line actually existing between the two countries shall be settled peacefully by the two parties through friendly consultations.

Article 6

The two parties have agreed that after the settlement of the Kashmir dispute between Pakistan and India, the sovereign authority concerned will reopen negotiations with the Government of the People's Republic of China on the boundary as described in Article. Two of the present agreement, so as to sign a formal boundary treaty to replace the present agreement, provided that in the event of the sovereign authority being Pakistan, the provisions of the present agreement and of the aforesaid protocol shall be maintained in the formal boundary treaty to be signed between the People's Republic of China and Pakistan.

Article 7

The present agreement shall come into force on the date of its signature.

Done in duplicate in Peking on the second day of March 1963, in the Chinese and English languages, both side being equally authentic.

79

Draft Resolution submitted by Ireland to the Security Council on 22 June 1962*

The Security Council,

Having heard the statements from the representatives of the Governments of India and Pakistan concerning the India-Pakistan question;

Having considered the report of the United Nations representative, Dr. F. Graham;

Expressing its best thanks to Dr. Graham for his efforts;

Noting with satisfaction the pledges made by the two parties to the effect that their Governments will not resort to force in settling this question;

Conscious of the responsibility of Security Council under the Charter for helping the parties to reach a peaceful solution of the question.

1. *Reminds* both parties of the principles contained in its resolution of 17 January 1948, and in the resolutions of the United Nations Commission for India and Pakistan dated 13 August 1948 and 5 January 1949.
2. *Urges* the Governments of India and Pakistan to enter into negotiations on the question at the earliest convenient time with a view to its ultimate settlement in accordance with Article 33 and other relevant provisions of the Charter of the United Nations.
3. *Appeals* to the two Governments to take all possible

measures to ensure the creation and maintenance of an atmosphere favorable to the promotion of negotiations.

4. *Urges* the Government of India and the Government of Pakistan to refrain from making any statements, or taking any action, which may aggravate the situation.

5. *Requests* the acting Secretary-General to provide the two Governments with such services as they may request for the purpose of carrying out the terms of the resolution.

*The Security Council voted on this Resolution on June 22, 1962 with the following result :

In favour : Chile, China, France, Ireland, United Kingdom of Great Britain and Northern Ireland, United States of America, Venezuela.

Against : Rumania, Union of Soviet Socialist Republic.

Abstaining : Ghana, United Arab Republic

One Permanent Member of the Security Council having cast a negative vote, the draft Resolution was not adopted.

80

Treaty between the Government of India and the Government of Pakistan concerning the most Complete and Satisfactory Utilisation of the Waters of the Indus System of Rivers

Karachi, 19 September 1960

PREAMBLE

The Government of India and the Government of Pakistan, being equally desirous of attaining the most complete and satisfactory utilisation of the waters of the Indus system of rivers and recognising the need, therefore, of fixing and delimiting, in a spirit of goodwill and friendship, the rights and obligations of each in relation to the other concerning the use of these waters and of making provision for the settlement, in a co-operative spirit, of all such questions as may hereafter arise in regard to the interpretation or application of the provisions agreed upon herein, have resolved to conclude a Treaty in furtherance of these objectives, and for this purpose have named as their plenipotentiaries :

The Government of India :

Shri Jawaharlal Nehru,
Prime Minister of India,

and

The Government of Pakistan :

Field Marshal Mohammad Ayub Khan, HP., H.J.,
President of Pakistan;

who, having communicated to each other their respective Full Powers and having found them in good and due form, have agreed upon the following Articles and Annexures :

ARTICLE I

Definitions

As used in this Treaty :

(1) The terms "Article and "Annexure" mean respectively an Article of, and an Annexure to, this Treaty.

Except as otherwise indicated, references to Paragraphs are to the paragraphs in the Article or in the Annexure in which the reference is made.

(2) The term "Tributary" of a river means any surface channel whether in continuous or intermittent flow and by whatever name called, whose waters in the natural course would fall into that river, *e.g.*, a tributary, a torrent, a natural drainage, an artificial drainage, a nadi, a nallah, a nai, a khad, a cho. The term also includes any sub-tributary or branch or subsidiary channel, by whatever name called, whose waters, in the natural course, would directly or otherwise flow into that surface channel.

(3) The term "The Indus," "The Jhelum," "The Chenab," "The Ravi," "The Beas" or "The Sutlej" means the named river (including Connecting Lakes, if any) and all its Tributaries : Provided however that

(i) none of the rivers named above shall be deemed to be a Tributary;

(ii) The Chenab shall be deemed to include the river Panjnad and

(iii) the river Chandra and the river Bhaga shall be deemed to be Tributaries of The Chenab.

(4) The term "Main" added after Indus, Jhelum, Chenab, Sutlej, Beas or Ravi means the main stem of the named river excluding its Tributaries, but including all channels and creeks of the main stem of that river and such Connecting Lakes as form part of the main stem itself. The Jhelum Main shall be

deemed to extend up to Verinag, and the Chenab Main up to the confluence of the river Chandra and the river Bhaga.

(5) The term "Eastern Rivers" means The Sutlej, The Beas and The Ravi taken together.

(6) The term 'Western Rivers" means The Indus, The Jhelum and The Chenab taken together.

(7) The term "the Rivers" means all the rivers, The Sutlej, The Beas, The Ravi, The Indus, The Jelum and The Chenab.

(8) The term "Connecting Lake" means any lake which receives water from, or yields water to, any of the Rivers; but any lake which occasionally and irregularly receives only the spill of any of the Rivers and returns only the whole or part of that spill is not a Connecting Lake.

(9) The term "Agricultural Use" means the use of water for irrigation, except for irrigation of household gardens and public recreational gardens.

(10) The terms "Domestic Use" means the use of water for :

(a) drinking, washing, bathing, recreation, sanitation (including the conveyance and dilution of sewage and of industrial and other wastes), stock and poultry, and other like purposes;

(b) household and municipal purposes (including use for household gardens and public recreational gardens) and

(c) industrial purposes (including mining, milling and other like purposes); but the term does not include Agricultural Use or use for the generation of hydro-electric power.

(11) The term "Non-Consumptive Use" means any control or use of water for navigation, floating of timber or other property, flood protection or flood control, fishing or fish culture, wild life or other like beneficial purposes, provided that, exclusive of seepage and evaporation of water incidental to the control or use, the water (undiminished in volume within the practical range of measurement) remains in, or is returned to, the same

river or its Tributaries; but the term does not include Agricultural Use or use for the generation of hydro-electric power.

(12) The term "Transition Period" means the period beginning and ending as provided in Article 11(6).

(13) The term' Bank" means the International Bank for Reconstruction and Development.

(14) The term "Commissioner" means either of the Commissioners appointed under the provisions of Article VIII(1) and the term "Commission" means the Permanent Indus Commission constituted in accordance with Article VIII(3).

(15) The term "interference with the waters" means :

(a) Any act of withdrawal therefrom; or

(b) Any man-made obstruction to their flow which causes a change in the volume (within the practical range of measurement) of the daily flow of the water : Provided however that an obstruction which involves only an insignificant and incidental change in the volume of the daily flow of water, now, for example, fluctuations due to afflux caused by bridge piers or a temporary by-pass, etc., shall not be deemed to be an interference with the waters.

(16) The term "Effective Date" means the date on which this Treaty takes effect in accordance with the provisions of Article XII, that is, the first of April 1960.

ARTICLE II

Provisions Regarding Eastern Rivers

(1) All the waters of the Eastern Rivers shall be available for the unrestricted use of India, except as otherwise expressly provided in this Article.

(2) Except for Domestic Use and Non-Consumptive Use, Pakistan shall be under an obligation to let flow, and shall not permit any interference with, the waters of the Sutlej Main and the Ravi Main in the reaches where these rivers flow in Pakistan and have not yet finally crossed into Pakistan. The Points of

final crossing are the following : (a) near the new Hasta Bund upstream of Suleimanke in the case of the Sutlej Main and (b) about one and a half miles upstream of the Syphon for the B-R-B-D Link in the case of the Ravi Main.

(3) Except for Domestic Use, Non-Consumptive Use and Agricultural Use (as specified in Annexure B), Pakistan shall be under an obligation to let flow, and shall not permit any interference with, the waters (while flowing in Pakistan) of any Tributary which in its natural course joins the Sutlej Main or the Ravi Main before these rivers have finally crossed into Pakistan.

(4) All the waters, while flowing in Pakistan, of any Tributary which, in its natural course, joins the Sutlej Main or the Ravi Main after these rivers have finally crossed into Pakistan shall be available for the unrestricted use of Pakistan : Provided however that this provision shall not be construed as giving Pakistan any claim or right to any releases by India in any such Tributary. If Pakistan should deliver any of the waters of any such Tributary, which on the Effective Date joins the Ravi Main after this river has finally crossed into Pakistan, into a reach of the Ravi Main upstream of this crossing, India shall not make use of these waters; each Party agrees to establish such discharge observation stations and make such observations as may be necessary for the determination of the component of water available for the use of Pakistan on account of the aforesaid deliveries by Pakistan, and Pakistan agrees to meet the cost of establishing the aforesaid discharge observation stations and making the aforesaid observations.

(5) There shall be a Transition Period during which, to the extent specified in Annexure H, India shall :

(i) limit its withdrawals for Agricultural Use,

(ii) limit abstractions for storages and

(iii) make deliveries to Pakistan from the Eastern Rivers.

(6) The Transition Period shall begin on 1st April 1960 and it shall end on 31st March 1970, or, if extended under the provisions of Part 8 of Annexure H, on the date up to which it has been extended. In any event, whether or not the replacement

referred to in Article IV(1) has been accomplished, the Transition Period shall end not later than 31st March 1973.

(7) If the Transition Period is extended beyond 31st March 1970, the Provisions of Article V(5) shall apply.

(8) If the Transition Period is extended beyond 31st March 1970, the provisions of Paragraph (5) shall apply during the period of extension beyond 31st March 1970.

(9) During the Transition Period, Pakistan shall receive for unrestricted use the waters of the Eastern Rivers which are to be released by India in accordance with the provisions of Annexure H. After the end of the Transition Period, Pakistan shall have no claim or right to releases by India of any of the waters of the Eastern Rivers. In case there are any releases, Pakistan shall enjoy the unrestricted use of the waters so released after they have finally crossed into Pakistan : Provided that in the event that Pakistan makes any use of these waters, Pakistan shall not acquire any right whatsoever, by prescription or otherwise, to a continuance of such releases or such use.

ARTICLE III

Provisions Regarding Western Rivers

(1) Pakistan shall receive for unrestricted use all those waters of the Western Rivers which India is under obligation to let flow under the provisions of Paragraph (2).

(2) India shall be under an obligation to let flow all the waters of the Western Rivers, and shall not permit any interference with these waters, except for the following uses, restricted (except as provided in item (c) (11) of Paragraph 5 of Annexure C) in the case of each of the rivers, The Indus, The Jhelum and The Chenab, to the drainage basin thereof :

(a) Domestic Use;

(b) Non-Consumptive Use;

(c) Agricultural Use, as set out in Annexure C; and

(d) Generation of hydro-electric power, as set out in Annexure D.

(3) Pakistan shall have the unrestricted use of all waters originating from sources other than the Eastern Rivers which are delivered by Pakistan into The Ravi or The Sutlej, and India shall not make use of these waters. Each Party agrees to establish such discharge observation stations and make such observations as may be considered necessary by the Commission for the determination of the component of water available for the use of Pakistan on account of the aforesaid deliveries by Pakistan.

(4) Except as provided in Annexure D and E, India shall not store any water of, or construct any storage works on, the Western Rivers.

ARTICLE IV

Provisions Regarding Eastern Rivers and Western Rivers

(1) Pakistan shall use its best endeavours to construct and bring into operation, with due regard to expedition and economy, that part of a system of works which will accomplish the replacement, from the Western Rivers and other sources, of water supplies for irrigation canals in Pakistan which, on 15th August 1947, were dependent on water supplies from the Eastern Rivers.

(2) Each Party agrees that any Non-Consumptive Use made by it shall be so made as not to materially change, on account of such use, the flow in any channel to the prejudice of the uses on that channel by the other Party under the provisions of this Treaty. In executing any scheme of flood protection or flood control each Party will avoid, as far as practicable, any material damage to the other Party, and any such scheme carried out by India on the Wejern Rivers shall not involve any use of water or any storage in addition to that provided under Article III.

(3) Nothing in this Treaty shall be construed as having the effect of preventing either Party from undertaking schemes of drainage, river training, conservation of soil against erosion and dredging, or from removal of stones, gravel or sand from the beds of the Rivers : Provided that

(a) in executing any of the schemes mentioned above,

each Party will avoid, as far as practicable, any material damage to the other Party;

(b) any such scheme carried out by India on the Western Rivers shall not involve any use of water or any storage in addition to that provided under Article III;

(c) except as provided in Paragraph (5) and Article VII(l)(b), India shall not take any action to increase the catchment area, beyond the area on the Effective Date, of any natural or artificial drainage or drain which crosses into Pakistan, and shall not undertake such construction or remodelling of any drainage or drain which so crosses or falls into a drainage or drain which so crosses as might cause material damage in Pakistan or entail the construction of a new drain or enlargement of an existing drainage or drain in Pakistan and

(d) should Pakistan desire to increase the catchment area, beyond the area on the Effective Date, of any natural or artificial drainage or drain, which receives drainage waters from India, or, except in an emergency, to pour any waters into it in excess of the quantities received by it as on the Effective Date, Pakistan shall, before undertaking any work for these purposes, increase the capacity of that drainage or drain to the extent necessary so as not to impair its efficacy for dealing with drainage waters received from India as on the Effective Date.

(4) Pakistan shall maintain in good order its portions of the drainages mentioned below with capacities not less than the capacities as on the Effective Date :

(i) Hudiara Drain

(ii) Kasur Nala

(iii) Salimshah Drain

(iv) Fazilka Drain

(5) If India finds it necessary that any of the drainages mentioned in Paragraph (4) should be deepened or widened in

Pakistan, Pakistan agrees to undertake to do so as a work of public interest, provided India agrees to pay the cost of the deepening or widening.

(6) Each Party will use its best endeavours to maintain the natural channels of the Rivers, as on the Effective Date, in such condition as will avoid, as far as practicable, any obstruction to the flow in these channels likely to cause material damage to the other Party.

(7) Neither Party will take any action which would have the effect of diverting the Ravi Main between Madhopur and Lahore, or the Sutlej Main between Harike and Suleimanke, from its natural channel between high banks.

(8) The use of the natural channels of the Rivers for the discharge of flood or other excess waters shall be free and not subject to limitation by either Party, and neither Party shall have any claim against the other in respect of any damage caused by such use. Each Party agrees to communicate to the other Party, as far in advance as practicable, any information it may have in regard to such extraordinary discharges of water from reservoirs and flood flows as may affect the other Party.

(9) Each Party declares its intention to operate its storage dams, barrages and irrigation canals in such manner, consistent with the normal operations of its hydraulic systems, as to avoid, as far as feasible, material damage to the other Party.

(10) Each Party declares its intention to prevent, as far as practicable, undue pollution of the waters of the Rivers which might affect adversely uses similar in nature to those to which the waters were put on the Effective Date, and agrees to take all reasonable measures to ensure that, before any sewage or industrial waste is allowed to flow into the Rivers, it will be treated, where necessary, in such manner as not to affect materially those uses :

Provided that the criterion of reasonableness shall be the customary practice in similar situations on the Rivers.

(11) The Parties agree to adopt, as far as feasible, appropriate measures for the recovery, and restoration to owners, of timber

and other property floated or floating down the Rivers, subject to appropriate charges being paid by the owners.

(12) The use of water for industrial purposes under Articles 11(2), 11(3) shall not exceed :

(a) in the case of an industrial process known on the Effective Date, such quantum of use as was customary in that process on the Effective Date;

(b) in the case of an industrial process not known on the Effective Date :

(i) such quantum of use as was customary on the Effective Date in similar or in any way comparable industrial processes; or

(ii) if there was no industrial process on the Effective Date similar or in any way comparable to the new process, such quantum of use as would not have a substantially adverse effect on the other Party.

(13) Such part of any water withdrawn for Domestic Use under the provisions of Articles 11(3) and 11(2) as is subsequently applied to Agricultural Use shall be accounted for as part of the Agricultural Use specified in Annexure B and Annexure C respectively; each Party will use its best endeavours to return to the same river (directly or through one of its Tributaries) all water withdrawn therefrom for industrial purposes and not consumed either in the industrial processes for which it was withdrawn or in some other Domestic Use.

(14) In the event that either Party should develop a use of the waters of the Rivers which is not in accordance with the provisions of this Treaty, that Party shall not acquire by reason of such use any right, by prescription or otherwise, to a continuance of such use.

(15) Except as otherwise required by the express provisions of this Treaty, nothing in this Treaty shall be construed as affecting existing territorial rights over the waters of any of the Rivers or the beds or banks thereof or as affecting existing property rights under municipal law over such waters or beds or banks.

ARTICLE V

Financial Provisions

(1) In consideration of the fact that the purpose of part of the system of works referred to in Article IV(1) is the replacement, from the Western Rivers and other sources, of water supplies for irrigation canals in Pakistan which, on 15th August 1947, were dependent on water supplies from the Eastern Rivers, India agrees to make a fixed contribution of Pounds Sterling 62,060,000 towards the costs of these works. The amount in Pounds Sterling of this contribution shall remain unchanged irrespective of any alteration in the par value of any currency.

(2) The sum of Pounds Sterling 62,060,000 specified in paragraph (1) shall be paid in ten equal annual installments on the 1st of November of each year. The first of such annual instalments shall be paid on 1st November 1960, or if the Treaty has not entered into force by that date, then within one month after the Treaty enters into force.

(3) Each of the instalments specified in Paragraph (2) shall be paid to the Bank for the credit of the Indus Basin Development Fund to be established and administered by the Bank, and payment shall be made in Pounds Sterling, or in such other currency or currencies as may from time to time be agreed between India and the Bank.

(4) The payments provided for under the provisions of Paragraph (3) shall be made without deduction or set-off on account of any financial claims of India on Pakistan arising otherwise than under the provisions of this Treaty : Provided that this provision shall in no way absolve Pakistan from the necessity of paying in other ways debts to India which may be outstanding against Pakistan.

(5) If, at the request of Pakistan, the Transition Period is extended in accordance with the provisions of Article 11(6) and of Part 8 of Annexure H, the Bank shall thereupon pay to India out of the Indus Basin Development Fund the appropriate amount specified in the table below :

TABLE

Period of Aggregate Extension Payment to of Transition Period	Payment of India
One year	stg. 3,125,000
Two years	stg. 6,406,250
Three years	stg. 9,850,000

(6) The provisions of Article IV(1) and Article V(1) shall not be construed as conferring upon India any right to participate in the decisions as to the system of works which Pakistan constructs pursuant to Article IV(1) or as constituting an assumption of any responsibility by India or as an agreement by India in regard to such works.

(7) Except for such payments as are specifically provided for in this Treaty, neither Party shall be entitled to claim any payment for observance of the provisions of this Treaty or to make any charge for water received from it by the other Party.

ARTICLE VI

Exchange of Data

(1) The following data with respect to the flow in, and utilisation of the waters of the Rivers shall be exchanged regularly between the Parties :

(a) Daily (or as observed or estimated less frequently) gauge and discharge data relating to flow of the Rivers at all observation sites.

(b) Daily extractions for or releases from reservoirs.

(c) Daily withdrawals at the heads of all canals operated by government or by a government agency (hereinafter in this Article called canals), including link canals.

(d) Daily escapages from all canals, including link canals.

(e) Daily deliveries from link canals.

These data shall be transmitted monthly by each Party to the other as soon as the data for a calendar month have been collected and tabulated, but not later than three months after the end of the month to which they relate : Provided that such of the data specified above as are considered by either Party to be necessary for operational purposes shall be supplied daily or at less frequent intervals, as may be requested. Should one Party request the supply of any of these data by telegram, telephone, or wireless, it shall reimburse the other Party for the cost of transmission.

(2) If, in addition to the data specified in Paragraph (1) of this Article, either Party requests the supply of any data relating to the hydrology of the Rivers, or to canal or reservoir operation connected with the Rivers, or to any provision of this Treaty, such data shall be supplied by the other Party to the extent that these are available.

ARTICLE VII

Future Co-operation

(1) The two Parties recognize that they have a common interest in the optimum development of the Rivers, and, to that end, they declare their intention to co-operate, by mutual agreement, to the fullest possible extent. In particular :

(a) Each Party, to the extent it considers practicable and on agreement by the other Party to pay the costs to be incurred, will, at the request of the other Party, set up or install such hydrologic observation stations within the drainage basins of the Rivers, and set up or install such meteorological observation stations relating thereto and carry out such observations thereat, as may be requested, and will supply the data so obtained.

(b) Each Party, to the extent it considers practicable and on agreement by the other Party to pay the costs to be incurred, will, at the request of the other Party, carry out such new drainage works as may be required in connection with new drainage works of the other Party.

(c) At the request of either Party, the two Parties may, by mutual agreement, co-operate in undertaking engineering works on the Rivers.

The formal arrangements, in each case, shall be as agreed upon between the Parties.

(2) If either Party plans to construct any engineering work which would cause interference with the waters of any of the Rivers and which, in its opinion, would affect the other Party materially, it shall notify the other Party of its plans and shall supply such data relating to the work as may be available and as would enable the other Party to inform itself of the nature, magnitude and effect of the work. If a work would cause interference with the waters of any of the Rivers but would not, in the opinion of the Party planning it, affect the other Party materially, nevertheless the Party planning the work shall, on request, supply the other Party with such data regarding the nature, magnitude and effect, if any, of the work as may be available.

ARTICLE VIII

Permanent Indus Commission

(1) India and Pakistan shall each create a permanent post of Commissioner for Indus Waters, and shall appoint to this post, as often as a vacancy occurs, a person who should ordinarily be a high-ranking engineer competent in the field of hydrology and water-use. Unless either Government should decide to take up any particular question directly with the other Government, each Commissioner will be the representative of his Government for all matters arising out of this Treaty, and will serve as the regular channel of communication on all matters relating to the implementation of the Treaty, and, in particular, with respect to :

(a) the furnishing or exchange of information or data provided for in the Treaty and

(b) the giving of any notice or response to any notice provided for in the Treaty.

(2) The status of each Commissioner and his duties and responsibilities towards his Government will be determined by that Government.

(3) The two Commissioners shall together form the Permanent Indus Commission.

(4) The purpose and functions of the Commission shall be to establish and maintain co-operative arrangements for the, implementation of this Treaty, to promote co-operation between the Parties in the development of the waters of the Rivers and, in particular :

(a) to study and report to the two Governments on any problem relating to the development of the waters of the Rivers which may be jointly referred to the Commission by the two Governments : in the event that a reference is made by one Government alone, the Commissioner of the other Government shall obtain the authorization of his Government before he proceeds to act on the reference;

(b) to make every effort to settle promptly, in accordance with the provisions of Article IX(1), any question arising there under;

(c) to undertake, once in every five years, a general tour of inspection of the Rivers for ascertaining the facts connected with various developments and works on the Rivers,

(d) to undertake promptly, at the request of either Commissioner, a tour of inspection of such works or sites on the Rivers as may be considered necessary by him for ascertaining the facts connected with those works or sites and

(e) to take, during the Transition Period, such steps as may be necessary for the implementation of the provisions of Annexure H.

(5) The Commission shall meet regularly at least once a year, alternately in India and Pakistan. This regular annual meeting shall be held in November or in such other month as may be agreed upon between the Commissioners. The Commission shall also meet when requested by either Commissioner.

(6) To enable the Commissioners to perform their functions in the Commission, each Government agrees to accord to the Commissioner of the other Government the same privileges and immunities as are accorded to representatives of member States to the principal and subsidiary organs of the United Nations under Sections 11, 12 and 13 of Article IV of the Convention on the Privileges and Immunities of the United Nations (dated 13th February 1946) during the periods specified in those Sections. It is understood and agreed that these privileges and immunities are accorded to the Commissioners not for the personal benefit of the individuals themselves but in order to safeguard the independent exercise of their functions in connection with the Commission; consequently, the Government appointing the Commissioner not only has the right but is under a duty to waive the immunity of its Commissioner in any case where, in the opinion of the appointing Government, the immunity would impede the course of justice and can be waived without prejudice to the purpose for which the immunity is accorded.

(7) For the purposes of the inspections specified in Paragraph (4) (c) and (d), each Commissioner may be accompanied by two advisers or assistants to whom appropriate facilities will be accorded.

(8) The Commission shall submit to the Government of India and to the Government of Pakistan, before the first of June of every year, a report on its work for the year ended on the preceding 31st of March, and may submit to the two Governments other reports at such times as it may think desirable.

(9) Each Government shall bear the expenses of its Commissioner and his ordinary staff. The cost of any special staff required in connection with the work mentioned in Article VII(1) shall be borne as provided therein.

(10) The Commission shall determine its own procedures.

ARTICLE IX

Settlement of Differences and Disputes

(1) Any question which arises between the Parties concerning the interpretation or application of this Treaty or the existence of any fact which, if established, might constitute a breach of this Treaty shall first be examined by the Commission, which will endeavour to resolve the question by agreement.

(2) If the Commission does not reach agreement on any of the questions mentioned in Paragraph (1), then a difference will be deemed to have arisen, which shall be dealt with as follows :

(a) Any difference which, in the opinion of either Commissioner, falls within the provisions of Part I of Annexure F shall, at the request of either Commissioner, be dealt with by a Neutral Expert in accordance with the provisions of Part 2 of Annexure F;

(b) If the difference does not come within the provisions of Paragraph (2) (a), or if a Neutral Expert, in accordance with the provisions of Paragraph 7 of Annexure F, has informed the Commission that, in his opinion, the difference, or a part thereof, should be treated as a dispute, then a dispute will be deemed to have arisen which shall be settled in accordance with the provisions of Paragraphs (3), (4) and (5) :

Provided that, at the discretion of the Commission, any difference may either be dealt with by a Neutral Expert in accordance with the provisions of Part 2 of Annexure F or be deemed to be a dispute to be settled in accordance with the provisions of Paragraphs (3), (4) and (5), or may be settled in any other way agreed upon by the Commission.

(3) As soon as a dispute to be settled in accordance with this and the succeeding paragraphs of this Article has arisen, the Commission shall, at the request of either Commissioner, report the fact to the two Governments, as early as practicable, stating in its report the points on which the Commission is in agreement

and the issues in dispute, the views of each Commissioner on these issues and his reasons therefore.

(4) Either Government may, following receipt of the report referred to in Paragraph (3), or if it comes to the conclusion that the report is being unduly delayed in the Commission, invite the other Government to resolve the dispute by agreement. In doing so it shall state the names of its negotiators and their readiness to meet with the negotiators to be appointed by the other Government at a time and place to be indicated by the other Government. To assist in these negotiations, the two Governments may agree to enlist the services of one or more mediators acceptable to them.

(5) A Court of Arbitration shall be established to resolve the dispute in the manner provided by Annexure G;

(a) upon agreement between the Parties to do so; or

(b) at the request of either Party, if, after negotiations have begun pursuant to Paragraph (4), in its opinion the dispute is not likely to be resolved by negotiation or mediation; or

(c) at the request of either Party, if, after the expiry of one month following receipt by the other Government of the invitation referred to in Paragraph (4), that Party comes to the conclusion that the other Government is unduly delaying the negotiations.

(6) The provisions of Paragraphs (3), (4) and (5) shall not apply to any difference while it is being dealt with by a Neutral Expert.

ARTICLE X

Emergency Provision

If, at any time prior to 31st March 1965, Pakistan should represent to the Bank that, because of the outbreak of large-scale international hostilities arising out of causes beyond the control of Pakistan, it is unable to obtain from abroad the materials and equipment necessary for the completion by 31st March 1973 of that part of the system of works referred to in

Article IV(1) which relates to the replacement referred to therein, (hereinafter referred to as the replacement element") and if, after consideration of this representation in consultation with India, the Bank is of the opinion that

(a) these hostilities are on a scale of which the consequence is that Pakistan is unable to obtain in time such materials and equipment as must be procured from abroad for the completion, by 31st March 1973, of the replacement element and

(b) since the Effective Date, Pakistan has taken all reasonable steps to obtain the said materials and equipment and, with such resources of materials and equipment as have been available to Pakistan both from within Pakistan and from abroad, has carried forward the construction of the replacement element with due diligence and all reasonable expedition,

the Bank shall immediately notify to each of the Parties accordingly. The Parties undertake, without prejudice to the provisions of Article XII (3) and (4), that, on being so notified, they will forthwith consult together and enlist the good offices of the Bank in their consultation, with a view to reaching mutual agreement as to whether or not, in the light of all the circumstances then prevailing, any modifications of the provisions of this Treaty are appropriate and advisable and, if so, the nature and the extent of the modifications.

ARTICLE XI

General Provisions

(1) It is expressly understood that

(a) this Treaty governs the rights and obligations of each Party in relation to the other with respect only to the use of the waters of the Rivers and matters incidental thereto and

(b) nothing contained in this Treaty, and nothing arising out of the execution thereof, shall be construed as constituting a recognition or waiver (whether tacit, by implication or otherwise) of any rights or claims whatsoever of either of the Parties other than those rights or claims which are expressly recognized or waived in this Treaty.

Each of the Parties agrees that it will not invoke this Treaty, anything contained therein, or anything arising out of the execution thereof, in support of any of its own rights or claims whatsoever or in disputing any of the rights or claims whatsoever of the other Party, other than those rights or claims which are expressly recognized or waived in this Treaty.

(2) Nothing in this Treaty shall be construed by the Parties as in any way establishing any general principle of law or any precedent.

(3) The rights and obligations of each Party under this Treaty shall remain unaffected by any provisions contained in, or by anything arising out of the execution of, any agreement establishing the Indus Basin Development Fund.

ARTICLE XII

Final Provisions

(1) This Treaty consists of the Preamble, the Articles hereof and Annexures A to H hereto, and may be cited as "The Indus Waters Treaty 1960".

(2) This Treaty shall be ratified and the ratifications thereof shall be exchanged in New Delhi. It shall enter into force upon the exchange of ratifications, and will then take effect retrospectively from the first of April 1960.

(3) The provisions of this Treaty may from time to time be modified by a duly ratified treaty concluded for that purpose between the two Governments.

(4) The provisions of this Treaty, or the provisions of this Treaty as modified under the provisions of Paragraph (3), shall continue in force until terminated by a duly ratified treaty concluded for that purpose between the two Governments.

In witness whereof the respective Plenipotentiaries have signed this Treaty and have hereunto affixed their seals.

Done in triplicate in English at Karachi on this Nineteenth day of September 1960.

For the Government of India	For the Government of Pakistan
(Sd/-)	(Sd/-)
JAWAHARLAL NEHRU	MOHAMMAD AYUB KHAN
	Field Marshal, H.P., H.J.

Dated : 19-09-1960

81

Trade Agreement between the Government of India and the Government of Pakistan

New Delhi, 21 March 1960

The Government of India and the Government of Pakistan with a view to developing, extending and consolidating trade and economic relations between the two countries have resolved to enter into the following Agreement :

Article I

The two Governments recognising the needs and requirements of each other in the context of their developing economies undertake to explore all possibilities for expansion and promotion of trade between the two countries on the basis of mutual advantage.

Article II

Each Government shall accord to the commerce of the country of the other Government treatment no less favourable than that accorded to the commerce of any third country.

Article III

The provisions of Article II shall not apply to the grant or continuance of any :

(a) privileges which are or will be granted by either of the two Governments in order to facilitate frontier trade;

(b) preferences, advantages, privileges or immunities accorded by either country to any third country prior to the 15th August, 1947, or in replacement thereof and

(c) any advantages accorded in connection with Customs Union or Free Trade Zone of which either may become a member.

Article IV

With regard to commodities mentioned In Schedules 'A' and 'B' attached to this Agreement, the two Governments shall facilitate imports and exports to each other's territories in accordance with their respective laws, regulations and procedures.

Article V

The Export and/or Import of goods not included in Schedules 'A' and `B' will also be permitted in accordance with the laws, regulations and procedures in force in either country from time to time.

Article VI

The two Governments further agree to enter by means of Protocols to this Agreement, into such Special Arrangements, including arrangements relating to Border Trade as may be considered by them to be necessary from time to time during the period of the validity of this Agreement to facilitate the movement of goods from one country to the other.

Article VII

The two Governments agree to accord, subject to their respective laws and regulations, reasonable facilities for the holding of trade fairs and exhibitions and visits of businessmen and Trade Delegations sponsored by the Governments concerned.

Article VIII

In order to facilitate the implementation of this Agreement, the two Governments shall consult each other as and when necessary, and also review the working of the Agreement at least once a year.

Article IX

This Agreement shall come into force from the date of

signature, and shall remain in force for a period of two years. The Agreement will be extended for a further period of one year unless either party gives to the other notice for its termination three months before the expiry of the said period of two years.

Done at New Delhi this twenty-first day of March, 1960 A.D. in two original copies in English language, both of which are equally authentic.

(Sd/-)	(Sd/-)
K.B. LALL	I.A. KHAN
For the Government of India.	For the Government of Pakistan.

Dated : 21-03-1960

SCHEDULE 'A'

EXPORTS FROM INDIA TO PAKISTAN

1. Coal 2. Stone boulders 3. Stones (Pakur) 4. Silbatta 5. Fire bricks 6. Lime and limestone 7. Mica 8. Bauxite 9. Barytes (white) 10. Pigments and dry colours 11. Dyeing and tanning substances 12. Chemicals 13. Drugs and medicines, including Ayurvedic and Unani Medicines 14. Mill board 15. Machinery and mill-work all sorts 16. Workshop equipment including hand tools and machine tools 17. Electric instruments, apparatus and appliances 18. Electric cables and wires 19. Fluorescent electric tubes 20. Electric insulation material 21. Accumulators and spare parts 22. Bicycles and spare parts 23. Scientific instruments, including laboratory glassware 24. Glass bottles, jars and phials 25. Iron and steel bolts, nuts and screws 26. Sanitary ware 27. Agarwood 28. Cinema films (exposed) 29. Canes and rattaris 30. Books, periodicals and newspapers 31, Essential oils 32. Sugar 33. Tea for blending 34. Coffee 35. Betel leaves 36. Biri tobacco 37. Biri leaves 38. Spices, all sorts 39. Fresh fruits 40. Catechu. 41. Potatoes 42. Buffalo horns 43. Conch shells 44. Gums and resins 45. Synthetic stones 46. Wood and timber 47. Fruit plants, seeds and bulbs 48. Iron and steel

49. Cement 50. Livestock 51. Gramophone records (in Indian and Pakistani languages and instrumental) 52. Hardware 53. Crockery and earthenware 54. Umbrella fittings 55. Khari salt 56. Cutch and gambier 57. Grouridmit H:P.S. 58. Hardwood and softwood 59. Tallow and wax 60. Sewing machines and spares 61. Coaltar and pitch 62. Typewriters 63. Rolling stock and accessories 64. Printing inks 65. Sports goods 66. Asbestos products.

SCHEDULE 'B'

EXPORTS FROM PAKISTAN TO INDIA

1. Raw jute 2. Jute cuttings 3. Raw cotton 4. Hides and skins 5. Betel leaves G. Betel nuts 7. Fresh and dried fruits 8. Coriander and methi seeds 9. Spices, including green spices 10. Honey, 11. Books and periodicals and newspaper 12. Cinema films (exposed) 13. Cement 14. Saltpetre 15. Machine tools 16. Bicycles and spare parts 17. Surgical instruments 18. Sports goods 19-Wood and timber, allsort. 20. Kapok (raw) 21. Livestock including horses 22. Asbestos products 23. Paints 24. Chuna khari pearls 25. Mother of pearl shells 26. Red beans 27. Black curnin seeds 28. Fresh fish 29. Dried and salted fish 30. Frozen fish 31. Eggs and poultry 32. Fruit plants, seeds and bulbs 33. Dhanicha seeds 34. Chuna Rhari pearls 35. Chrome ore 36. Newsprint 37. Paper 38. Gaur meal 39. Gaur gum 40. Fresh vegetable. 41. Gramophone records 42. Forest Produce (specified items only) 43. Drugs and medicines including Ayurvedic and Unani medicines.

PROTOCOL NO. 1 : In pursuance of Article VI of the Trade Agreement between the Government of India and the Government of Pakistan, the two Governments have agreed to enter into the following Special Payments Agreement to facilitate, on a self-balancing basis, the exchange between the two countries of the commodities mentioned in Annexure I thereto.

1. All payments in respect of the sale and purchase of the commodities listed in the Schedules at Annexure I up to the

values mentioned therein, shall be made by Pakistan and India in nonconvertible Indian Rupees.

2. For the exclusive purpose of facilitating transactions in respect of the sale and purchase of the commodities listed in the said Schedules, payments shall be made through Account 'A' opened by the National Bank of Pakistan, Karachi, with the State Bank of India, New Delhi, in accordance with the provisions of the Limited Payments Agreement between the Governments of Pakistan and India, dated the 3rd December, 1959.

3. All transactions in the commodities listed in the said Schedules for purposes of Account 'A' shall be valued either on F.O.R. or C & F basis depending on the terms of the contracts entered into.

4. Account 'A' shall be self-balancing Account with a swing limit of Rs. 50 lakhs (Rupees fifty lakhs only) on either side. When the outstanding amount in Account 'A' exceeds the swing limit, the country running an import surplus may suspend imports temporarily, while the country running an import deficit shall take steps to expedite imports, so that the imbalance is rectified. The rate of interest and technical details for the operation of Account 'A' shall be in accordance with Annexure 11.

5. In order to facilitate the implementation of this Arrangement, the two Governments shall review the working of this Arrange and other consequential problems arising therefrom at the expiry of six months from the date of signature and compare the debits and credits on either side to devise such measures as may be mutually agreed upon to rectify the imbalance, if any, in favour of one or the other country.

6. In case of any change in the parity rate of the Indian rupee, the balance in Account 'A' shall be adjusted in proportion to the change in the rate.

7. If at the close of the currency of this Arrangement, there remains any amount outstanding in Account 'A' to the credit of either Government, the same shall be liquidated by the import

of goods mentioned in the Schedules by the country concerned except that if a small balance not exceeding, say Rs. 1,000 (Rupees one thousand only), remains unadjusted for six months after the termination of this Arrangement, this amount may be adjusted by a remittance from Pakistan if the account is in debit or a remittance from India if the account is in credit.

8. Values for the export and import of the commodities have been shown in Schedules 'I' and 'II' of Annexure I to this Arrangement. These values are valid for a period of one year, except that in the case of the initial year, the values shall be deemed to take effect from the 3rd December 1959. The list of commodities and values thereof in the Schedules may be amended from time to time by mutual consent.

9. This Arrangement supersedes the Limited Payments Agreement, dated the 3rd December 1959, 1 and shall form Protocol No. 1 to the Trade Agreement, dated the 21st March 1960. It will remain in force for the duration of the said Trade Agreement. Provisions of this Protocol shall apply mutatis mutandis to the transactions entered into in accordance with the provisions of the Limited Payments Agreement.

10. This Protocol is signed in New Delhi on the 21st day of March 1960, in two original copies in English language, both of which are authentic.

(Sd/-)	(Sd/-)
K.B. LALL	I.A. KHAN
For the Government of India.	For the Government of Pakistan.

Dated : 21-03-1960

ANNEXURE II

Banking Agreement between the State Bank of India and the National Bank of Pakistan. For Financing the movement of goods under the Protocol to the Trade Agreement between the

Government of India and the Government of Pakistan signed on March 21, 1960.

The National Bank of Pakistan, Local Principal Office, Karachi, shall maintain a special non-convertible Indian Rupee Account with the State Bank of India, New Delhi for the purpose of making and receiving of all payments in respect of the sale and purchase of commodities covered by the Protocol to this Arrangement signed on the 21st March, 1960. This Account shall be styled "NATIONAL BANK OF PAKISTAN CLEARING ACCOUNT 'A'."

2. All claims or adjustments in respect of goods exchanged under this Protocol as also all bank charges shall be settled through the said Account.

3. This Account shall have a swing limit of Rs. 50 lakhs (Rupees fifty lakhs only) on either side subject to the proviso that all outstanding Letters of Credit and other commitments on the part of either the National Bank of Pakistan or the State Bank of India shall be honoured, even if the balance, debit or credit, exceeds the said limit. The balance in the Account, both credit and debit, shall carry interest at 2½ per cent per annum on a daily product basis, and this interest shall be credited or debited monthly to the said Account under advice to the National Bank of Pakistan.

PROCEDURE

4. Exports from Pakistan to India.

The Offices of the National Bank of Pakistan handling export documents will send these documents under a covering schedule to the concerned office of the State Bank of India in India and will at the same time send a copy of this schedule to the State Bank of India, New Delhi.

5. Exports from India to Pakistan.

The Offices of the National Bank of Pakistan opening Letters of Credit will advise the credits through the concerned offices of the State Bank of India in India and will send a copy of each such Letter of Credit to the State Bank of India, New Delhi.

Collecting Offices of both National Bank of Pakistan and State Bank of India will advise the respective remitting offices on the other side of the payment of each bill received for collection. Copies of such advices issued by offices of the State Bank of India will in each case be sent to the National Bank of Pakistan, Local Principal Office, Nicol Road, Karachi.

The State Bank of India, New Delhi, will send weekly statements of account to the National Bank of Pakistan, Local Principal Office, Karachi. The statements will indicate the relative bill and Letter of Credit number against each item posted in the statement, and also the name of the office of the National Bank of Pakistan concerned.

PROTOCOL No. II : In pursuance of Article VI of the Trade Agreement between the Government of India and the Government of Pakistan, the two Governments have agreed to enter into, by means of this Protocol, Special Arrangements in respect of the commodities specified below

TABLE

This protocol is signed in New Delhi on the twenty first day of March 1960 in two original copies in English Language, both of which are equally authentic.

(Sd/-)
K.B. LALL
For the Government
of India.

(Sd/-)
I.A. KHAN
For the Government
of Pakistan.

Dated : 21-03-1960

LETTERS

No. 1

GOVERNMENT OF INDIA,
MINISTRY OF COMMERCE AND INDUSTRY,

New Delhi, 21 March 1960

Dear Mr. Khan,

During the course of the discussions leading to the conclusion of the Trade Agreement between the two countries, it was suggested with reference to Article 11 thereof that the following letter be exchanged between the two countries :

"With reference to Article 11 of the Trade Agreement concluded between the Government of India and the Government of Pakistan on 21st March 1960, it was suggested that if the Government of either country enters into a bilateral arrangement with any third country for any commodity in the export of which the other country has a substantial interest, the Government entering into the bilateral arrangement shall give due consideration to and safeguard the interests of the other country to the extent practicable.

I shall be grateful if you could kindly confirm that the above correctly sets out the understanding reached between us".

You undertook to place the above suggestion before your Government for consideration and communicate their views as soon as practicable.

I shall be grateful if you would kindly acknowledge this letter.

Yours sincerely,

(Sd/-)
K.B. LALL

Mr. I. A. KHAN, Leader, Pakistan Trade Delegation, New Delhi.

No. 2

New Delhi, 21 March 1960

Dear Shri Lall,

I write to acknowledge having received your letter which reads as follows (Letter No. 1 not reproduced).

My Government's decision on your suggestion will be communicated to you as soon as practicable.

Yours sincerely,

(Sd/-)
I.A. KHAN

Mr. K.B. LALL, Government of India, New Delhi.

No. 3

GOVERNMENT OF INDIA,
MINISTRY OF COMMERCE AND INDUSTRY,

New Delhi, 21 March 1960

Dear Mr. Khan,

In the course of our discussions which resulted in the conclusion of the Trade Agreement which was signed today, we reviewed the working of the Limited Payments Agreement which was signed between the two countries in Karachi on the 3rd December, 1959. It was agreed to expand the scope of Special Payments facilities and to increase the swing limit from Rs. 25 lakhs to Rs. 50 lakhs. The amplified Arrangement has been signed today as a Protocol in pursuance of Article VI of the Trade Agreement. In order, however, to give a smooth start to extended exchanges of goods through Special Payments Agreement, it has been agreed that for a period of six months from today, the reference in paragraph 4 of the Protocol concerning the swing limit shall remain in abeyance.

I shall be grateful if you kindly confirm .hat the above correctly sets out the understanding reached between us.

Yours sincerely,

(Sd/-)
K.B LALL

Mr. I.A. KHAN, Leader, Pakistan Trade Delegation, New Delhi.

82

Agreement between Governments of India and Pakistan regarding Procedures to end Disputes and Incidents along the Indo-West Pakistan Border Areas

New Delhi, 11 January 1960

1. West Pakistan-Punjab border. Of the total of 325 miles of the border in this sector, demarcation has been completed along about 252 miles. About 73 miles of the border has not yet, been demarcated due to differences between the Governments of India and Pakistan regarding interpretation of the decision and Award of the Punjab Boundary Commission presented by Sir Cyril Radcliffe as Chairman of the Commission. These differences have been settled along the lines given below in a spirit of accommodation :

(i) The Sarja Marja, Rakh Hardit Singh and Pathanke (Amritsar-Lahore border). The Governments of India and Pakistan agree that the boundary between West Pakistan and India in this region should follow the boundary between the Tehsils of Lahore and Kasur as laid down under Punjab Government Notification No. 2183-E, dated 2nd June 1939. These three villages will in consequence fall within the territorial jurisdiction of the Government of Pakistan.

(ii) Chak Ladheke (Amritsar-Lahore border). The Governments of India and Pakistan agree that the delineation of the boundary will be as shown in the map of the Kasur Tehsil by Sir Cyril Radcliffe and Chak Ladheke will in consequence fall within the territorial jurisdiction of the Government of India.

(iii) Ferozepur (Lahore-Ferozepore border). The Governments of India and Pakistan agree that the West Pakistan-Punjab (India) boundary in this region is along the district boundaries of these districts and not along the actual course of the river Sutlej.

(iv) Suleimank, (Ferozepur-Montngoamgerreye border). The Governments of India and Pakistan agree to adjust the district boundaries in this region as specified in the attached schedule and as shown in the map appended thereto as Annexure

2. West Pakistan-Bombay border-Exploratory discussions regarding the boundary dispute in the Kutch-Sind region showed that the differences between the Governments of India and Pakistan could not be settled. Both Governments have decided to study the relevant material and hold discussions later with a view to arriving at a settlement of this dispute.

3. Detailed Ground Rules for the guidance of the Border Security forces along the Indo-West Pakistan frontier) prepared as a result of the deliberations of the Conference (Annexure 11) will be put into force by both sides immediately. These Rules will be reviewed and brought up-to-date after the boundary has been finally demarcated and the return of areas in adverse possession of either country has, been effected in the West Pakistan-Punjab (India) sector. Similar action will be taken in respect of the other two sectors in due course.

4. The Governments of India and Pakistan agree to give top priority to completion of demarcation along the West Pakistan-Punjab (India) sector in accordance with the settlements arrived at during this conference. Both Governments will direct their Surveyors General to complete the demarcation and the fixing of pillars in this sector by the end of April, 1960. Return of areas held in adverse possession by either country in this sector will be completed by 15th October, 1960. Necessary preparatory

work to this end should be undertaken immediately by all concerned.

(Sd/-)	(Sd/-)
M.J. DESAI,	J.G. KHARAS,
Commonwealth Secretary,	Joint Secretary,
Ministry of External Affairs,	Ministry of Foreign Affairs
Government of India.	and Commonwealth Relations,
	Government of Pakistan.

Dated : 11-01-1960.

SCHEDULE : REFERRED TO IN PARA 1 (IV)

1. The boundary between Pakistan and India in the vicinity of Suleimanke headworks will be along the line marked A B C D E F G H I J K L M in the map at Annexure 1. The points A and M represent the junction of this section of the boundary with the boundary between Ferozepur and Montgomery districts. The portion A B C D E F will follow the boundary of the original area acquired for the Suleimanke Headworks subject to the modification in respect of the reach D to F as specified in para 2. From F to G it will follow the alignment of the existing Left Marginal Bund. From G to H it will follow the dotted straight line shown in the map as closely as practicable subject to such adjustments in alignment at site as may be required from technical considerations to be decided mutually after carrying out necessary surveys. From H to K *viz.*, RD 47,500, the boundary will follow the alignment of the existing marginal bund. From K to L it will follow the alignment of the existing new Hasta bund. From L it will run in a straight line to the apex point of the bulge in the district boundary, as shown on the map.

2. The boundary will run at a distance of 50 feet from the outer toe of the existing Left Marginal Bund in all the reaches where the boundary as defined in para I above runs along it, *i.e.*, from D to G and from H to K. In the reach from G to H it would similarly be placed 50 feet from the outer toe of the proposed

bund. In the reach K to L, the boundary will run at a distance of 100 feet from the eastern toe of the existing new Hasta bund.

3. The two parties recognise that they have common and mutual interest in the proper upkeep and maintenance of the Left Marginal Bund at Suleimanke, and to that end, they declare their intention to co-operate by mutual agreement to the fullest possible extent. In particular,

(1) Each party will maintain in its territory according to the following specifications the portion of the Left Marginal Bund that will lie in Pakistan or continue to be in India :

(i) Top width-25 feet

(ii) Side slope on the River side-3 to 1

(iii) Outer slope-2 to I

(iv) Free Board above the highest flood level on record as on 10-1-1960, 5 feet minimum.

(2) Each party will carry out annual river survey in its own territory upto the conventional distance upstream of the Barrage at Suleimanke, and exchange it with the other party.

(3) The representatives of either party will be allowed to inspect the Left Marginal Bund in the territory of the other party at regular intervals that may be mutually fixed or at any time when either party makes a special request. Such inspections will be made jointly by the representatives of both parties, and each party will afford all necessary facilities to the other party.

(Sd/-)	(Sd/-)
S.N. RAVIKANT, C.E. Irrigation, Punjab, India.	M. MAHBOOB, Chief Engineer, Irrigation West Pakistan.
(Sd/-) M.J. DESAI.	(Sd/-) J.G. KHARAS.

Dated : 10-01-1960

ANNEXURE

GROUND RULES FOR BORDER GUARDS

In pursuance of the directive given to the sub-committee these ground rules were formulated by Lt. Gen. P.N. Thapar, GOC-in-C, Western Command (India) and Lt. Gen. Bakhtiar Rana, SQA, MC Corps, Commander, Pakistan. In their deliberations they were assisted from the Pakistan side by Brig. Said-ud-Din, Director-General, West Pakistan Rangers, Brig. Tikka Khan and Mr. M.S. Koreishi, PFS, Under Secretary, Ministry of Foreign Affairs, and on the Indian side by Shri Bhagwan Singh Rosha, IPS, DIG, PAP., Brig. Gurbakhsh Singh, Shri Govardhan, IPS, IG. Rajasthan, Shri V.G. Kanetkar, IP., DIG., Bombay and Shri M.M. Sen, I.C.S., Deputy Secretary, Ministry of Defence. The ground rules formulated in this paper are applicable to the West Pakistan-Punjab (India), West Pakistan-Rajasthan and West Pakistan-Bombay border.

On this border the security forces of both the countries are located at some places in close proximity to each other, and to avoid any untoward incident and resulting tension, it is necessary that pending Pakistan Border Issues (West Pakistan) 11 Jan. 1960, 305 the determination of the final boundary and the exchange of the territories, in adverse possession of the two Governments, the security forces of the two respective countries should observe the ground rules as laid down hereinafter.

On this frontier the *de facto* boundary is generally known to the security forces of both sides and the local population. In case of disputes arising in any sector, regarding the de facto boundary the status quo will be maintained by the local post commanders and a working boundary in the areas under dispute, should be decided upon by the officers mentioned in paragraph 4 below and jointly recorded in a descriptive manner and clearly identified on the ground.

This working boundary will be decided upon by the undermentioned assisted by appropriate Civil Officers :

(i) West Pakistan/Punjab (1) Border between the Director General,

West Pakistan Rangers/rep. and the D.T.G., P-.A.P, Punjab (India)/rep.,

West Pakistar./Rajasthan Border between the Director General,

West Pakistan Rangers/rep. and D.I.G., RAC/rep.,

(iii) West Pakistan/Bombay Border between the Director General,

West Pakistan Rangers/rep., DIG., (HQ)/rep.,

The *de facto* boundary may or may not coincide with the *dejure* international boundary and the observance of the *de facto* boundary by both sides will not commit the two Governments in any manner in respect of their *dejure* claim.

Neither side will have any permanent or temporary border security forces or any other armed personnel within 150 yards on either side of this *de facto* boundary and no picket forward posts or observation posts will be established within this area.

Notwithstanding the provisions of paragraph 6 above, both sides may :

(a) go right up to the de facto boundary in hot pursuit of an offender; (b) send patrols within the zone specified above upto the *de facto* boundary, provided :

The each side will inform the other about the actual patrol beat or any changes thereto if it falls within 50 yards of the boundary.

(b) patrols are small in numbers, *i.e.*, not exceeding a section of one and ten;

(iii) patrols invariably move with flags and

(iv) only personal weapons are carried by the patrols (no L.M.Gs. will be carried);

(c) retain such pickets, forward posts and observation posts as are already established until the de jure boundary is finalised and return of territories under adverse possession takes place. A list of such posts on both sides will be exchanged by 1-2-60.

New posts within the 150 yards belt on either side will only be established by mutual agreement.

Defensive works existing within 150 yards on either side of the de facto/working boundary not included in the list mentioned in para 7(c) above must be destroyed or filled up by 15-3-1960 and reports to this effect will be exchanged by both sides.

Notwithstanding the provisions of paragraph 6 to 8 above, in areas regarding which disputes of title are already pending with the respective Governments for a decision, the status quo inclusive of defence and security measures will be strictly maintained until such time as the de jure boundary is finalised and the return of territories in adverse possession of the two countries takes place.

It will be the duty of the border security forces on either side to prevent armed civilians entering the 300 yards stretch of the border (150 yards on either side of the working boundary).

Border security forces of both sides are charged with the responsibility of preventing smuggling in their respective areas. Therefore, it is incumbent upon them to arrest smugglers of any nationality, whether armed or unarmed, and to deal with them under the law of the land.

In the case of local population, inadvertent crossings are likely to take place along with border. The border security forces, after satisfying themselves that the crossing was done inadvertently, shall immediately return the persons concerned to the opposite commanders at officers level.

Whenever the personnel of the border forces of either country inadvertently stray across the border line information about it should be immediately conveyed to the nearest post of the other side and the personnel must be handed back without delay to their nearest post along with their arms and ammunition etc., if any, through Gazetted Officers/Upper Subordinates of both sides.

Bonafide governmental bodies *e.g.*, survey parties, etc., while operating in the border area shall not be interfered with. The programme of such parties will be notified to both sides by the Government concerned-at least a month ahead. Such parties will report to the nearest post of their own country before starting the work.

Whenever any cattle are alleged to have been lifted across the border a report, to be lodged with the opposite border post commander to whom the details such as the tracks of the cattle and of the criminals involved will be handed over. The Border Post Commanders concerned will acknowledge receipt of the report and then inform the nearest Police Station in their own country who will make all efforts to recover the cattle. After recovery the cattle must be handed back immediately to the Police Officers on the opposite side.

Grazing of unattended cattle on the border shall be discouraged. In the case of stray cattle these will be returned immediately by the Border Post Commanders to their opposite numbers after having satisfied themselves that the cattle have in actual fact strayed from across the border.

The SPs. of Border Districts will also attend where necessary the monthly border meetings for the purpose of exchange of cattle and discussing border crimes.

The duties of the Sub-centres/Wing Commanders/SPs. and lower Commanders in their respective areas of responsibility shall be as under :

(a) They will maintain close liaison with their opposite numbers.

(b) They will, by frequent visits, make themselves known to the Border Security Forces of the opposite side.

(c) They will receive all complaints regarding border violation/tension. They will immediately hold a joint enquiry not later than 24 hours of the information report. Where this is not possible due to long distances and difficulties of communications, the joint enquiry should be held as soon as possible.

(d) Where two border posts are situated in close proximity

to each other and it is possible for them to communicate by flags, any commander who wishes to meet his counterpart, will wave a flag of the specifications given in paragraph 23 below and will proceed to the border unarmed without any escort to a pre-arranged place. The opposite commander or the senior officer on seeing the flag, will acknowledge the signal and proceed to the place of meeting also with a flag unarmed and without escort. The use of flags shall be introduced by 15-2-1960.

Where the posts are separated by a long distance, contact will be established in the following manner :

A party consisting of I and 6 armed with their personal weapons for their own protection and carrying the appropriate flag will proceed to the post of the other side. On arrival within 300 yards of this post, they will establish a temporary base and send forward two men unarmed with the appropriate flags to make necessary contact.

(e) Nationals of both the countries, while cultivating land upto the de facto boundary of the country concerned shall not be interfered with by the border security forces of the other side.

(f) If a national of one country lays a fresh claim to land across the *de facto* border and takes any step in furtherance of that claim which is objected to by the other side, the two commanders will hold a joint enquiry on the spot and restrain the person from enforcing his claim until the matter is settled.

Where, due to the change in the course of a river, territory of one country is thrown on the other side, such change will not affect either the dejure or de facto position of the territory.

It is felt that the tension on the borders will be greatly minimised if there is close personal touch between commanders of the two border security forces and therefore the following periodic meetings are recommended :

(a) Wing Comdrs Rangers (Pak)/ Monthly at the SPs. of PAP/RAC (India) border. Special Reserve Police, Bombay, (India).

(b) Officers mentioned in para 4 As required above or their representatives shall also meet. These officers will be authorised by their respective Governments to settle the disputes on the spot as far as possible.

The military commanders shall also meet as and when the situation demands and whenever they consider it necessary.

If unfortunately, in spite of this, firing occurs, the other side shall refrain from replying. The local commanders will get in touch with each other by telephone and will meet with a view to bringing about a cease-fire forthwith. After every firing incident, it is necessary for both sides to carry out a joint investigation, fix responsibility and submit their respective reports for information of their higher authorities.

In order to maintain close liaison between the border forces of the two countries, it is essential that adequate telephone and other communications are provided at various levels.

All pickets and patrols on both sides will have flags of the following description

Pickets :

Pole Cloth Size 7 ft 4×3 feet

Colours India .... Orange.

Patrols :

Pole cloth 3 feet 2×2l/2 feet

Pakistan Blue.

At night flags will be substituted by light signals or signal by torches as mutually arranged between the post commanders.

The areas :

Whenever there is a joint enquiry by DCs. or Commissioners on the two sides, the respective commanders of security forces shall also attend the meeting and submit for the information of the respective higher commanders their assessment of the situation created by the particular incident.

Finally, we recommend :

(a) that the press on both sides should be persuaded to exercise restraint and not to publish exaggerated reports or material which is likely to inflame the feelings of the population on both sides. Should incorrect reports be published, contradictions at a governmental level should be issued at the earliest opportunity;

(b) that after the *dejure* boundary has been finalised and the return of territories in adverse possession has been effected these ground rules should be reviewed in order to bring them up-to-date.

(Sd/-)	(Sd/-)
BSADKH-TIAR RANA,	P.N. THAPAR,
Lt. Gen., S-Q.A., M.C.,	Lt. Gen., G.O.C. in-C,
Corps Commander,	Western Command,
West Pakistan.	India.

Dated : 9-01-1960.

83

Limited Payments Agreement between the Governments of India and Pakistan

Karachi, 3 December 1959

The Government of India and the Government of Pakistan animated by the desire to develop and strengthen trade between the two countries and promote closer economic relations, have agreed to the exchange of certain commodities on a self-balancing basis under the following Payments Agreement. This Agreement shall be in addition to the normal trade under the existing Trade Agreement between the two countries.

Article I

All payments in respect of the sale and purchase of the commodities listed in the schedules at Annexure I upto the values mentioned therein, shall be made by Pakistan and India in nonconvertible Indian rupees.

Article II

For the exclusive purpose of facilitating such payments, the National Bank of Pakistan, Karachi, shall open a separate Clearing Account (hereinafter referred to as Account 'A' with the State Bank of India.

Article III

Payments in respect of the sale and purchase of the commodities listed in the said schedules, shall be cleared through Account 'A'.

Article IV

All transactions in the commodities listed in the said schedules for the purposes of Account 'A' shall be valued either on FOR or C&F basis depending on the terms of the contracts entered into.

Article V

Account A' shall be a self-balancing Account with a swing limit of Rs. 25 lakhs (Rupees Twenty five lakhs only) on either side. When the outstanding amount in Account 'A' exceeds the swing limit, the country running an import surplus may suspend imports temporarily, while the country running an import deficit shall take steps to expedite imports so that the imbalance is rectified. The rate of interest and technical details for the operation of Account 'A' shall be as settled between the National Bank of Pakistan and the State Bank of India as per Annexure 11.

Article VI

In order to facilitate the implementation of this Agreement, the two Governments shall review the working of this Agreement and other consequential problems arising therefrom at the expiry of three months from the date of signature and compare the debits and credits on either side to devise such measures as may be mutually agreed upon to rectify the imbalance, if any, in favour of one or the other country.

Article VII

In case of any change in the parity rate of the rupees on either side, the balance in Account 'A' shall be adjusted in proportion to the change in the rate.

Article VIII

If at the close of the currency of this Agreement, there remains any amount outstanding in Account 'A' to the credit of either Government, the same shall be liquidated by the import of goods mentioned in the schedules by the country concerned except that if a small balance not exceeding say Rs. 1,000/- (Rupees one thousand only) remains unadjusted for six months after the termination of this Agreement, this amount may be adjusted by a remittance from Pakistan if the account is in debit or a remittance from India if the account is in credit.

Article IX

The list of commodities in the schedules may be amended from time to time by mutual consent.

Article X

This Agreement shall be valid for a period of one year with effect from the date of signature and may be extended for such further period as may be mutually agreed upon.

Article XI

This Agreement is signed in Karachi on the third day of December 1959 in two original copies in the English language, both of which are authentic.

For and on behalf of the Government of India.

(Sd/-)

K.R.F. KHILNANI
Leader,
Indian Trade Delegation.

For and on behalf of the Government of Pakistan.

(Sd/-)

I.A. KHAN
Leader,
Pakistan Trade Delegation.

84

Agreement between Governments of India and Pakistan regarding Procedures to end Disputes and Incidents along the Indo-East Pakistan Border Areas

New Delhi, 23 October 1959

1. The Governments of India and Pakistan re-affirm their determination to implement the Nehru-Noon Agreement in full, the legal and other procedures necessary for implementation being devised as expeditiously as possible. It was agreed that all preliminary work short of actual work in the field should be undertaken now by both sides so that demarcation to implement the Nehru-Noon Agreement can be carried out expeditiously as soon as the requisite legal procedures are devised. It was also agreed that India, while framing the legislation, if required, to effect transfer of territorial jurisdiction consequent on demarcation, will make a provision in the said legislation which will give government necessary authority to effect such transfers in connection with boundary disputes that may be settled.

2. Detailed Ground Rules for the guidance of the Border Security forces along the Indo-East Pakistan frontier prepared as a result of the deliberations of the Conference-copy attached. Appendix 1 will be put into force by both sides immediately. The decisions taken at the Conference of Chief Secretaries in August 1959 for constant contact between the border authorities on both sides with a view to maintaining peaceful conditions,

which have been further elaborated at the Conference, (Appendix 11) should also be implemented by issue of detailed instructions by the Governments concerned.

It was also agreed that the Chief Secretaries will jointly review the progress of demarcation every quarter.

3. Detailed programmes for demarcation work for the field season should be prepared as usual. Provisions made in the Ground Rules for speeding up demarcation work and for consequential exchange of territorial jurisdiction should be strictly observed. Exchange of all areas already demarcated along the Indo-East Pakistan boundary should take place before 30th June, 1960, subject to the necessary legal and constitutional procedures being worked out.

4. West Bengal-East Pakistan Boundary. Over 1200 miles of this boundary have already been demarcated. As regards the boundary between West Bengal and East Pakistan in the areas of Mahananda, Burung and Karatoa rivers, it was agreed that demarcation will be made in accordance with the latest cadastral survey maps supported by relevant notifications and record-of-rights.

5. Tripura-East Pakistan Boundary. Exploratory discussions revealed that the problem had not been carefully studied as all the material on each side had not been examined and there was divergence of opinion as to whether the Kar-Creed maps or the revenue survey maps should be taken as the basis of demarcation. It was agreed that copies of the relevant records available with both sides should be supplied to each other and facilities given to see the originals and the experts on both sides should, within a period of two months, be ready with their appreciation of the records and indicate :

(i) the difference in the area involved if either the Kar-Creed or revenue survey maps were adopted as the basis of demarcation;

(ii) their respective positions as to how the boundary should run in the upper and lower reaches of the Feni river with necessary evidence in support of their view.

The two Governments or their representatives will, on receipt of this material, discuss the matter further and decide what should be adopted as the basis of demarcation in these various regions of the Tripura-East Pakistan Border.

6. Assam-East Pakistan Boundary. The three pending disputes have been settled along the lines given below in a spirit of accommodation :

(i) The dispute concerning Bagge Award III has been settled by adopting the following rational boundary in the Patharia Forest Reserve region :

From a point marked X (H522558) along the Radcliffe Line BA on the old Patharia Reserve Boundary as shown in the topographical map sheet No. 83D/5, the boundary line shall run in close proximity and parallel to the cart road to its south to a point A (H5 31554); thence in a southerly direction up the spur and along the ridge to a hill top marked B (H523529); thence in a south-easterly direction along the ridge down the spur across a stream to a hill top marked C (H532523); thence in a southerly direction to a point D (H530517); thence in a south-westerly direction to a flat top E (H523507); thence in a southerly direction to a point F (H524500); thence in a south-easterly direction in a straight line to the midstream point of the Gandhai Nala marked G (H540494); thence in south-westerly direction up the midstream of Gandhai Nala to a point H (H533482); thence in a south-westerly direction up a spur and along the ridge to a point I (H517460); thence in a southerly direction to a point on the ridge marked J (H518455); thence in a south-westerly direction along the ridge to a point height 364 then continues along the same direction along the same ridge to a point marked K (H500428); thence in a south and south-westerly direction along the same ridge to a point marked L (H496420); thence in a south-easterly direction along the same ridge to a point marked M (H499417); thence in a south-westerly direction along the ridge to a point on the bridle path with a height 587; then up the spur to the hill top marked N (H487393); then in a south-easterly and southerly direction along the ridge to the hill top with height 692; thence in a southerly direction down the spur to a point on Buracherra marked 0 (H484344); thence in a south-westerly direction up the spur along the ridge to the trigonometrical survey station with height 690; thence in a southerly direction along the ridge to a point height 490 (H473292); thence in a straight line due south to a point on the eastern boundary of the Patharia Reserve Forest marked Y (H473263), along the Radcliffe Line BA.

The line described above has been plotted on two copies of topographical map sheets Nos. 83 D/5, 83D/6 and 83D/2.

The technical experts responsible for the ground demarcation will have the authority to make minor adjustments in order to make the boundary alignment agree with the physical features as described.

The losses and gains to either country as a result of these adjustments with respect to the line marked on the map will be balanced by the technical experts.

(ii) the dispute concerning Bagge Award IV in the Kushiyara river region has been settled by adopting the thana boundaries of Beani Bazar and Karlmganj as given in Assam Government Notification No. 5133-H dated 28th May, 1940, as the India-East Pakistan boundary in this region, relevant portion of line BA given in the Radcliffe map being varied accordingly.

(iii) Tukergram. The East Pakistan-India boundary in this region given by Sir Cyril Radcliffe as the boundary between the districts of Sylhet and Cachar is confirmed. India's territorial jurisdiction in the whole of Tukergram village will be immediately restored.

7. Use of Common Rivers. The need for evolving some procedures for the purpose of mutual consultations in regard to utilisation of water resources of common rivers was recognised by both sides.

The Indian Delegation assured that India will raise no objection to the development activities in connection with the Karnafuli dam project in East Pakistan on consideration of submergence of some area in India. It was agreed that immediate steps should be taken for the demarcation of that portion of the boundary where some area might be permanently flooded when the Karnafuli dam in East Pakistan is raised to its full height so that the Governments of Pakistan and India can, in the light of the resulting area flooded, discuss how the claims of the Government of India regarding the loss, if any, caused by the flooding of the Indian territory should be settled.

8. Impartial Tribunals. It was agreed that all outstanding boundary disputes on the East Pakistan — India and West Pakistan-India border raised so far by either country should be referred to an impartial tribunal consisting of three members, for settlement and implementation of that settlement by demarcation on the ground and by exchange of territorial jurisdiction, if any. Any dispute which may have been referred to the tribunal can be withdrawn by mutual agreement.

It was also agreed that the decision of the tribunal shall be by majority and final and binding on both the parties.

9. It was agreed that neither country will train its border rivers so as to cut into the territory of the other.

10. Press. It was agreed that efforts should be made by both countries to advise their press from time to time to exercise restraint and assist in the maintenance and promotion of friendly relations between India and Pakistan. It was also agreed that false or exaggerated reports in the press, which are likely to worsen Indo-Pakistan relations, should be contradicted by the Governments concerned.

(Sd/-)	(Sd/-)
J.G. KHARAS	M.J. DESAI
Acting Foreign Secretary,	Commonwealth Secretary,
Ministry of Foreign Affairs &	Ministry of External Affairs,
Commonwealth Relations,	New Delhi.
Karachi.	

Dated : 23-10-1959.

APPENDIX I

"GROUND RULES" formulated by The Military Sub-Committee of The Indian and Pakistan Delegations :

As instructed by the leaders of the two delegations the military sub-committee met on the 17th October, 1959. In pursuance of the directive, this joint paper was written by Major General Umrao Khan, S. Pk., G.O.C. 14th Division, East Pakistan, and Lt. General S.P.P. Thorat, D.S.O., G.O.C.-in-Chief, Eastern Command, India. From the Pakistan side Mr. S.M Koreishi, P.F.S., Under Secretary, Ministry of Foreign Affairs and from the Indian side Brigadier Ghasi Ram, Commander, 181 Inf. Bde. also attended the meeting.

For the sake of clarity the paper is divided into two parts-part I deals with the basic requirements which will have direct bearing on the implementation of the "Ground Rules" which are outlined in part II. We earnestly feel that unless the basic requirements are fulfilled, the implementation of the "Ground Rules" will not be as effective as we would like them to be.

The Ground Rules formulated in this paper deal with the Indo-East Pakistan border.

PART I

2. During the general discussions between the two delegations held from the 15th to 19th October, 1959, it was agreed :

(a) That legal provision must be made for effecting the exchange of territories after demarcation has taken place, whereever it becomes necessary.

(b) That the boundary should be demarcated as early as administratively possible. The progress of demarcation should be reviewed every quarter by the Governments of Pakistan and India with reference to the Field programmes settled by the D.L.Rs and necessary action taken to resolve difficulties, if any, and to expedite progress of demarcation work. In case of a dispute, the disputed portion may be left out, the dispute being reported cartographically and in writing to the Chief Secretaries of the Governments concerned who would resolve the dispute or refer to the Central Government concerned and the demarcation should proceed from where the disputed area ends.

(c) That following demarcation, exchange of territories in sizeable stretches of the border should by agreement take place without waiting for the entire length of the border to be demarcated.

To implement this it was agreed that the transfer of territorial jurisdiction should take place on an agreed date which shall not be later than the 31st of December of the year in which demarcation has been completed by the 31st of May. The State Government shall make every attempt to speedily transfer the territorial jurisdiction of these areas in respect of which the following processes have been completed :

(i) The mechanical part of the process of demarcation would be deemed to be completed when the final traverse has been done after construction of pillars and the position of the pillars has been jointly checked and proved by the D.L.Rs concerned;

(ii) Necessary time should be allowed to the farmers to harvest their crops before the transfer of territorial jurisdiction and

(iii) Before the transfer of territorial jurisdiction, the authorities on the two sides should collect data on the populated and farm areas and on properties held by individuals. This will enable the Governments concerned to exchange these data and ensure that special responsibility is placed on the local commanders and/or police and other officials to provide full protection to the person and property of the people so that their interests are not prejudiced by the transfer of jurisdiction on the agreed date.

PART II

3. On the Indo-East Pakistan border the security forces of both the countries are located in close proximity of each other.

Owing to a variety of reasons there have been occasional firings across the border. The causes which usually lead to firing are :

(a) Often, border security forces on both sides do not know where the International Boundary lies on the ground. Therefore, when nationals of the other country cross into what they think is their territory, fire is opened to prevent the ingress.

(b) Where the boundary in the riverine area is criss-cross and portions of land on the home side of the river are owned by the other country, fire is opened when these lands are cultivated or attempts are made to dispossess their rightful owners.

(c) When a char land is formed after the floods, whether in the bed of the river or as an accretion of the mainland, attempt is made by nationals of both countries to seize the newly formed char lands. This leads to claims and counter-claims as to which side owns the char lands. Firing is resorted to support claims of the respective sides.

(d) When the river falls on the international boundary, fishing and navigational disputes occur and fire is opened to stop cattle lifting or other raids by local inhabitants on either side.

(e) Occasionally fire is opened because of suspected movement in the vicinity of border security posts-this happens usually at night.

(f) sometimes a build-up of border security forces leads to a race between the two countries and tempers are frayed. A “trigger-happy” person lets off a round and this develops into a shooting match.

4. The problem is how to prevent such firings.

Most of the causes for the firing can be eliminated or at least considerably lessened if the security forces on either side 'keep out' of each other's way. (This does not apply in the case of commanders as stated in para 6 to 8 below).

5. We think that the possibilities of fire being opened will be considerably reduced if border security forces on both sides observe the following simple rules :

(a) Where the international boundary is not properly demarcated by pillars, a "working boundary" which can be easily identified on the ground should be decided between the commanders of the border security forces of both sides. The working boundary will be decided upon as under :

(i) Assam East Pakistan Border : Between D.G., E.P.R., and Commander 181 Inf. Bde.

(ii) West Bengal East Pakistan Border : Between D.G., E.P.R., and I.G.P. West Bengal Border.

(iii) Tripura East Pakistan Border : Between D.G., E.P.R., and I.G.P. Tripura.

(b) The working military boundary may or may not coincide with the International boundary and its acceptance by both sides will not commit the two Governments in any manner in respect of their dejure claims. The working military boundary should, if necessary, be marked in some simple manner and the demarcations should be shown jointly and recorded on one inch maps.

(c) After an identifiable boundary line whether real or working has been demarcated, neither side will have any permanent or temporary border security forces or any other armed personnel within 150 yards on either side of this line. Also no permanent posts will be constructed till the final demarcation has been done.

(d) This will not prevent either side from patrolling up to the 'real' or 'working' boundary provided :

(i) Where possible adequate warning is given to the other side;

(ii) Patrols are small in numbers, *i.e.*, not exceeding a section (1 & 10); Patrols will invariably move with flags;

(iii) Nothing but non-automatic small arms are carried by the patrol.

(e) If defensive works of any nature including trenches exist in the stretch of 300 yards (150 yards on each side of the working boundary) they must be destroyed or filled up.

(f) It will be the duty of the border security forces on either side to prevent armed civilian entering the 300 yards stretch of the border (150 yards on either side of the working boundary).

(g) Border security forces of both sides are charged with the responsibility of preventing smuggling in their respective areas. Therefore it is incumbent upon them to arrest smugglers of any nationality, whether armed or unarmed, and to deal with them under the law of the land.

(h) Wherever the boundary "real" or "working" runs through mid-stream of a river, the facilities to use the main channel will be provided by both sides. The following procedure will be adopted to regulate traffic and ensure that the nationals of both the countries are not harrassed :

(i) Joint check-posts will be established on the bank if possible or in the main channel where it leaves or enters the mid-stream boundary.

(ii) A check will be made and manifests of commodities will be prepared at the Joint Check-post. Manifests signed by Joint Check-posts will be accepted as the permit to use the main channel for navigation purposes only.

(iii) The boats using the main channel in the other country will not be allowed to touch the bank or exchange goods or engage in any other transaction with the nationals of other side.

(i) Border forces on both sides shall on no account participate in any quarrels between nationals of the two countries living on the border. If nationals of one country ingress the working boundary and enter illegally and commit or attempt to commit an offence, the border security forces would be at liberty to take appropriate action in the exercise of the "right of private defence," preferably without resorting to fire. In case fire has been opened the local commander will intimate his action to opposite commander and to his own higher authorities.

(j) In case of inadvertent crossings, after satisfying themselves that the crossing was done inadvertently, the border security forces shall immediately return the persons concerned to the opposite commanders at the officers level. Similarly, the cattle straying across the border will be handed over to the authorities on the other side.

(k) Certain bona ride governmental bodies, *e.g.*, survey parties, forest guards etc. will be operating in the near vicinity of the international borders. Border security forces shall not interfere with their working-in fact they are expected to help. The existence of such parties will be notified to both sides, by the departments concerned.

6. For the practical implementation of the above, the border on both sides shall be divided into Sectors/Sub-sectors. The existence and the Headquarters of these sub-sectors will be intimated to each other and attempt should be made to link the Headquarters of both sides with telephone.

7. The sub-sector commanders should be of the rank of Capt./Major or of equivalent ranks in the police.

8. The duties of the Sector/Sub-sector/Post Commanders in their respective areas of responsibility shall be as under

(a) They will maintain close liaison with their opposite numbers.

(b) They will, by frequent visits, make themselves known both to the Border Security Forces of the opposite side and to own local populations.

(c) They shall receive all complaints regarding territorial disputes referring to title to any land, immovable property lying on the other side of the border, char lands, navigation facilities and difficulty of harvesting. They will immediately hold a joint enquiry not later than 24 hours of the information report.

(d) They will immediately enforce a status-quo *e.g.* if a national of one country lays a fresh claim to land and takes any step in furtherance of that claim which is objected to by the other side, then the two commanders will hold a joint enquiry on the spot and restrain the person from enforcing his claim until the matter is settled at the appropriate level.

(e) The two commanders shall be responsible for referring disputes to the appropriate authorities and for seeing that they are progressed with a view to bringing the disputes to a final settlement.

(f) Similarly the military Commanders on both sides will keep in close touch with the progress of Survey parties working in their areas. Where in their opinion the progress is not according to the programme or work is stopped on account of difference of opinion or for any other reason, immediate reports by quickest means will be submitted to the G.O.C.-in-C./G.O.C. concerned who will report the matter to their respective Governments with a copy to the Chief Secretary concerned.

9. We suggest that the tension on the borders will be greatly minimised if there is close personal touch between commanders of the two border security forces, particularly military commanders on either side. We recommend that they should meet periodically to discuss matters of mutual interest. Sector Commanders or their senior representatives will normally meet each other at the time of routine DMs/DCs' meetings. The brigade commanders shall also meet as and when the situation demands and whenever they consider it necessary. In any case when it is apprehended that trouble is likely to occur they must meet. We further recommend that in case the situation is likely to become serious, the G.O.C. 14th Div., East Pakistan and

G.O.C.-in-C., Eastern Command or their representatives of sufficiently high rank should meet to discuss the situation and evolve means of eliminating the tension.

10. We attach great importance to such contacts for we feel that they will contribute substantially towards the good relations between the two forces, and help in removing misunderstanding about moves by both sides.

11. If in spite of this, unfortunately firing does start, the other side shall refrain from replying. The local commanders will get in touch with each other by telephone and will meet with a view to implementing the cease-fire forthwith. After every firing incident, it is necessary for both sides to carry out an investigation, fix the responsibility and submit the report for information to their higher authorities.

12. Communications : In order to maintain close liaison between the border forces of the two countries, it is essential that adequate telephone and other communications are provided at various levels.

13. Telephone : G.O.C.-in-C., Eastern Command and G.O.C. 14th Div., East Pakistan, should be able to talk to each other directly without any formality. Similarly, D.G., E.P.R. and Comdr., 181 Inf. Bde., I.G.P. West Bengal and I.G.P., Tripura should be able to talk to each other whenever necessary. Telephones between the two opposing Coy/Wing Headquarters and between important border posts of either side should also be installed, which will be done as early as possible, in any case, not later than January 1960.

14. Communication by Flags. In the absence of telephone conversation/contact whenever any Commander on either side wishes to meet his counterpart, he will wave a flag, of the specifications given below and will proceed to the border unarmed without any escort to a pre-arranged place. The opposite Commander or the Senior Officer present on seeing the flag hoisted, will acknowledge the signal and proceed to the place of meeting, also unarmed and without escort. The use of flags shall be introduced by 15 November, 1959.

15. All pickets and patrols on both sides will have flags of the following description :

PICKETS SIZE : POLE/7ft. CLOTH/4 × 3 ft.

PATROLS SIZE : POLE/3ft. CLOTH/2 × 2 1/2ft.

Colours Indian : Orange. Pakistan : Blue.

16. At night flags will be substituted by light signals (two red very lights) or signal by torches as arranged between the two commanders.

17. In the past tension has mounted on false rumours and exaggerated reports to such a pitch that the movement of extra forces and reinforcements to the affected areas was undertaken. Repetition of such moves in future is inadvisable from all points of view. To prevent such contingencies in the future, it is necessary that whenever there are reports of concentration and build up of forces on either side, Military Commanders of all levels, including the G.O.C.-in-C, Eastern Command and G.O.C. 14 Div., East Pakistan should meet and ascertain the authenticity of the reports if necessary even by a visit to the affected area. Similarly joint inspection will also be applicable to any fresh digging which is likely to create unnecessary misunderstandings.

18. Whenever there is a joint enquiry by DMs. or Commissioners on the two sides, the respective overall commanders of security forces shall also attend the meeting and submit for the information of the higher respective military commanders their assessment of the situation created by the particular incident.

19. Finally, we think that much harm is caused by alarming reports which are occasionally published in the press. We recommend that the press on both sides be persuaded to exercise restraint and not to publish material which is likely to inflame the feelings of the population on both sides. Should incorrect reports be published we recommend that

contradiction on a governmental level be issued at the earliest opportunity.

(Sd/-)	(Sd/-)
Lt. Gen., S.P.P., THORAT, D.S.O., G.O.C.-in C., Eastern Command, India.	Major-Gen., UMRAO KHAN S.Pk., G.O.C., 14 Div., East Pakistan.

Dated : 20-10-1959.

APPENDIX II

MONTHLY MEETINGS

It was agreed that with regard to the meetings of DMs./SPs. with their opposite numbers in the two countries the following additional provision should be made :

(a) Monthly meetings should be held in the second week of every month;

(b) Invitations for the meetings should issue alternatively from each side, beginning with India;

(c) In case a date in the second week cannot be fixed due to unavoidable reasons it must be fixed within the following week on a mutually agreed date;

(d) When a border incident occurs and it becomes necessary for the two DMs./SPs. to meet, either of them can ask his counter-part to meet him at a particular place. Immediately on receipt of the request for a meeting the invited D.M. should proceed to the appointed place within 24 hours. If he cannot present himself personally due to unavoidable circumstances, he may send his S.D.O./S.P. or the local Magi strate/ A.S.P. as may be appropriate under the circumstances;

(e) If for any reason a move cannot be made within 24 hours the matter should be reported by both sides to their Chief Secretaries. The Governments of West Bengal, Assam, Tripura and East Pakistan should issue instructions to their officers that these instructions should be scrupulously followed;

(f) It was agreed that so far as Tripura and the bordering Pakistan districts are concerned, the monthly meeting should be held between the S.P., Tripura, and the D.I.G. of Chittagong Range.

DAWKI

As regards Dawki, Sonatilla/Latangtilla the decision taken at the Chief Secretaries, Conference was reviewed. It was decided that this should be dealt with under the Ground Rules which provide for withdrawal of BOPs from within 150 yards of the "real" or "working" boundary.

85

Agreement between India and Pakistan on *ad hoc* Transitional Arrangements for the Irrigation use of the Water of the Indus System of Rivers

Washington, 17 April 1959

Whereas representatives of India and of Pakistan, together with representatives of the International Bank, are engaged in the preparation of a comprehensive plan for the irrigational use of the waters of the Indus system of rivers, and

Whereas by agreements dated June 21, 1955, October 31, 1955 and September 24, 1956, the Government of India and the Government of Pakistan agreed upon ad hoc transitional arrangements for the periods April 1 to September 30, 1955; October 1, 1955 to March 31, 1956; and April 1, 1956 to March 31, 1957 respectively, and

Whereas it is considered desirable that ad hoc transitional arrangements should be made for the period April 1, 1959 to March 31, 1960,

Now therefore, the Government of India and the Government of Pakistan agree as follows :

A. For the Period April 1 to October 15

1. Except as provided in paragraphs 2, 3, and 7 below, India agrees to limit withdrawals from river flow (for direct use in canals or for storage) in Indian territory, in each water-accounting period specified in paragraph 10 of this Agreement, to the equivalent of the following :

(a) 10, 250 cusecs from April 1 to July 10, 12,000 cusecs from July 11 to August 31, 10,500 cusecs during September, and 10,000 cusecs from October I to 15 from the Sutlej, as at Rupar, plus

(b) 3,500 cusecs during April, 4,500 cusecs during May, 5,500 cusecs from June 1 to September 30, and 5,100 cusees from October 1 to 15 from the Sutlej and Beas combined; as at Ferozepore, provided that the withdrawal from the Beas component does not exceed 16% of that component (during the period October I to October 15 the Beas component shall be as corrected for gains and losses between Ferozepore and Islam), plus

(c) Any Ravi supplies (after having given effect to paragraph 9 of this Agreement) transferred to the Beas and received at Ferozepore.

2. In addition to the withdrawals that India would be entitled to make under paragraph 1 above, India may make further withdrawals equivalent to amounts related to Pakistan's ability to replace. These amount, by water-accounting periods, shall be the aggregate of (a) and (b) below limited to amounts related to the effective capacities of the link canals, such amounts being as defined under (c) below.

(a) 80% of the equivalent (at Ferozepore) of any Ravi supplies escaped below Madhopur.

(b) 80% of the gross amount, determined as below :

When the discharge at Merala is below the floor discharge shown in column 2 of the following table, the gross amount, as at Ferozepore, shall be zero. When the discharge at Merala reaches or exceeds the ceiling discharge shown in column 3 of the Table, the gross amount as at Ferozepore shall be the amount shown in column 4 of the table. For discharges at Merala between those shown in columns 2 and 3, the gross amount, as at Ferozepore, shall be the proportional intermediate amount.

TABLE

Period		Floor Discharge at Merala	Ceiling Discharge at Merala	Gross amount as at Ferozepore, corresponding to the ceiling discharge	Effective capacity as at Ferpzepre
	(Col. 1)	(Col. 2)	(Col. 3)	(Col. 4)	(Col. 5)
April	1-10	11,100	16,800	4,300	8,600
	11-20	9,800	20,200	8,600	9,700
	21-30	10,000	23,300	11,900	11,900
May	1-10	15,700	30,100	13,000	13,000
	11-20	17,000	32,100	13,000	13,000
	21-31	19,500	34,100	13,000	13,000
June	1-10	16,500	30,900	13,000	13,000
	11-20	19,800	34,300	13,000	13,000
	21-30	19,200	33,500	13,000	13,000
July	1-10	17,700	31,900	13,000	13,000
	11-20	19,700	34,400	13,000	13,000
	21-31	18,200	32,500	13,000	13,000
August	1-10	11,900	25,900	13,000	13,000
	11-20	13,000	26,900	13,000	13,000
	21-31	16,300	29,700	13,000	13,000
September	1-10	18,000	32,000	12,000	12,000
	11-20	18,700	33,000	12,000	12,000
	21-30	20,200	34,000	12,000	12,000

(c) The limiting amount shall be 80% of the effective capacity shown in column 5 above.

(d) During October 1 to 15, India may make additional withdrawals, over and above those specified in paragraphs 1 and 2 (a) above, of 400 cusecs as at Ferozepore. If, during this period, river supplies in Pakistan are sufficiently good to permit the transfer of further additional amounts, Pakistan will cause such supplies to be transferred and will, through its Special Commissioner, notify the Indian Special Commissioner of the amounts which may be made available as additional replacement supplies.

In addition to the withdrawals that India would be entitled to make under paragraph 1 and 2 above, India may make another withdrawals to the extent and in the circumstances specified below :

3. (a) When, in any water accounting period the supplies at Ferozepore below (including withdrawals by the Dipalpur Canal), plus the amounts specified for India under paragraph 2 above, exceed the amounts set out below, India may withdraw the equivalent of 50% of the excess (provided that this quantity, viz. 50% of the excess, shall be reduced, but not below zero, by the equivalent at Ferozepore of the amounts, if any, stored during that period) and will allow the balance to escape below Ferozepore :

Period (Ferozepore Dates)		Amount
April	1-10	7,000 cusecs
	11-20	7,000 cusecs
	21-30	8,000 cusecs
May	1-10	8,000 cusecs
	11-20	11,000 cusecs
	21-31	13,000 cusecs
June	1-10	16,000 cusecs
	11-20	19,000 cusecs
	21-30	26,000 cusecs
July to August 31		30,000 cusecs
September	1-10	28,000 cusecs
	11-20	25,000 cusecs
	21-30	19,000 cusecs
October	1-10	13,000 cusecs
	11-15	9,500 cusecs

(b) (i) When there is an escapage below Islam, India may withdraw equivalent to the amount of the escapage.

(ii) If, during a water-accounting period, the equivalent at Ferozepore of the actual delivery at the tail of the Balloki-Suleimanke Link is less than the effective capacity (column 5 of the table under paragraph 2(b) and there is an escapage below Khanki or below Balloki not due to an operational emergency, India may withdraw additional amounts, limited to the unused effective capacity or to the equivalent of the escapage, whichever is less. If the escapage has been due to an operational emergency, Pakistan will take steps to discontinue the escapage as soon as the emergency is over.

There shall be no restriction on Indian withdrawals when, during any water accounting period, the aggregate of (i), (ii) and (iii) below exceeds 35,000 cusecs (without correction for gains and losses) between April I and August 31, 30,000 cusecs (without correction for gains and losses) in September and 25,000 cusecs (corrected for gains and losses between Ferozepore and Islam) during the first fifteen days of October :

(i) The supply at Ferozepore below (including withdrawals by the Diplapur Canal).

(ii) The equivalent (at Ferozepore) of any Ravi supplies escaped below Madhopur.

(iii) Between April 1 and September 30, the appropriate gross amount under paragraph 2(b) above, and, during the October 1 to 15, the amount under paragraph 2(d) above.

The aggregate of 10 and (iii) will be limited to the effective capacity shown in column 5 of the Table under paragraph 2(b) above.

B. For the Period October 16 to March 31

4. Except as provided in paragraphs 5, 6 and 7 below, India agrees to limit canal withdrawals in Indian territory in each water accounting period specified in paragraph 10 of this Agreement to the equivalent of the following :

(a) 10,000 cusecs from the Sutlej, as at Rupar, plus

(b) 3,500 cusecs during the last sixteen days of October and 2,720 cusecs thereafter from the Sutlej and Beas combined, as at Ferozepore, provided that the withdrawal from the Beas component corrected for gains and losses between Ferozepore and Islam does not exceed 21% of that component, as so corrected, plus

(c) Any Ravi supplies (after having given effect to paragraph 9 of this Agreement) transferred to the Beas and received at Ferozepore.

5. In addition to the withdrawals that India would be entitled to make under paragraph 4 above, India may make further withdrawals equivalent to amounts related to Pakistan's ability to replace. These amounts shall be such amounts, if any, as may be agreed upon between the Special Commissioners.

6. In addition to the withdrawals that India would be entitled to make under paragraphs 4 and 5 above, India may make further withdrawals to the extent and in the circumstances specified below :

(a) When there is an escapage below Islam (except during the annual closure at Islam headworks) India may withdraw amounts equivalent to the amount of the escapage.

(b) There shall be no restriction on Indian withdrawals from the Sutlej and Beas when, during any water accounting period specified in paragraph 10 of this Agreement, the supply at Ferozepore below, corrected for gains and losses between Ferozepore and Islam, including withdrawals of Dipalpur Canal, plus the amounts specified in paragraph 5 above, exceeds 10,000 cusecs.

C. General

7. India may utilise the stored water in any manner it likes.

8. The water-account required under paragraph 10 of this Agreement will, during the period April 1 to July 10 (Ferozepore dates), be prepared with due allowance for time-lag as set out in Annex I to this Agreement. During the period July 11 to March 31, such water account will be prepared on the basis of identical dates at various points of river supply and canal withdrawals, without any allowance for time-lag. During the period April 1 to September 30, the corrections to be applied for gains and losses shall be as set out in Annex I to this Agreement.

During the period October 1 to March 31, there shall be no allowance for gains or losses, except for those in the reach from Ferozepore to Islam. For this reach, the gains and losses shall be the actual gains and losses, calculated without any allowance for time-lag.

If, at any time between the closure of the Suleimanke Barrage (about the middle of October) and December 25, any supplies are released below Suleimanke, the Special Commissioners will agree .on an estimate of the gains which would have accrued in the reach from Suleimanke to Islam but for such release and these estimated gains will be used in the water-account instead of the actual gains or losses but not beyond December 25. This provision will not apply if the release is made when the supply reaching Suleimanke is in excess of 6,000 cusecs or when the supply reaching Islam falls below 350 cusees, in which event the actual gains or losses will be adopted for purposes of the water-account.

9. India will continue to supply the existing withdrawals of C.B.D.C. as hitherto.

10. Each calendar month will be divided into three periods (Ist to 10th, 11th to 20th and 21st to the end of the month) for the purposes of the water-account, except October which will be divided into four periods (Ist to 10th, 11th to 15th, 16th to 20th and 21st to 31st). An attempt will be made to balance the water-account for each of the periods specified above but any excess or deficit in Indian withdrawals in any such period will be carried over to the next period for adjustment.

11. (1) The Governments of India and Pakistan will each nominate a Special Commissioner, who shall be charged with the responsibility of supervising, in India and in Pakistan respectively, the implementation of this Agreement. Each Government may, if it so desires, appoint a Deputy Special Commissioner to assist the Special Commissioner.

(2) The two Commissioners will consult with each other, on the request of either, and each Commissioner will furnish to the Commissioner of the other Government the data specified in

Annex II to this Agreement. On the request of the Commissioner of the other Government, each Government will afford to the Commissioner of the other Government, or his Deputy, all reasonable access to the irrigation works concerned.

(3) In the event of any serious damage to irrigation works arising from causes beyond the control of the Government of Pakistan, which would have the effect of diminishing the supplies in the Balloki-Suleimanke Link, there shall be consultation between the Special Commissioners as to whether or not any modification should be made in the terms of paragraph 2 of this Agreement on account of such an emergency, and also with regard to the steps to be taken to restore this position to normal.

(4) In the event of any dispute arising with respect to the implementation of this Agreement, which cannot be resolved by discussion between the Special Commissioners, the matter will be referred to the representatives of the two Governments (participating with the International Bank in the Indus Water Talks) either of whom may, if he considers it necessary, enlist the good offices of the International Bank.

12. This Agreement will be without prejudice to any rights or claims of either Government, and will imply no commitments other than those specified herein for the period covered by the Agreement.

13. This Agreement applies to the period April 1, 1959 to March, 31, 1960. If, at any time during the currency of this Agreement, the International Bank should give notice to the two Governments of its withdrawals from the work of preparation of a comprehensive plan for the irrigation use of the waters of the Indus system of rivers, this Agreement shall cease to have effect as from a date three months after the date of the Bank's withdrawal, or from 31st March, 1960, whichever is earlier.

Done at Washington, D.C., this 17th day of April, 1959, in three counterparts, of which one shall be retained by each of the parties to this Agreement and the third deposited in the archives of the International Bank for Reconstruction and Development.

For the Government of India,	For the Government of Pakistan,
(Sd/-)	(Sd/-)
N.D. GULHATI	AZIZ AHMED
Additional Secretary to the Government of India, Ministry of Irrigation and Power.	Ambassador of Pakistan to the United States of America.

Dated : 17-04-1959

ANNEX I

A. Time-Lag (Days)

	April	May 1 to July 10
Rupar to Ferozepore	4	3
Harike to Ferozepore	1	1
Ferozepore to Suleimanke	3	2
Madhopur to Balloki	6	4
Balloki to Suleimanke	1	1
Suleimanke to Islam	4	3
Madhopur to Ferozepore *via* Beas	4	3

B. Equivalent at tail Balloki-Suleimanke Link (B.S. Link) of supplies below Madhopur

	Supplies below Madhopur (Cusecs)	Equivalent at tail B.S. Link (Cusecs)
Below	750	0
	750	150
	1,000	400
	1,500	750
	2,000	1,000
	16,000	8,000
	24,000	12,000

For intermediate values of the supplies below Madhopur, the equivalent at tail B.S. Link will be worked out proportionately.

The above values apply to the period April 1 to August 20. From August 21 to September 30, any discharge below Madhopur will be assumed to reach the tail of the B.S. Link without loss.

C. Equivalent at Ferozepore of supplies at tail Balloki-Suleimanke Link (B.S. Link)

Supplies at tail B.S. Link (Cusecs)	Equivalent at Ferozepore (Cusecs)
Nil	Nil
1,000	1,000
2,000	2,200
3,000	3,200
4,000	4,300
5,000	5,400
6,000	6,500
7,000	7,600
8,000	8,600
9,000	9,700
10,000	10,800
11,000	11,900
12,000	13,000

For intermediate values of the supplies at tail Balloki-Suleimanke Link, the equivalent at Ferozepore will be worked out proportionately.

The above values applies to the period from April 1 to August 31. During September, no loss or gain will be taken into account.

D. Sutlej Component at Ferozepore corresponding to discharge below Rupar

Discharge of the Sutlej below Rupar (Cusecs)	Sutlej Comp. at Ferozepore (Cusecs)
0	0
1,000	640
1,500	960
2,000	1,280
3,000	1,920
5,000	3,200
7,500	5,400
10,000	7,600
15,000	12,000
20,000	16,400
30,000	25,200
40,000	34,000
50,000	42,800
100,000	86,800

For intermediate values of the discharges below Rupar, the Sutlej component at Ferozepore will be worked out proportionately.

The above values apply for the period April 1 to August 31 (Ferozepore dates). During September, the Sutlej component at Ferozepore will be taken to be the same as the discharge below Rupar.

E. Equivalent at Ferozepore of withdrawals by Grey Canals or of withdrawals at Harike

Grey Canal withdrawals or withdrawals at Harike (Cusecs)	Equivalent at Ferozepore (Cusecs)
0	0
1,000	900
2,000	1,800
3,000	2,700
4,000	3,600
5,000	4,500

For intermediate values of the Grey Canal withdrawals or of the withdrawals at Harike, the equivalents at Ferozepore will be worked out proportionately.

The above values will apply for the period from April 1 to August 31. During September, the equivalent at Ferozepore will be taken to be the same as the actual Grey Canal withdrawals or the actual withdrawals at Harike.

ANNEX II

1. The following data will be exchanged for the period April 1, 1959, to March 31, 1960. This will be transmitted in duplicate by the Special Commissioners by air mail on a daily basis :

(a) Data to be furnished by Pakistan :

(1) Discharge of River Jhelum downstream of Mangla.

(2) Discharge at head of Upper Jhelum Canal.

(3) Discharge (combined) of old escapes on Upper Jhelum Canal.

(4) Discharge (combined) of Silt-Extractors on Upper Jhelum Canal.

(5) Discharge of River Jhelum below Rasul.

(6) Discharge of River Chenab downstream of Merala.

(7) Discharge at head of Merala-Ravi Link.

(8) Discharge at head of Upper Chenab Canal.

(9) Discharge at tail of Upper Jhelum Canal.

(10) Discharge of River Chenab below Khanki.

(11) Discharge at head of Lower Chenab Canal.

(12) Discharge of Chhenawan Escape.

(13) Discharge (combined) of all distributaries on Merala-Ravi Link.

(14) Discharge at head of Merala-Ravi Sub-Link.

(15) Discharge at tail of Merala-Ravi Link.

(16) Discharge at head of Bambanwala-Ravi-Bedian-Dipaipur Link.

(17) Discharge of Bambanwala-Ravi-Bedian Link escape into River Ravi.

(18) Discharge at tail of Bambanwala-Ravi-Beclian-Dipalpur Link.

(19) Discharge of River Ravi at Shabdara.

(20) Discharge at tail of Upper Chenab Canal.

(21) Discharge of Deg Nallah.

(22) Discharge of River Ravi downstream of Balloki.

(23) Discharge at head of Balloki-Suleimanke Link.

(24) Discharge at head of Lower Bari Doab Canal.

(25) Discharge of River Ravi upstream of Balloki.

(26) Discharge passed from Balloki-Suleimanke Link into Dipalpur Canal.

(27) Discharge at tail of Ballold-Suleimanke Link.

(28) Discharge at tail of Montgomery-Pakpattan Link.

(29) Discharge of River Sutlej upstream of Suleimanke.

(30) Discharge of River Sutlej downstream of Suleimanke.

(31) Discharge at head of Pakpattan Canal.

(32) Discharge at head of Eastern Sadiqia Canal.

(33) Discharge at head of Fordwah Canal.

(34) Discharge of River Sutlej upstream of Islam.

(35) Discharge of River Sutlej downstream of Islam.

(36) Discharge at head of Mailsi Canal.

(37) Discharge at head of Bahawal Canal.

(38) Discharge at head of Quimpur Canal.

(b) Data to be furnished by India :

(1) Discharge of river Sutlej at Bhakra.

(2) Discharge of river Sutlej at Olinda.

(3) Discharge of river Sutlej upstream of Rupar.

(4) Discharge at head of Bhakra Main Line.

(5) Discharge at head of Sirhind Canal.

(6) Discharge of Bist Doab Canal.
(7) Discharge of river Sutlej below Rupar.
(8) Discharge of Eastern Bein into Sutlej.
(9) Discharge of river Sutlej at Usafpur.
(10) Discharge of river Beas at Dera Gopipur.
(11) Discharge at head of Shah Nahar Canal.
(12) Discharge of river Beas at Mirthal.
(13) Discharge of river Beas at Mandi (plain).
(14) Discharge of Western Bein into Beas.
(15) Discharge at head (combined) of Grey canals.
(16) Discharge upstream of Harike.
(17) Discharge at head of Ferozepore feeder.
(18) Discharge of Makhu Canal.
(19) Discharge at head of Sirhind feeder.
(20) Discharge downstream of Harike.
(21) Discharge of river Sutlej upstream of Ferozepore.
(22) Discharge at head of Bikaner Canal.
(23) Discharge at head of Eastern Canal.
(24) Discharge at head of dipalpur Canal.
(25) Discharge of river Sutlej Downstream of Ferozepore.
(26) Gauge in river Ravi at Mukesar, if observed.
(27) Discharge of river Ravi upstream of Madhopur.
(28) Discharge at head of Upper Bali Doab Canal (including escapages).
(29) Escapages from Upper Bari Doab Canal into River Ravi.
(30) Escapages from Upper Bari Doab Canal into river Beas.
(31) Discharge at head of Upper Bari Doab Canal (excluding escapages).
(32) Discharge of river Ravi downstream of Madhopur.
(33) Discharge at head of Madhopur-Beas Link.

(34) Discharge at tail of Madhopur-Beas Link.

(35) Discharge of river Sutlej above Bhakra Reservoir, when observation arrangements have been established.

(36) Discharge of streams discharging into Bhakra Reservoir, when observation arrangements have been established.

(37) Reservoir level at Bhakra Dam.

(38) Pond level at Nangal Dam.

(39) Discharge at head of Nangal Canal.

(40) Pond level at Harike.

(41) Discharge of escapages (combined) from Nangal Canal into river Sutlej.

2. In addition, the following data will be transmitted by telegram on a daily basis :

(a) To be furnished by India :

(1) Discharge of River Sutlej downstream of Rupar.

(2) Discharge of River Ravi downstream of Madhopur.

(3) Discharge at head of Upper Bari Doah Canal.

(4) Discharge of River Sutlej downstream of Ferozepore.

(5) Discharge at head of Dipalpur Canal.

(6) Discharge of River Sutlej above Bhakra when observation arrangements have been established.

(7) Reservoir level at Bhakra.

(8) Discharge at head of Bhakra Main Line.

(9) Discharge at head (combined) of all canals at Rupar.

(10) Discharge at head (combined) of all canals at Harike.

(11) Discharge at head (combined) of Eastern and Bikaner canals at Ferozepore.

(b) To be furnished by Pakistan :

(1) Discharge at tail of Upper Jhelum Canal.

(2) Discharge of River Chenab upstream of Merala.

(3) Discharge of River Chenab downstream of Ehanki.

(4) Discharge of River Ravi downstream of Balloki.

(5) Discharge of River Sutlej downstream of Suleimanke.

(6) Discharge at head (combined) of all canals at Suleimanke.

(7) Discharge at tail of Balloki-Suleimanke Link.

(8) Discharge of River Sutlej downstream of Nam.

(9) Discharge at head (combined) of all canals at Islam.

3. India will supply Pakistan with the following Capacity Curves :

(a) For Bhakra Reservoir.

(b) For Nangal Pond.

(c) For Harike Pond.

86

Agreement between India and Pakistan on Border Disputes (East Pakistan)

New Delhi, 10 September 1958

In accordance with the directives issued by the two Prime Ministers, the Secretaries discussed this morning the following disputes :

West Bengal — East Pakistan

(1) Bagge Awards in disputes I and 11.

(2) Hilli.

(3) Berubari Union No. 12.

(4) Demarcation of Indo-Pakistan frontier so as to include the two chitlands of old Cooch Behar State adjacent to Radcliffe Line in West Bengal.

(5) 24-Parganas-Yhulna-Jessore 24-Parganas. Boundary disputes.

Assam-East Pakistan.

(6) Pakistan claim to Bholaganj.

(7) Piyain and Sumra-Boundary disputes.

Tripura-East Pakistan.

(8) Tripura land under Pakistan railway and Tripura land to the west of the railway line at Bhagalpur.

(9) Feni river-Boundary dispute.

West Bengal-East Pakistan.

(10) Exchange of enclaves of the old Cooch Behar State- in Pakistan and Pakistan enclaves in India. Claim to territorial compensation for extra area going to Pakistan.

2. As a result of the discussions, the following agreements were arrived at :

(1) Bagge Awards on disputes I and II.

It was agreed that the exchange of territories as a result of demarcation should take place by 15 January, 1959.

(2) Hilli.

Pakistan Government agrees to drop this dispute. The position will remain as it is at present in accordance with the Award made by Sir Cyril Radcliffe and in accordance with the line drawn by him on the map.

(3) Berubari Union No. 12.

This will be so divided as to give half the area to Pakistan, the other half adjacent to India being retained by India. The division of Berubari Union No. 12 will be horizontal starting from the north-east corner of Dobiganj thana. The division should be made in such a manner that the Cooch Behar enclaves between Pachgar thana of East Pakistan and Berubari Union No. 12 of Jalpaiguri thana of West Bengal will remain connected as at present with Indian territory and will remain in India. The Cooch Behar enclaves lower down between Beda thana of East Pakistan and Berubari No. 12 will be exchanged along with the general exchange of enclaves and will go to Pakistan.

(4) Pakistan Government agree that the two chitlands of the old Cooch Behar State adjacent to Radcliffe Line should be included in West Bengal and the Radcliffe Line should be adjusted accordingly.

(5) 24-Parganas-Khulna 24-Parganas — Jessore Boundary disputes

It is agreed that the mean of the two respective claims of India and Pakistan should be adopted, taking the river as a guide, as far as possible, in tho case of the latter dispute. (Ichamati river).

(6) Pakistan Government agrees to drop their claim on Bholaganj.

(7) Piyain and Surma river regions to be demarcated in accordance with the relevant notifications, cadastral survey maps and, if necessary, record of rights. Whatever the result of this demarcation might be, the nationals of both the Governments to have the facility of navigation on both of these rivers.

(8) Government of India agrees to give in perpetual right to Pakistan the land belonging to Tripura State to the west of the railway line as well as the land appurtenant to the railway line at Bhagalpur.

(9) The question of the Feni river to be dealt with separately after further study.

(10) Exchange of old Cooch Behar enclaves in Pakistan and Pakistan enclaves in India without claim to compensation for extra area going to Pakistan, is agreed to.

3. The Secretaries also agreed that the question of giving effect to the exchange of territory as a result of the demarcation already carried out should be given early consideration.

(Sd/-)

M.S.A. BAIG,
Foreign Secretary,
Ministry of Foreign Affairs and
Commonwealth Relations,
Government of Pakistan.

(Sd/-)

M.J. DESAI,
Commonwealth Secretary,
Ministry of External Affairs,
Government of India.

Dated : 10-09-1958.

87

The India-Pakistan Question, Australia, Columbia, Philippines, U.K., U.S.A. Joint Draft Resolution*

The Security Council,

Having received and noted with appreciation the report of Mr. Gunnar V. Jarring, the Representative of Sweden, on the mission undertaken by him pursuant to the Security Council resolution of 21 February 1957;

Expressing its thanks to Mr. Jarring for the care and ability with which he has carried out his mission;

Observing with appreciation the expressions made by both parties of sincere willingness to co-operate with the United Nations in finding peaceful solution;

Observing further that the Governments of India and Pakistan recognize and accept the commitments undertaken by them in the resolutions of the United Nations Commission for India and Pakistan dated 13 August 1948 and 5 January 1949, which envisage the determination of the future status of the State of Jammu and Kashmir in accordance with the will of the

* The Representative of the U.S.S.R. said in the Security Council on 21 November, 1957 that he would oppose this Joint Draft Resolution (S/3911). The President deferred the consideration of the question without putting the draft resolution to vote. Subsequently, certain amendments were introduced by the Representative of Sweden to the Joint Draft Resolution and this Draft Resolution as amended (S/3920) was adopted by the Security Council on 2-12-1957, vide Resolution No. 126 (1957).

people through the democratic method of a free and impartial plebiscite, and that Mr. Jarring felt it appropriate to explore what was impeding their full implementation;

Concerned over the lack of progress towards a settlement of the dispute which his report manifests;

Considering the importance which it has attached to demilitarization of the State of Jammu and Kashmir as one of the steps towards a settlement;

Recalling its previous resolutions and the resolutions of U.N.C.I.P. on the India-Pakistan question;

1. *Requests* the Government of India and the Government of Pakistan to refrain from making any statements and from doing or causing to be done or permitting any acts which might aggravate the situation and to appeal to their respective people to assist in creating and maintaining an atmosphere favorable to the promotion of further negotiations;
2. *Requests* the United Nations Representative for India and Pakistan to make any recommendations to the parties for further action which he considers desirable in connection with Part I of the U.N.C.I.P. resolution of 13 August 1948, having regard to his third and fifth reports and the report of Mr. Jarring, and to enter into negotiations with the Governments of India and Pakistan in order to implement Part II of the U.N.C.I.P. resolution of 13 August 1948, and in particular to reach agreement on a reduction of forces on each side of the cease-fire line to a specific number, arrived at on the basis of the relevant Security Council resolutions and having regard to the fifth report of the United Nations Representative for India and Pakistan;
3. *Calls upon* the Governments of India and Pakistan to co-operate with the United Nations Representative in order to formulate an early agreement on demilitarization procedures, which should be

implemented within three month of such an agreement being reached;

4. *Authorizes* the United Nations Representative to visit the sub-continent for these purposes and

5. *Instructs* the United Nations Representative to report to the Security Council on his efforts as soon as possible.

88

Draft Resolution (2 December 1957)

The Security Council,

Having received and noted with appreciation the report of Mr. Gunner V. Jarring, the Representative of Sweden, on the mission undertaken by him pursuant to its resolution 123 (1957) of 21 February 1957,

Expressing its thanks to Mr. Jarring for the care and ability with which he has carried out his mission;

Observing with appreciation the expressions made by both parties of sincere willingness to co-operate with the United Nations in finding peaceful solution;

Observing further that the Governments of India and Pakistan recognize and accept the commitments undertaken by them in the resolutions of the United Nations Commission for India and Pakistan dated 13 August 1948 and 5 January 1949, which envisage the determination of the future status of the State of Jammu and Kashmir in accordance with the will of the people through the democratic method of a free and impartial plebiscite, and that Mr. Jarring felt it appropriate to explore what was impeding their full implementation;

Concerned over the lack of progress towards a settlement of the dispute which his report manifests;

Considering the importance which it has attached to demilitarization of the State of Jammu and Kashmir as one of the steps towards a settlement;

Recalling its previous resolutions and the resolutions of U.N.C.I.P. on the India-Pakistan question;

1. *Requests* the Government of India and the Government of Pakistan to refrain from making any statements and from doing or causing to be done or permitting any acts which might aggravate the situation and to appeal to their respective people to assist in creating and maintaining an atmosphere favorable to the promotion of further negotiations;
2. *Requests* the United Nations Representative for India and Pakistan to make any recommendations to the parties for further appropriate action with a view to making progress towards the implementation of the resolutions of the U.N.C.I.P of 13 August 1948 and 5 January and towards a peaceful settlement;
3. *Authorizes* the United Nations Representative to visit the sub-continent for these purposes and
4. *Instructs* the United Nations Representative to report to the Security Council on his efforts as soon as possible.

*The Security Council voted on this Resolution on 2-12-1957 with the following result :

Infavour : **Australia, China, **Columbia. **Cuba, France, **Iraq, **Philippines, **Sweden, U.K. and U.S.A.

Against : None.

Abstaining : U.S.S.R.

**Non-Permanent Members of the Security Council.

89

Resolution 123 (1957) adopted by the Security Council at its 774th Meeting on 21 February 1957. (Document No. S/3793, dated the 21 February 1957)

The Security Council,

Recalling its resolution 122 (1957) of 24 January 1957, its previous resolutions and the resolutions of the United Nations Commission for India and Pakistan on the India-Pakistan question,

1. Requests the President of the Security Council, the representative of Sweden, to examine with the Governments of India and Pakistan any proposals which, in his opinion, are likely to contribute towards the settlement of the dispute, having regard to the previous resolutions of the Security Council and of the United Nations Commission for India and Pakistan; to visit the sub-continent for this purpose; and to report to the Security Council not later than 15 April 1957;
2. Invites the Governments of India and Pakistan to co-operate with him in the performance of these functions;
3. Requests the Secretary-General and the United Nations Representative for India and Pakistan to render such assistance as he may request.

*The Security Council voted on this Resolution on 21-2-1957 with the following result :

In favor **Australia, China, **Columbia, **Cuba, France, **Iraq, **Philippines, **Sweden, U.K., U.S.A.

Against : None

Abstaining : U.S.S.R.

**Non-Permanent Members of the Security Council.

90

The India-Pakistan Question, Australia, Cuba, United Kingdom of Great Britain and Northern Ireland and United States of America : Joint Draft Resolution* (20 February 1957)

The Security Council,

Recalling its resolution of 24 January 1957, its previous resolutions and the resolutions of the United Nations Commission for India and Pakistan on the India-Pakistan question;

Having taken into consideration the statements of the representatives of the Governments of India and Pakistan;

Concerned at the lack of progress in settling the dispute;

Considering the importance which it has attached to the demilitarization of the State of Jammu and Kashmir as a step towards the settlement of the dispute;

Noting that demilitarization preparatory to the holding of a free and impartial plebiscite under United Nations auspices has not been achieved in accordance with the resolutions of the United Nations Commission for India and Pakistan;

Noting the proposal of the representative of Pakistan for the use of a temporary United Nations force in connection with demilitarization;

Believing that, insofar as it might contribute towards the achievement of demilitarization as envisaged in the resolutions of the United Nations Commission for India and Pakistan and towards the pacific settlement of the dispute, the use of such a force would deserve consideration;

1. *Requests* the President of the Security Council, the representative of Sweden, to examine with the Governments of India and Pakistan proposals which, in his opinion, are likely to contribute to the achievement of demilitarization or to the establishment of other conditions for progress towards the settlement of the dispute, having regard to the previous resolutions of the Security Council and of the United Nations Commission for India and Pakistan, and bearing in mind the statements of the representatives of the Governments of India and Pakistan and the proposal for the use of a temporary United Nations force;
2. *Authorizes* him to visit the sub-continent for this purpose;
3. *Requests* him to report to the Security Council as soon as possible but not later than 15 April 1957;
4. *Invites* the Governments of India and Pakistan to co-operate with him in the performance of these functions;
5. *Requests* the Secretary-General and the United Nations representative for India and Pakistan to render such assistance to him as he may request.

*The Security Council voted on this Resolution (S/3787) on February 20, 1957 with the following result :

Infavour : Australia, China, Columbia, Cuba, France, Iraq, Philippines, United Kingdom of Great Britain and Northern Ireland, United States of America.

Against Union of Soviet Socialist Republics.

Abstaining : Sweden.

The President (Mr. Jarring, the Representative of Sweden) announced the result in the following words :

"There were 9 votes in favor, one against and one abstention. Since the negative vote was cast by a member of the Council the joint draft resolution has not been adopted".

91

Resolution 122 (1957) adopted by the Security Council at its 765th Meeting on 24 January 1957*

The Security Council,

Having heard statements from representatives of the Governments of India and Pakistan concerning the dispute over the State of Jammu and Kashmir,

Reminding the Governments and authorities concerned of the principle embodied in its resolutions 47 (1948) of 21 April 1948, 51 (1948) of 3 June, 1948, 80 (1950) of 14 March 1950 and 91 (1951) of 30 March 1951, and the United Nations Commission for India and Pakistan resolutions of 13 August 1948 and 5 January 1949, that the final disposition of the State of Jammu and Kashmir will be made in accordance with the will of the people expressed through the democratic method of a free and impartial plebiscite conducted under the auspices of the United Nations,

1. *Reaffirms* the affirmation in its resolution 91 (1951) and declares that the convening of a Constituent Assembly as recommended by the General Council of the "All Jammu and Kashmir National Conference" and any action that Assembly may have taken or might attempt to take to determine the future shape and affiliation of the entire State or any part thereof, or action by the parties concerned in support of any such action by the Assembly, would not constitute a disposition of the State in accordance with the above principle;

Decides to continue its consideration of the dispute.

*The Security Council voted on this Resolution on 24-1-1957 with the following results :

Infavour : **Australia, China, **Columbia, **Cuba, France, **Iraq, **Philippines, **Sweden, U.K. and U.S.A.

Abstaining : U.S.S.R.

**Non-Permanent Members of the Security Council.

92

Trade Agreement between India and Pakistan

New Delhi, 22 January 1957

The Government of India and the Government of Pakistan being desirous of strengthening and developing commercial relations between their respective countries have agreed as follows :

Article I

The two Governments recognising the needs and requirements of each other for foreign exchange in the context of their developing economies and having regard to the present disequilibrium in their trade and payments position undertake to explore all possibilities for expansion of trade between the two countries on the basis of mutual advantage.

Article II

With regard to the commodities/goods mentioned in Schedules 'A' and 'B' attached to this Agreement, the two Governments shall facilitate imports from and exports to each other's territories to the extent permitted by their respective laws, regulations and procedures.

Article III

Imports and exports of the commodities/goods mentioned in Schedules 'A' and V shall normally take place through ordinary commercial channels, except where either Government finds it necessary to buy or sell part or whole of the quantity/value of any item on Government account.

Article IV

With respect to commodities/goods not included in Schedules 'A' and 'B' export or import shall also be permitted in accordance with the laws, regulations and procedures in force in either country from time to time.

Article V

Each Government shall accord to the commerce of the country of the other Government treatment no less favourable than that accorded to the commerce of any third country.

Article VI

The provisions of Article V shall not apply to : (a) any advantage which either country has accorded or may accord at any time during the period of validity of this Agreement to other bordering countries in order to facilitate frontier traffic,

(b) any advantages accorded in connection with a customs union or free zone of which either country may become a member,

(c) preferences or advantages accorded by either country to any third country prior to the 15th August 1947 or in replacement thereof.

Article VII

The two Governments recognising the need for entering into special arrangements as contemplated by Article XXIV (11) of the General Agreement on Tariffs and Trade agree to enter into such arrangements. The commodities covered by such special arrangements and the nature and scope thereof are set out in Schedule 'C'.

Article VIII

In order to meet the day-to-day requirements of the people living within a ten mile belt of the border between West Bengal, Assam and Tripura on the one hand and East Pakistan on the other and with a view to providing facilities to these people to dispose of their goods, border trade shall be allowed in the commodities specified in accordance with Schedule 'D' to this Agreement.

Article IX

In order to facilitate the implementation of this Agreement the two Governments shall consult with each other as and when necessary and in any case review the working of the Agreement every six months.

Article X

Subject to the approval of the Governments of India and Pakistan this Agreement shall come into force with effect from the 1st February 1957. It shall remain in force up to the 31st January 1960, provided that after the expiry of the first year it may be terminated by either party giving six months notice in writing to the other. The schedules attached to the Agreement will be subject to revision by mutual consultation before the commencement of the years 1958 and 1959. Done at New Delhi, this Twenty-second day of January 1957.

(Sd/-)	(Sd/-)
S. RANGANATHAN	A.M. AHMED
For the Government of India.	For the Government of Pakistan.

Dated : 22-01-1957

SCHEDULE 'A'

EXPORTS FROM INDIA TO PAKISTAN

S. No. of Commodities/goods. 1. Coal. 2. Stone Boulders. S. Stones (Pakur). 4. Silpatta. 6. Fire bricks. 6. Lime and lime stone. 7. Mica. 8. Bauxite. 9. Barytes (white). 10. Pigments and dry colours. 11. Dyeing and tanning substances. 12. Chemicals. 13. Drugs and medicines, including Ayurvedic and Unani Medicines. 14. Mill board and straw board. 15. Machinery and Mill work *e.g.*, textile machinery, Agricultural machinery, Sugar cane crushing machinery. Rice flour and oil crushing machinery, Printing machinery, Centrifugal pumps. 16. Workshop equipment including hand tools and machine tools. 17. Electric instruments apparatus appliances. 18. Electric cables and wires. 19. Fluorescent electric tubes. 20. Electric insulation material. 21. Accumulators and batteries. 22. Bicycles and spare parts. 23. Scientific instruments, including laboratory glassware. 24. Glass bottles, jars and phials. 25. Iron steel bolts, nuts and screws. 26. Sanitary ware. 27. Agarwood. 28, Canes and rattans. 29. Cinema films. 30. Books, periodicals and newspapers. 31. Essential oils. 32. Sugar. 33. Tea for blending. 34. Coffee. 35. Betel leaves. 36. Biri and hukka tobacco. 37. Biri leaves. 38. Spices. 39. Fresh fruits. 40. Catechu. 41. Potatoes. 42. Buffalo homs. 43. Conch shells. 44. Gurns and resins. 45. Synthetic stones.

SCHEDULE 'B'

EXPORTS FROM PAKISTAN TO INDIA

S. No. of Commodities/goods. 1. Raw jute. 2. Hides and skins. 3. Fish including dried fish, poultry and eggs. 4. Betel leaves. 5. Betel nuts. 6. Fresh and dried fruits. 7. Coriander and methi seeds. 8. Spices. 9. Honey. 10. Books and periodicals, and newspapers. 11. Cinema films. 12. Cement. 13. Salt petre. 14. Machinetools. 15. Bicycles and spare parts. 16. Surgical instruments. 17. Sports goods. 18. Wood and timber all sorts, other than hard wood.

SCHEDULE 'C'

SPECIAL ARRANGEMENTS

Sr. No.	Commodities/ goods	Quantity/Value (per year except where otherwise specified)	Remarks
1	2	3	4
1.	Coal	30,000 tons per month	For export from India to West Pakistan by rail only. (Provided supplies are not interrupted by causes beyond human control such as strikes, accidants floods, etc.)
		55,000 tons per month	For export from India to East Pakistan by rail and river. (Provided supplies are not interrupted by causes beyond human control such as strikes, accidants floods, etc.)
		15,000 tons per month	For export from India to Pakistan by sea or river. (Provided supplies are not interrupted by causes beyond human control such as strikes, accidants floods, etc.)
2.	Stone boulders	Approximately 1,000 tons per week from source of supply on the Eastern Railway broad guage side and approximately 300 tons a day from Source of supply on North Eastern Railway meter gauge Side in Assam.	For Export from India to East pakistan. The movement will be subject to agreement between the Railways concerned regarding details in respect of rate and mode of payment, supply of rolling stock, locomotives, railway staff and other contingencies.
3.	Hard wood	15,00 tons of sal and teak and 1,000 tons of gurjan wood (standard sizes).	For export from India to East Pakistan.
		500 tons of sal and teak (standard sizes).	For export from India to West Pakistan.
4.	Soft wood	2,000 tons of kail (standard sizes).	For export from India to West Pakistan by river Chenab only.
5.	Potato seeds	Rs. 5 lakhs.	For export from India to Pakistan.
6.	Coal tar	P.M.	For export from India to Pakistan.
7.	Bell metal	P.M.	For export from India to East Pakistan.
8.	Antimony	P.M.	For export from India to Pakistan.
9.	Raw jute	Quantity to be indicated by the end of September each year.	
10.	Antimony ore	P.M.	For export from Pakistan to India.
11.	Sandal wood	P.M.	For export from East Pakistan to India.
12.	Chillies, garlic and ginger.	P.M.	For export from East Pakistan to India.

(Contd.)

SCHEDULE 'C' (*Contd.*)

1	2	3	4
13.	Cinema films	10 Bengali films, 7 Urdu/Hindi films.	For import into Pakistan from India on the basis of outright sale. Imports into India from Pakistan will be licensed freely on the basis of outright sale.
14.	Forest produce	P.M.	(i) For export to East Pakistan from India (excluding timber and bamboo). (ii) For export from East Pakistan to India, such items as timber, unspecified agar-wood, thatching grass, bamboo, hogla leaves and golepatta.
15.	Livestock	P.M.	For export from India to East Pakistan and for export from West Pakistan to India.
16.	Gram	P.M.	For Export from India to East Pakistan and for export from West Pakistan to India of equal quantity.
17.	Cement	50,000 tons. 50,000 tons.	For export from India to East Pakistan For export from West Pakistan to India.
18.	Sulphuric acid	1,000 tons. 1,000 tons.	For export from India to East Pakistan For export from West Pakistan to India.
19.	Salt (rock and sea)	P.M.	For export of rock salt from West Pakistan to India and export of sea salt from India to East Pakistan.

N.B. — The two Governments shall permit import/export up to at least the quantity/value specified above, actual imports and exports depending upon terms, delivery periods, specifications, etc. being mutually agreed upon between exporters and importers on either side.

SCHEDULE 'D'

PROVISIONS RELATING TO BORDER TRADE REFERRED TO IN ARTICLE VIII OF THE AGREEMENT

These facilities shall apply only to the trade across the Land Customs frontiers between West Bengal, Assam and Tripura on the, one hand and East Pakistan, on the other.

2. Those facilities shall be available only to persons holding 'A' category visas.

3. As from the expiry of a period of six months from the date of entry into force of this Agreement, however, all such persons may cross the border for this purpose only once a day in each direction and only through such routes as may be authorised in this behalf. Each Government will, after such consultation with the other as may be necessary, be free to

prescribe an adequate number of such routes having regard to the requirements of bona fide border trade.

4. The carriage of goods covered by the Schedule shall be free from import, export and exchange control restrictions as well as customs duties and customs formalities except those required for purposes of paragraph six below.

5. The persons engaged in border trade may carry in cash a sum not exceeding Rs. 5 in Indian currency when going from India to Pakistan and a similar amount in Pakistan currency when going from Pakistan to India.

6. Either Government may maintain such checks and such preventive measures, including the right to search, as are considered necessary to ensure that these concessions are not exceeded or abused.

ANNEXURE

I. LUSHAI HILLS CHITTAGONG HILL TRACTS SECTORS

For export from Lushai Hills to Chittagong Hill tracts		For export from Chittagong Hill tracts to Lushai Hills	
Name of Commodities	Quantities allowed to be carried	Name of Commodities	Quantities allowed to be carried
1. Til seeds	Head load	1. Gur	Head load
2. Raw cotton	Do.	2. Kerosene oil	One bottle
3. Chillies	Do.	3. Pulses	5 seers
4. Forest produce (including timber, unclassed agarwood, cane thatching grass, Firewood and bamboos).	Do.	4. Washing soap 5. Onion 6. Garlic 7. Fish, fresh 8. Fish, dried 9. Poultry 10. Eggs	½ seer 5 seers 5 seers 10 seers 5 seers Four One dozen
5. Fresh fruits	Do.	11. Vegetables	Head Load
6. Bay leaves	Do.	12. Milk	5 seers
7. Milk	5 seers	13. Milk products (excluding ghee)	2 seers
8. Milk products (excluding ghee)	2 seers	14. Betel nuts 15. Betel leaves	1 seer 5 seers
		16. Earthenware	Head load
		17. Tea	1lb

II. KHASI JAINTIA AND GARO HILLS — SYLHET, MYMENSINGH SECTOR

For export from Khasi, Jaintia and Garo Hills to Sylhet and Mymensingh		For export from Sylhet and Mymensingh to Khasi, Jaintia and Garo Hills	
Name of Commodities	Quantities allowed to be carried	Name of Commodities	Quantities allowed to be carried
1. Fresh fruits	Head load	1. Fish, fresh	10 seers
2. Vegetables (including potatoes)	Do.	2. Fish, dried	5 seers
3. Betel leaves	5 seers	3. Poultry	4 seers
4. Forest produce (including timber, unclassed agarwood, cane, thatching grass, firewood and bamboos	Head Load	4. Eggs	One dozen
		5. Vegetables	Head load
		6. Betel nuts	1 seer
		7. Betel leaves	5 seers
		8. Spices	2 seers
		9. Milk	5 seers
5. Ginger, turmeric and tejpatta	Do.	10. Milk products (excluding ghee)	2 seers
6. Milk	5 seers	11. Fresh fruits	Head load
7. Milk products (excluding ghee)	2 seers		
8. Lime and lime stone	Head load		

III. CACHAR-SYLHET SECTOR

For export from Cachar to Sylher		For export from Sylher to Cachar	
Name of Commodities	Quantities allowed to be carried	Name of Commodities	Quantities allowed to be carried
1. Forest produce (including timber, unclassed agarwood, cane, thatching grass, firewood and bamboos).	Head load	1. Fish, fresh	10 seers
		2. Fish, dried	5 seers
		3. Poultry	Four
		4. Eggs	1 dozen
		5. Soap (Washing)	½ seer
		6. Spices (including ginger)	2 seers
2. Kerosene oil	1 bottle	7. Onion	5 seer
3. Vegetables (including potatoes)	Head load	8. Garlic	5 seers
4. Fresh fruits	Head load	9. Fresh fruits	Head load
5. Milk	5 seers	10. Vegetables	Do.
6. Milk products (excluding ghee).	2 seers	11. Milk	5 seers
7. Soap (washing)	½ seer	12. Milk products (excluding ghee)	2 seers
		13. Kerosene oil	1 bottle

IV. TRIPURA EAST BENGAL SECTOR

For export from Tripura to East Bengal		For export from East Bengal to Tripura	
Name of Commodities	Quantities allowed to be carried	Name of Commodities	Quantities allowed to be carried
1. Vegetables (including Potatoes).	Head load	1. Poultry Four	
		2. Eggs	1 dozen
2. Milk	5 seers	3. Milk	5 seers
3. Milk products (excluding ghee).	2 seers	4. Milk products (excluding ghee)	2 seers
4. Forest produce (including timber, unclassed agarwood, cane, thatching grass, firewood and bamboos).	Head load	5. Fish, fresh	10 seers
		6. Fish, dried	5 seers
		7. Vegetables	Head load
		8. Onion	5 seers
		9. Garlic	5 seers
		10. Coconut (dry and green).	1 dozen
5. Til seeds	Do.	11. Betel nuts	1 seer
6. Fresh Fruits	Do.	12. Betel leaves	5 seers
7. Gram	5 seers	13. Spices (including (chillies)	2 seers
8. Pulses	5 seers	14. Kerosene oil	1 bottle
9. Kerosene oil	1 bottle		

V. RANGPUR (EAST PAKISTAN) — ASSAM (BORDERING DISTRICT OF RANGPUR)/COOCH BEHAR/JALPAIGURI (WEST BENGAL) SECTOR

Export from Assam (Bordering District of Rangpur) Cooch Behar, Jalpaiguri (West Bengal) to Rangpur (East Pakistan)		Export from Rangpur (East Pakistan) to Assam (Bordering District of Rangpur) Cooch Behar, Jalpaiguri (West Bengal)	
Name of Commodities	Quantities allowed to be carried	Name of Commodities	Quantities allowed to be carried
1. Fresh fruits	Head load	1. Fish, fresh	10 seers
2. Vegetables (including potatoes)	Do.	2. Fish, dried	5 seers
		3. Poultry	Four
3. Spices	2 seers	4. Eggs	One dozen
4. Fire wood	Head load	5. Milk	5 seers
5. Milk	5 seers	6. Milk products (excluding ghee)	2 seers
6. Milk products (excluding ghee).	2 seers	7. Gur	
7. Tobacco	1 seer	8. Tobacco	Head load
8. Washing soap	½ seer	9. 1 seer	
9. Bamboo	Head load	10. Coconuts	1 dozen
10. Thatching grass	Head load	11. Betel nuts	1 seer
		12. Betel leaves	5 seers
		13. Spices	2 seers
		14. Salt	1 seer
		15. Fodder for cattle	Head load
		16. Bamboo	Do.
		17. Thatching grass	Do
		18. Hogla leaves	Do
		19. Firewood	Do.

VI. REST OF EAST PAKISTAN AND REST OF WEST BENGAL

Export from Rest of West Bengal to Rest of East Pakistan		Export from Rest of East Pakistan to Rest of West Bengal	
Name of Commodities	Quantities allowed to be carried	Name of Commodities	Quantities allowed to be carried
1. Fresh fruits	Head load	1. Fish, fresh	10 seers
2. Vegetables (including potatoes)	Do.	2. Fish, dried	5 seers
		3. Poultry	Four
3. Spices	2 seers	4. Eggs	One dozen
4. Milk	5 seers	5. Coconuts	One dozen
5. Milk products (excluding ghee)	2 seers	6. Spices	2 seers
		7. Betel leaves	5 seers
6. Gram	5 seers	8. Betel nuts	1 seer
7. Pulses	5 seers	9. Bamboo	Head load
8. Firewood	Head load	10. Thatching grass	Do.
9. Bamboos	Do.	11. Fodder for cattle	Do.
10. Thatching grass	Do.	12. Golpatta	Do.
11. Simul cotton	Do.	13. Milk	5 seers
12. Washing soap	½ seer	14. Milk products (excluding ghee)	2 seers
		15. Fresh fruits	Head load
		16. Vegetables	Do.
		17. Hogla leaves	Do.
		18. Fire wood	Do.
		19. Gram	5 seers
		20. Pulses	5 seers
		21. Broomsticks	Head load
		22. Simul cotton	Do.

LETTERS

No. 1

GOVERNMENT OF INDIA
MINISTRY OF COMMERCE AND CONSUMER INDUSTRIES,

New Delhi, 22 January 1957

My Dear Aziz Ahmed,

During the course of discussions between our two Delegations which resulted in a fresh Trade Agreement between India and Pakistan which was signed today, matters relating to Ziratia tenants were also discussed. It was agreed that the question of facilities to Ziratia tenants was connected with the prevention of smuggling and improvement of facilities for the transit of foodgrains through East Pakistan to Tripura. As a result of these discussions, the following understanding was reached : (1) The Ziratia tenants residing on either side of the

Tripura East Pakistan border, who have land on either side of the border within a ten mile belt, shall continue to be allowed to take across the border within a reasonable period after the harvest 40 maunds of paddy per family or the total produce of such land cultivated by them, whichever is less. (2) The representatives of the two Governments shall meet before the end of February 1957 with a view to devising as early as possible measures to improve the facilities for the movement of foodgrains through East Pakistan to Tripura. The steps set out in the attached enclosure, which have been suggested by the Indian Delegation will among others be considered in this behalf. (3) As from the expiry of a period of six months after 31st January 1957, all Ziratia tenants may cross the border with paddy only through such routes as may be authorised in this behalf. Before the expiry of this period, the representatives of the two Governments will meet to consult with each other about the routes to be prescribed for the purpose and measures necessary for the implementation of the provisions in (1) above without the concessions envisaged therein being abused. (4) The two Governments shall, before the end of November 1957, enter into consultation with each other for reviewing the implementation of the arrangements relating to Ziratia tenants and the improvements made in the transit facilities through East Pakistan into Tripura. 2. I shall be grateful if you will confirm that the above correctly sets out the understanding that was reached between us.

Yours sincerely,

(Sd/-)
S. RANGANATHAN.

AZIZ AHMED, Esquire,
Secretary, Ministry of Commerce,
Government of Pakistan.

ENCLOSURE REFERRED TO IN SHRI RANGANATHAN'S LETTER TO MR. AZIZ AHMED REGARDING ZIRATIA TENANTS

SUGGESTIONS FOR IMPROVEMENT OF MOVEMENT FACILITIES BETWEEN EAST PAKISTAN AND TRIPURA

1. The Liaison Officer of the Indian Railway at Shantahar may be provided with the assistance of one more Inspector who may be posted at Akhaura. These two Officers should look after the timely transit of wagons for Tripura.

2. Clearance facilities should be provided at Kasba Railway Station.

3. A Siding from Kasba Railway Station inside Tripura territory should be provided.

4. Sidings into Tripura territory should be provided by extension from Balla and Belonia Railway Stations.

5. Demurrage for non-clearance of goods arriving by M.G. Wagons at Akhaura, Balla and Belonia should not be charged so long as the responsibility for delay does not lie on the consignee. Particularly no demurrage should be charged on M.G. Wagons which bring only part of goods transhipped from M.G. Wagons and not allowed to be cleared till the remaining component M.G. Wagons have arrived.

6. Certificate of short delivery should be given at points of destination in East Bengal territory in respect of goods cleared for Tripura.

7. Railway out Agency should be provided at Agartala.

No. 2.

DELEGATION OF PAKISTAN

New Delhi, 22 January 1957

My Dear Ranganathan,

I write to acknowledge the receipt of your letter of today's date which reads as follows : (Not reproduced).

I confirm that the above sets out the position correctly.

Yours sincerely,

(Sd/-)
AZIZ AHMED.

Shri S. RANGANATHANI, I.C.S.,
Secretary to the Government of India,
Ministry of Commerce and Consumer Industries, New Delhi.

No. 3.

GOVERNMENT OF INDIA
MINISTRY OF COMMERCE AND CONSUMER INDUSTRIES

New Delhi, 22 January 1957

My Dear Aziz Ahmed,

We have exchanged letters today regarding the concessions to Ziratia tenants. I write this letter to seek confirmation of the following three points which arose during the discussions :

(1) With reference to paragraph 1 (2) of that letter we agreed that the discussions between the representatives of the two Governments in regard to improvement of transit facilities to Tripura through East Pakistan need not necessarily be confined to improvement in transit facilities in relation to food-grains only.

(2) With reference to paragraph 1(4) of that letter you

maintained that the fact that the transit facilities through East Pakistan to Tripura, were in the judgment of the Government of India inadequate would not justify their withdrawing the facilities for the Ziratia tenants. I, however, made it clear to you that it was my understanding that in the event of the improvement in the transit facilities through East Pakistan to Tripura, not being adequate in the opinion of the Government of India, the Government of India will be free to reconsider the entire arrangements relating to the Ziratia tenants.

(3) We also agreed that these arrangements regarding Ziratia tenants set out in the correspondence referred to above, will come into effect after ratification by our respective Governments.

Yours sincerely,

(Sd/-)
S. RANGANATHAN.

AZIZ AHMED, Esqr., Secretary,
Ministry of Commerce,
Government of Pakistan.

No. 4.

DELEGATION OF PAKISTAN

New Delhi, 22 January 1957

My Dear Ranganathan,

I write to acknowledge the receipt of your letter of today's date which reads as follows : (Not reproduced).

I confirm that the above sets out the position correctly.

Yours sincerely,

(Sd/-)
AZIZ AHMED.

Shri S. RANGANATHAN, I.C.S.,
Secretary to the Government of India,
Ministry of Commerce and Consumer Industries, New Delhi.

No. 5.

GOVERNMENT OF INDIA
MINISTRY OF COMMERCE AND CONSUMER INDUSTRIES

New Delhi, 22 January 1957

My Dear Aziz Ahmed,

During the course of the discussions between our two delegations which resulted in a fresh Trade Agreement between India and Pakistan, the difficulties being experienced by the persons residing in the border areas between India and East Pakistan, resulting from the non-issue of 'A' category visas in sufficient numbers and the present complicated procedure followed in issuing them were discussed. It was agreed that these questions should be discussed at an early date between representatives of the two Governments, with a view to resolving these difficulties. I should be grateful if you would kindly confirm that the foregoing correctly sets out the understanding reached between us.

Yours sincerely,

(Sd/-)

S. RANGANATHAN.

AZIZ AHMED, Esqr., Secretary,
Ministry of Commerce,
Government of Pakistan, Camp : New Delhi.

No. 6.

DELEGATION OF PAKISTAN

New Delhi, 22 January 1957

My Dear Ranganathan,

I write to acknowledge the receipt of your letter of today's date which reads as follows : (Not reproduced). I confirm that the foregoing correctly sets out the understanding reached between us.

Yours sincerely,

(Sd/-)

AZIZ AHMED.

Shri S. RANGANATHAN, I.C.S,
Secretary to the Government of India,
Ministry of Commerce and Consumer Industries, New Delhi.

93

Excerpts from Speech by Mr. V.K. Krishna Menon at Eleventh Session 611th Plenary Meeting, 6 December 1956

Our neighbours from Pakistan also made reference to India in regard to Kashmir. Now Kashmir is still on the agenda of the Security Council. We put it there. We came here with a complaint of aggression. I have no desire, therefore, to go into great detail about it. I had the pleasure of hearing the distinguished lady, who was a countrywoman of ours until ten years ago, for whom we have very great affection and regard, speak to us 592nd meetings and I can only echo her sentiments : we want to see the end of aggression in Kashmir.

The Foreign Minister of Pakistan has made certain references to our military expenditure. This is a matter of some concern to us, because we are discussing problems of disarmament, the attitude of countries in regard to military expenditure and things of that kind. There are two sets of figures available, one-the figures of the budget of the Government of India, and the other-the figures collected by the United Nations. They do not vary in substance; they are calculated upon a different basis, and, at the risk of boring the Assembly with figures, I think it is necessary for us to state this, because the Foreign Minister of Pakistan told us that 70 per cent of the national budget of Pakistan was devoted to military expenditure and that the same was the case in India. I do not question the right of the Foreign Minister of Pakistan to speak of his country; I have no objection to his speaking about us when the facts are right.

First of all, with regard to Pakistan, this 70 per cent is not the real figure, since it does not take into account the large volume of foreign military aid arising from Pakistan's military alliance with the United States, or whatever other amounts may result from its other military alliances. But assuming that it is 70 per cent, I would like that to be compared with our figures.

The total revenue budget of India for the year 1956 to 1957 is 5,500 million rupees, which works out at $1,100 million. Our defence expenditure for that period is $408 million, or 37.6 per cent of our budget, which is just over half of the 70 per cent that was mentioned.

But I think I shall be very unfair to the Government of India, and in part to myself, therefore, if I leave it at that. These figures do not represent the real picture, because the budget I gave was the revenue budget, without taking into account capital expenditure. If you take the whole budget of India, including our capital expenditure, it comes to $1,400 million for the year 1956 to 1957, and the total defence expenditure, both current and capital, is $434 million, making 18.6 percent of our total budget.

These figures are available in the United Nations and anybody can check them. That is to say, if we take the capital expenditure on the nation-building side, as well as the capital expenditure on the replenishment of the army, navy and air force, then you will get the figure of 18.6 per cent. But if you say that we are trying to distort these figures or present them to our advantage, you can take the other ones, that is to say the merely current expenditure on both sides, without capital expenditure. But do not forget that this so-called capital expenditure is part of our national planning budget, and includes education and various community projects on which the Government of India spends somewhere around $300 million a year.

Therefore, the figures which have been given are entirely wrong and likely to carry a mistaken impression. It is all the more galling to us, because we are very stern advocates of the lowering of military expenditure and of disarmament, and in that connection I would like to read out the figures for the previous years.

Before 1939, the proportion of military expenditure was 33 per cent; in the year 1946 to 1947, that is, when we took over in the last year of British administration, military expenditure was 46 per cent; in the year 1949 to 1950, it came down to 29 per cent, and each year it has gone down a little so that we have now, in the year 1956 to 1957, reached the present figure of 18.6 per cent of our capital and current expenditure, or, as I said before, 37.6 per cent on the other basis. I mention this because we do not like to be presented to the world as a country that is armed to the teeth and is starving our people in order that we may acquire or keep weapons. Ours is perhaps one of the few countries of the world where from 1947 onwards military expenditure has gone down in spite of the fact that military equipment, the greater part of which has to be secured from other countries, is increasing in cost. All I desire to say now about Kashmir is that a third of the territory is unlawfully, against the decision of the United Nations, occupied by Pakistan forces. In the interests of peace we have kept behind the cease-fire line-there are incidents now and then but nothing very serious, there are United Nations observers there-and I think the problem with regard to Kashmir is the vacation of this aggression. The fact that that part of India is now under foreign occupation-although it is under the occupation of a neighbour with whom we want to remain on very good terms-is still not very agreeable to us. I think I will leave it there.